Chasing The Frontier

Chasing The Frontier

Scots-Irish in Early America

Larry J. Hoefling

iUniverse, Inc.
New York Lincoln Shanghai

CHASING THE FRONTIER
Scots-Irish in Early America

Copyright © 2005 by Larry J. Hoefling

iUniverse books may be ordered through booksellers or by contacting:

iUniverse
2021 Pine Lake Road, Suite 100
Lincoln, NE 68512
www.iuniverse.com
1-800-Authors (1-800-288-4677)

ISBN-13: 978-0-595-35914-1 (pbk)
ISBN-13: 978-0-595-80368-2 (ebk)
ISBN-10: 0-595-35914-0 (pbk)
ISBN-10: 0-595-80368-7 (ebk)

Printed in the United States of America

Contents

Foreword

A T THE TIME THIS PROJECT was first undertaken, there were relatively few recent writings regarding the Scots-Irish, or Scotch-Irish, as they were then more frequently described. Many local histories included information on the Scots-Irish in those areas where they settled in the greatest number, with the majority of those written in the early part of the twentieth century.

In his book, *The Scotch-Irish, A Social History*, James G. Leyburn noted a lack of material regarding the migration of the Lowland Scots to Northern Ireland in the early 1600's, and the later exodus from there to the American colonies. His description of the background and social climate that led to the massive emigrations is likely the most comprehensive work on the Scots-Irish. Leyburn cites the Revolutionary War as the social event that marks the assimilation of the group of immigrants into the American culture.

While there is no question the pre-Revolutionary separatism of the Scots-Irish was ever equaled after that time, there is evidence that the characteristics of that group were still present in several areas of the country at a much later date. Certainly, the Scots-Irish were influenced by the habits and customs of their neighbors, and there was no hesitation among them to find marriage partners among the English and German pioneers of the time. Still, there were those whose marriages were to the sons and daughters of the Scots-Irish, and whose children were raised in communities where Scots-Irish ancestry was prevalent. While the American Revolution may have aided the Scots-Irish in shedding the immigrant label that so many newcomers to this country faced, there were numbers in whom the early traits and characteristics of the Scots-Irish could be seen many years after the Revolution.

This effort is not to contradict Leyburn's premise, but only to examine the lives and culture of the Scots-Irish in the years after the Revolutionary War, as the influences of the young country continued to affect them, and as they continued to influence others around them.

The term Scotch-Irish was used in the initial manuscript, and a number of bound copies use the term in both the title and the pages. An email correspondent pointed out to me that the term Scotch better described a whiskey than a group of people, a position that I could hardly argue. Still, it was not until some years later that the expression Scots-Irish began to appear more appropriate, and it may be the sensitivity to political correctness that would compel me to edit the entire manuscript in that fashion, while the passage of time has seemed to allow me to more easily acquiesce to those with differing opinions.

I owe a debt of gratitude to all those who made suggestions and offered research advice, including the library staff at the Tulsa City-County Library, and those at Cass County (MO), Casey County (KY), Lexington (KY), Stanford (KY), Latter Day Saints FHC (Tulsa), Sapulpa (OK), Staunton (VA), and Salisbury (NC). Also, those staff members at governmental agencies who were most helpful, including Augusta County (VA) Clerk, Cass County (MO) Historical Society, Genealogical Society of Rowan County (NC), Harrison-Rockingham Historical Society (VA), Holt County (MO) Recorder, Kentucky Genealogical Society, Lincoln County (KY) Clerk, the University of Kentucky, and the North Carolina State Archives. Additionally, my appreciation for assistance above and beyond by the late Katherine G. Bushman of Staunton, VA; the late Maxine Heidrich of Cass County, MO; Barbara Lowrey, Kathy Huber, Betty Black, Sam and Margaret Baughman, Madeline Hilbert of Dayton, VA; James Kluttz of Landis, NC; Mr. and Mrs. Gary Lynn of Hustonville, KY; Evelyn Stallings of Salisbury, NC; Gaither Shrumm of Lincolnton, NC; Lucille Ullery of Freeman, MO, and the many others whose names should be included, as well as those whose patience and encouragement served so well; and a special and sincere thanks to Martha Lee Huston Hoefling, for the unflagging support, time, effort, and words of encouragement over the many years this project has taken.

Larry Hoefling, May 2005

Introduction

THERE IS NO SIMPLE DESCRIPTION that can be applied to the Scots-Irish, or Scotch-Irish, as they are also known. Many encyclopedias include neither term, although a recent Internet search returned 1,080,000 references to Scotch-Irish, and 1,970,000 Scots-Irish. The search engine results indicate a greater usage of the lately devised term Scots-Irish. Although neither moniker was used in their time, both are found today in the US and in Europe.

Any race or nationality undertaking a migration to foreign soil would leave behind many of the characteristics of their homeland after spending a century or more in the new country. Additionally, new characteristics of social, cultural, and economic interaction would be developed based on their lives in the new setting. Those who have become identified as the Scots-Irish made such migrations twice in less than two hundred years.

Those who settled the Great Plantation of King James in the early 1600's emerged as a different race in Northern Ireland than those countrymen left behind in Scotland. After spending just over a century in what was called Ulster, there was a massive migration of those same families to the American colonies. To paraphrase James G. Leyburn in his study of the migration, the Scots-Irish in Northern Ireland no longer resembled the Scottish, and were never truly Irish.

The difficulty in categorizing the Scots-Irish applies as well to their morals, attitudes, and demeanor in the colonies, and later the US. Those with identifiable Scots-Irish ancestry range from religious leaders and politicians to backwoodsmen whose very descriptions have become slurs and epithets. While they were building churches and passing laws prohibiting swearing, the Scots-Irish were also wagering on horse races and getting into confrontations with anyone who threatened them. Some phrases describing the Scots-Irish as a class would come as high praise to any group, and conversely, other descriptions would shame even the most shameless. Just when there appears to be a constant among them, yet another variation appears.

There are truths about the Scots-Irish that cannot be disputed. As a minority in colonial America, they were represented in great numbers, largely on the frontiers. The minority percentage was no insignificant number, with estimates ranging upwards of thirteen percent of the population. They were strong in their opinions, even when those points of view were questionable at best. They sided with the rebel cause during the revolution, and were present in great numbers at some of the most important junctures in the battle for independence. It is also true that those holding Scots-Irish ancestries who take particular pride in their many accomplishments must also acknowledge the many mistakes and social blunders that must be attributed to the group.

Not the least among those errors was the Scots-Irish intemperance of the many Native Indian tribes whose traditional homelands were encroached upon by the frontier settlers. The early-day Quakers had established reasonable and fairly respected relationships with several Nations in an effort to lead lives in peaceful coexistence. Most of the Scots-Irish frontiersmen held no interest in coexistence. There is plenty of anecdotal evidence that the Scots-Irish loved a feud, and had the time and inclination to pursue several at once.

It is also a truth that the Scots-Irish originated in the Scottish Lowlands, rather than the Highlands of modern day romance. During the period that the Ulster Province was opened to settlement by King James, there were vast differences between the Scottish people that could generally be defined by geography. While both cultures were held in disdain by the English of the time, both later made marks in a number of social arenas, and the Scots-Irish had a significant impact in a number of areas in an extremely short length of time.

Beliefs that the Scots-Irish migration involved only the poorest and least cultured are debatable. The incredible number of families that took part in the migration from Northern Ireland to the American colonies in the period just before the Revolutionary War would indicate that all manner of classes would be included. There are accounts of entire parishes booking passage for the New World, which would include not only the poorest of the congregation, but the affluent and ministry as well. The founding of churches and schools in the colonies was not the work of a headless class. Many of those same institutions are still thriving. Some of the educational principals espoused by the early Scots-Irish became models.

On the other hand, there are those who assert that the Scots-Irish were nothing more than what has been called 'poor white trash.' No cultures exist without social and legal standards and none maintain perfect records in upholding those standards. It is incorrect to portray the Scots-Irish as exemplary citizens in every aspect, but it is equally wrong to assume that they were all rascals, scoundrels, and backwoods yokels.

This effort is an attempt to color the area between those two extremes with details of the lives of descendents of the original settlers of the Ulster Plantation. It is hoped that a presentation of the social climate and customs of the times will add to a greater appreciation of the Scots-Irish frontier families in early America.

CHAPTER ONE

The Lowland Scots

THEY WERE POOR, HUNGRY, and scratching out desperate lives in the rugged country of seventeenth century Scotland, but within the course of several generations, they would become the prolific and hardy settlers of a new continent who would help shape the destiny of an emerging nation. They were of no less intelligence than the citizens of other European countries, but their isolation and the lawlessness of the region left them dramatically entrenched in conditions more closely approximating those found at the height of the Middle Ages; having never been exposed to the basic agricultural techniques commonly used in other parts of the world, farms of the Scottish lowlands barely yielded enough to eat, much less provide the seeds for the next year's planting. The clans from the highlands raided the lowland communities with regularity, sometimes for provisions, women, or cattle, but often simply for sport. Yet, despite the destitute conditions that marked their origins, within the short span of one hundred years those men and women who later came to be termed Scots-Irish would make a dramatic impact on not only the European community, but the society of the American colony as well.

Scotland was an isolated frontier in the 1600's. It was a time when the families with the largest number of young men were the strongest, and were considered as ruling clans. The ability to govern Scotland was continually compromised by the infighting between the various clans, which not only contributed to the local lawlessness, but also ruled out any possibility of forging alliances against a common foe. The Scots were constantly at odds with their British neighbors, and the English were successful in granting favors to one group or another to effectively eliminate a unified Scotland.

In its most simplistic representation, the country could be divided geographically into two distinct north and south regions, separated at a narrow section of land between the Firth of Clyde and the Firth of Forth, which was roughly from Edinburgh to Glasgow, although the coastal regions of the northeast would likely be less aligned with the highlands than the lowlands. To the north of that line was a true wilderness of mountains and glens inhabited by the barbaric Gaelic speaking tribes or clans. In that region, there were no towns or villages to speak of, only communities of clans and their associated families. The lowlands offered a more accessible terrain, but was only scarcely better suited to the requirements of agriculture. The best farmland was situated along the eastern edge of the lowlands, but its proximity and landscape made it the target of raiders from both England and the highlands. The remainder of the south territory was comprised of a thin, stony soil, with numerous marshes and bogs that prohibited farming except on the irregular and sloping sides of the rocky hills.

Among the lowlanders, a more impoverished existence could scarcely be imagined. The thin soil was irregular and rocky, and the types of crops planted did not lend themselves to the geography. Homes were crudely constructed with any available materials, largely grasses and peat, since timber was scarce. By the late 1500's the forests of the Scottish lowlands had been all but eliminated, and although strict laws were passed in an effort to conserve living trees and encourage new plantings, there was no enforcement. As a result, species of wildlife indigenous to the forests were forced into the highlands, including large animals such as wolves and wild boars, which previously had been hunted in great numbers.

Despite a romantic notion that persists regarding early day Scottish life, there was little about it that might have been considered glamorous, much less desirable. Forays into the country by residents of the more civilized countries of the world brought descriptions of abject poverty and filthy living conditions, and the Scots of the time were viewed as little more than throwbacks to medieval times. The infrequent tours into the lands of Scotland were similar in nature to the later safaris into the wilds of the African continent, and were equally uncomfortable and often dangerous.

In the lowlands, towns were often no more than communities of families living in service to the landholder, often termed freeholders or *lairds*, and occupations were those that were required of the laird in exchange for the protection he

provided. Tenant farmers eked out livings by tilling the rocky soil and tending what little livestock they could acquire. The arrangement was little different that that of medieval fiefdoms, and the feudal Scots were the much-used serfs in servitude to the gentry. It was an arrangement understood by both parties, and there was little prospect for social or cultural advancement among the citizenry, and little disappointment or unrest, since nothing beyond the status quo was promised or expected. They were not lacking in ambition to better themselves, there simply was no avenue for the average family to pursue a better life. In Scotland, a man's place was a man's place, *born to till the earth, the earth ye till until ye die.*

The towns of Edinburgh and Glasgow had greater populations and their residents held allegiances to no laird, but the housing was little better and the residents were no less filthy or poverty-stricken than their rural counterparts whose farms occupied the higher ground between bogs and marshes. Lacking the knowledge to drain the standing water, tenants used the crudest of instruments to till the rocky hillsides. It was generally understood that Scottish ground was not intended for farming, and accounts imply a simple acceptance of that as fact. The majority of lowland Scots never saw a prosperous farm, and grew traditional crops such as barley and a grain called gray oats—which were believed to be the only suitable crops for the poor Scottish soil—although both crops had long been abandoned by farmers in other parts of the world as unsatisfactory. During the rare season when a harvest was larger than normal, it was still of scant nutritional value. After completing the meager harvest, paying due to the landlord, and setting aside grain for next year's planting, little was left to allow them to survive the winter.

Traveling was not unheard of; there was a constant demand for soldiers and sailors in the service of European countries, and a large percentage of the lowland farmers spent at least some time as mercenaries. It was from these adventurers that the Scots could hear of the state of the world, and were able to make comparisons to their own frugal lives. They were tales of wealth and beauty that could be found beyond the Southern Uplands, the kind of which was only occasionally spotted throughout the Kingdom of the Scots, a softness that was clean to the touch, a healthy, living scent, that could be breathed in and exhaled. The stories they told became songs to which the villagers danced; tales became legends that were retold on cold winter nights, as families huddled in the sooty silence of an earthen shanty.

Even with knowledge of prosperity abroad, there was an implicit belief that the station of the Scot was determined, and the latter day notions of ambition and aspirations to a higher class were simply concepts to which the Scots had never been introduced. The feudal system introduced into Scotland in the twelfth century was the only social structure known to the lowlanders, who lived and died on the same lands as their ancestors.

Most of the niceties that their European contemporaries enjoyed were objects of wonder to the lowlanders, who often were introduced to such items at the markets and traveling fairs, but were generally priced out of the reach of the common tenant farmer. Paper and glass were almost unknown in much of the country, and even such things as mortar were rarely used in the construction of the common structures.

The rolling hills were covered with grasses and peat, which managed to grow despite the rocky terrain. The Scottish Parliament forbade the cutting of trees, a law that was nearly impossible to break since the forests had long since disappeared under the axe. Lacking wood, the farmers had to establish shelters without boards or timbers; there were none to be burned for heat in the fire, none for the construction of chairs, and none in the walls. There was no cement to hold the rocks in place, so the wide gaps between the stones were filled with mud and straw and moss to keep out the wind. The floor was the bare earth. Bedding consisted of heather mats, and when the family gathered in the evening, they sat on the ground or on smooth stones. Each evening, a fire was built from peat or dried moss and it burned in the center of their single room; the smoke eventually found its way out an opening left in the turf that served as the roof. The grass roof would be checked regularly and when it was dried to the point that it was apt to burn, the tenant and his family rummaged for new stones or pulled down the old ones to build a new shelter, and used the remaining dried grasses and peat of the old house as fuel.

In a society without ready money, livestock was a dear possession and a constant chore for the tenant farmers. Given the scarcity of wood, there were no fences to pen the animals, and the tenant who owned a cow or pig would bring it inside the house to keep it from straying.

When the wail of the laird's horn sounded, the tenant-farmers were obliged to take up what arms they could find—usually rocks and stones—and assist in protecting the community from attack. Just as often, the call was for an attack on a neighboring laird, and although the tenants made for ragged troops, they were able to provide themselves a degree of protection. Animals were often carried off during the raids, and sometimes houses were pulled down. Retribution and vengeance regularly followed. As the farmer's most prized possessions, cattle were usually the subjects of the raids. Life in the south Lowlands of Scotland was difficult, and protecting the livestock and raiding the neighbors were among the few sources of local excitement.

Danger was a part of the raids, although the weapons used were crude, and often, less than deadly. Stones were thrown as the raiding party approached, and larger stones at close range could be used as clubs. With a scarcity of raw materials, effective weaponry was out of the reach of those in most communities and reserved for those well beyond the peasant class. Despite the primitive nature of their attack, men were often carried back home from the raids to sons and grieving wives, who buried them in graves beneath the rocky hillside. The danger involved brought an excitement that made the raids all the more appealing. There were few distractions in the lives of the villagers and the raids served that purpose well; as a result, there was little safety to be found anywhere in the Lowlands, except what the lairds and their tenant armies could provide.

Scotland was a land in constant turmoil, and not all was due to politics and feuds. The Black Death had ravaged the country on numerous occasions, dating back hundreds of years, and neither the Scottish parliament nor Queen Elizabeth could control the effects of poverty and crime. The government had little effect on the lairds, men sufficiently removed from any other authorities who held reign as though they were nobles. The Scottish Parliament made feeble attempts, but the laws they enacted had little actual effect on the farms, the tenants, or the simple lives of the commoners. The feudal system was well established and each Scot was born into his or her station. There was no middle class to speak of; nobility sired nobility, the lairds kept their lands, and the peasant farmers generally remained as such.

When Queen Elizabeth died in 1603, it ended her several attempts to bring the Scots and Irish into an alignment with English culture and politics. Although her troops managed individual victories, overall her intended policies met with little success; the clans of Ireland were no different than Scotland's Highlanders— and neither group tended farms nor were inclined to herd livestock. They spent their days fighting amongst themselves and preying upon others, taking what they needed to survive. There were exceptions in both countries, but as a rule, Ireland and Scotland were considered by the rest of the world to be lawless, poverty-stricken, hinterlands—visited only by the hardiest adventurers.

Despite the poverty, frequent illness, and constant threat of attack by neighboring lairds, the Scots were high-spirited, and laughter was heard regularly. On holidays, the musicians played their instruments and sang while the villagers danced and cheered. Times were hard, but their lot had been cast, and they made the best of their place in the accepted social order. It might be expected that the drudgery and common existence of the lowland Scots would beat them into a morose and despairing populace, but there is every indication that just the opposite was true. Accounts of the time indicate there was a general sense of happiness and a happy-go-lucky attitude, expressed in dance and song, as in a singing riddle transcribed by a contemporary.

> *I hov a young suster fer beyondyn the se;*
> *many be the drowryis that sche sente me.*
> *Sche sente me the cherye withoutyn ony ston,*
> *and so sche dede the dowe withoutyn ony bon.*
> *Sche sente me the storye withoutyn ony ende;*
> *and so sente the babye withoutyn ony cryen.*
>
> *How schulde ony cherye be withoute ston?*
> *How schulde ony dowe be withoute bon?*
> *How schulde ony storye be withoute ende?*
> *How schulde ony babye be withoute cryen?*
>
> *Quan the cherye was a flour than hadde it non ston;*
> *Quan the dowe was on egge it hadde no bon.*
> *The storye of aere love schall havyn non end;*
> *The babye quan sleepye than hadde no cryen.*

Cherries without stones, dove without bone, story without end, baby without crying—lyrics to typical puzzle verses sung by the Lowlanders. The fact that the tenant farmers had occasion to sing at all came as a surprise to many of the adventurers who returned from excursions into the wilds of Scotland. *Cherries without stones*, and celebrations without cause.

Shortly before the death of Queen Elizabeth, the Catholic Church, which had been firmly entrenched all across Europe, was shaken by a series of religious reformers. In Scotland, the greatest figure in the Reformation was John Knox, and he had awakened the sleeping minds of the lowlanders with his message of change. The change brought with it at least a spiritual desire among lowlanders to better themselves and to make better lives for their children. Changes in the politics and changes in the church were bringing out words from men who had never thought to speak their minds; there were discussions of matters that had never been discussed, the lives of men and women, their place and purpose, their religion, and their education. To be sure, there were still fights among the lairds and there were occasions to defend themselves against the Highlanders, who were still completely and happily mired in medieval times. For the lowlanders though, the doors of civilization were about to be thrown wide open. Beckoning from beyond the threshold was King James, who called to the Scots to join his "planting" of Ireland.

While the Scots lived in virtual isolation from the rest of the world, they were no further removed than their Irish neighbors. For five hundred years, the English had tried to introduce their brand of civilization to the Irish, never with much success. At various times, lands were given to Englishmen in hopes that their influence would tame the Irish, who wanted nothing to do with the English or English ways. Invariably, British settlers took up the Irish cause, as well as Irish customs and, more often than not, even their accent.

Ireland was divided into four kingdoms; the northernmost was Ulster, ruled by Tyrone and Tyrconnell, two clan leaders who joined in a revolt against the English that lasted eight years. In 1603, just before the death of Queen Elizabeth, the two clan leaders were finally subdued and fled Ireland. Their lands—some three million acres—were declared escheated, or forfeited, and ownership reverted to the English Crown.

King James ascended the throne in 1603, and immediately recognized an opportunity to at last bring Ireland into the realm. He issued an edict that granted land to English and Scottish lords and landed gentry, with instructions that any colonization would be by Protestant subjects, and not the "mere Irish." Not all the land was suitable, but in 1609, nearly a quarter of a million acres was made available for colonization.

The Scots were extended the invitation through the Scottish Privy Council, which related that the King, out of his "unspeikable love and tindir affectioun" for his Scottish subjects, would allow them to apply for a land grant. The offer was of special benefit to Scots, the edict continued, since their homes "lye so neir to that coiste of Ulster." There were others who thought the King's generosity had a more practical aspect, among them, Stewart of Donaghdee, a Presbyterian minister.

"The king had a natural love to have Ireland planted with Scots," he said. "Beside their loyalty, of a middle temper, between the English trader and the Irish rude breeding,…a great deal more like to adventure to plant Ulster than the English."

Never before had such an opportunity been presented to the humble farmers. Before the invitation to join the "Great Plantation" of King James, few Scotsmen had left their homeland; emigration involved huge risks and a financial consideration beyond the reach of most Scots. In considering a move to Ulster, the risk was greatly diminished and the land was practically free. A Scotsman could take his chance in the new country, knowing that he could send for his family if all went well, and if it didn't, it was only a short boat ride back home.

The Presbyterian movement that swept through Scotland, coincided with the Reformation in England which established the Anglican Church as the official religion of that land. Only Ireland remained under the influence of the Roman Catholic Church, and King James saw the "Great Plantation" as an opportunity to transplant Protestantism there. It would be a chance for the English to finally draw Ireland into the fold. For the desperate Scots, it represented a long denied avenue to improve their lives. The "Great Plantation" of Ireland would benefit everyone—except the Irish.

The colonization of Ulster, the northernmost of the kingdoms of Ireland, was a tremendous success. Six months after the offering was made, seventy-seven Lowlanders asked to colonize. By 1611, that number had been reduced to fifty-nine, who were accepted as colonists, and were awarded over 80,000 acres. Those awarded the lands were called "undertakers," and to cultivate, they recruited men from Scotland, and more than a few Irishmen joined in the settlement, although the King had expressly forbidden it.

For many Scottish families, the lands of Ulster now represented a lifeline to survival, since Scottish lairds had begun a practice that required the payment of a rental fee—or feu—along with a share of the harvest. Many of the tenant farmers were unable to raise the money. Dispossessed of their homes, they gathered family and livestock to leave the lands farmed for generations by their ancestors. They could find another farm on Scottish soil even thinner and more rock-laden than what they had left, or consider crossing the North Channel.

It was not a tough decision. Word spread quickly of the early successes of the Plantation. Food was cheap, the soil was rich, and livestock flourished. Men could determine their own destinies in Ulster, and not be a victim of the whims of the laird. By the time the stories had been repeated often enough, even those who had not been evicted felt the lure of the King's Plantation.

Drawn too were the Covenanters and their neighbors. When the English Crown tried to change the Presbyterian faith in Scotland to bring it more in line with the Church of England, a group of traditionalists—the Covenanters—had rebelled. Although most Scottish Presbyterians had little or no difficulty accepting the changes, the Covenanters simply refused. They began meeting in the woods to practice their faith and when the Crown sent soldiers to hunt them down, the Covenanters battled fiercely. Some Scots who lived nearby opted to get away from the fighting and try a new start in Ulster. Eventually, the Covenanters were defeated, and thousands of them joined their countrymen in crossing the channel for Ulster.

Soon, there was a steady stream of families waiting to make the crossing. The villagers gathered their few belongings and their animals and made their way to the coast, where boats carried them to Ulster. In addition to inviting the Scots, King James offered land to his English subjects as well. They were fewer in number but as they arrived and began tilling the soil, the Scots learned from their English neighbors how to drain the bogs and reveal the rich soil beneath the plains. The lands worked by the Scotsmen in Ulster proved to be successful enterprises almost immediately, and the good news brought subsequent waves of immigrants to the Irish colony. There were no more gray oats. The English farmers shared a South American crop brought back by Sir Walter Raleigh called the potato. Eventually, the Ulster harvest was so bountiful that it became a staple not only in Ulster, but also over all of Ireland and was referred to as the "Irish Potato." Early American colonists knew little or nothing of the crop until the Scots-Irish immigrants introduced it in 1718.

The early success of the Ulster Plantation allowed men to bring their families to join them, and communities began forming; as more families made settlements, the Scot's new-found need for religious teaching required the establishment of churches. Presbyterian ministers in Scotland saw the opportunity for new congregations and made the move as well. For the Scotsman and his family in Ireland—the *Scotch-Irish,* or *Scots-Irish*—religious devotion took on a fervor that had never before been experienced, anywhere in the world. Presbyterianism was not only the official religion of Scotland, it had also become a central point in the lives of the countrymen. Presbyterianism became the focus of the common man; it was the source for conversation and inspiration among neighbors and families. Church meetings lasted all day, and some members of the congregations traveled more than a day to attend services. To read the teachings—and increasingly—to prepare young men for the ministry, public schools were formed. Those Scots who moved to Ulster continued in their newfound desire for education, as did their descendants who emigrated to America, and brought with them their religion. The Presbyterian churches, schools, and colleges, were among the first founded in the American colonies.

A home in Ulster was very near paradise for the former tenant farmers. For protection from the "wild Irish," leases required the Scottish settlers to build a house for themselves and a "bawn" for the livestock. Compared to their grass and dirt structures in Scotland, a family home in Ulster was nothing short of a castle. Built of rock, the houses not only consisted of several rooms, but several stories as well. As homes of the new Ulstermen began to dot the landscape, their construction styles began to favor those of the English. Although the homes of Scotsmen generally lacked amenities such as artwork or decorative landscaping, they were solid structures, and comparable to those of the English. In the early days of the Ulster Plantation, cattle and sheep were herded into the bawn each night, to guard against theft and predatory animals.

Wolves roaming the Irish countryside proved to be one of the primary dangers of the new homeland. Unlike the Lowlands, much of Ulster was forested, and farms nearest the woods were in constant danger of losing livestock. Men were paid a bounty of six pounds for the killing of each female wolf, a practice that was continued for decades, and by the time the bounty was discontinued the wolf population in Ireland had been completely eliminated.

The other danger to the Ulstermen also lay hidden in the forests. Few of the "wild Irish" were allotted lands in their own or other Irish counties, and as a result, most of the original tenants were dispossessed of their homes. They were forced to flee into the woods, and the Scots called them widcairns, or wood-kerns; men who had no lands to farm and were forced to live by raiding the farms of colonists. Like that offered for the head of a wolf, bounties were placed on the capture of widcairns and many were simply shot without the benefit of a trial. In later years, the practice was changed to allow captured widcairns to leave the country rather than face execution for their alleged crimes.

In spite of the difficulties caused by living in the midst of hostile Irish, Scotsmen continued to pour into Ulster. In ten year's time, fifty thousand Scots and Englishmen had settled the counties of Northern Ireland. Before 1670, there were more than twenty families named Houston, a dozen of which were located in County Antrim alone, where a grant could include "all that 18 score acres of land in Ballygally." David Houston, of County Antrim, had entered the Presbyterian ministry, and by 1689, he had developed a sizable congregation so fervent in its following that they became known as "Houstonites." He preached through Counties Antrim, Down, and Londonderry until just before his death in 1696.

There were Scot families named Gay, who pronounced their name Guy, as well as families named Hamilton, Campbell, Cunningham, Anderson, Wilson, McDonald, McClung, McKee, and McGinnis, among the numerous others who joined those tilling the rich Ulster soil. The Scots-Irish who were among the earliest settlers in parts of Lancaster County, Pennsylvania are those whose 100 years leases had come due in the first years after 1710, including Allen, Allison, Anderson, Bailey, Baston, Bayley, Beach, Bealey, Black, Blazer, Bringham, Brown, Brownlow, Bryan, Buchanan, Buey, Campbell, Clark, Cloud, Cook, Couch, Cunningham, Davison, Doaks, Dunning, Galbraith, Gardner, Hairston, Harris, Howard, Hutchinson, Inless, Kelley, Kyle, Lowrey, Maris, Mayfort, McFarland, McKee, Middleton,

Mitchell, Monday, Moore, Scott, Smith, Sterret, Stewart, Taylor, Walker, White, Wilkins, Wood, and Work. Many of the Scots-Irish surnames have Anglo-Saxon origins, attributed to early settlers in the lowlands and Northumberland by men of those races. Among the English who weathered the hardships of starting anew in Ireland were the Stephensons; many others from the English settlements found life too difficult compared to the life they had left behind.

The successes of the colonists increased as well. Sheep were well suited to the fields of Northern Ireland, and the residents learned the art of making a woolen cloth. The manufacture of the cloth became so widespread that in a short time, it became a product for export. No longer were men forced to work the land; trades became an important aspect of the many communities. They became shoemakers and sheriffs, tailors and planters. Where ambition had previously held no opportunity for fulfillment, the transplanted Scots found in Ulster more opportunities than they could have imagined. Crops did well, livestock prospered, communities and churches flourished, and the woolen exports even provided an income.

The Scots in Ulster emerged from medieval subsistence farmers to citizens of a civilized society, involved in education and commercial enterprise—whose children would never again suffer the aimless distractions of an unfulfilled life—and had done it all within the span of a single generation.

For almost one hundred years the colonists of Ulster lived increasingly productive lives, with only occasional and temporary setbacks. What had been a barren wilderness in 1610 when the lands were opened had been transformed by the industry of the Scots into a contemporary civilization. While lacking some of softer aspects of other European cultures, it was cosmopolitan in comparison to the near-barbaric existence on the Scottish Lowlands.

It may have been their very success that contributed to the demise of life in Ulster for the transplanted Scots.

In the early 1700's, there had already been some discussion of America among the families of Ulster. They colonized once already, and it had proven greatly beneficial. Numerous reports of prosperity in America had made their way across the Atlantic, and the lure was strong enough to lead some to abandon Ulster during some of the early hard times. By 1717, men from Ulster, as well as a few from Scotland, including some who had been transported after the highlands uprising, were present all the American colonies. It was that year the "Great Migration" from Ulster began.

England had placed restrictions on the importation of Irish goods as early as 1671, in an effort to lessen competition. It had some effect on the Ulster trade industry, but it was a series of droughts in the early 1700's that brought the flourishing economy to a halt. For six straight years, beginning in 1714, the lack of adequate rainfall ruined crops and the cost of food among townspeople became exorbitant.

Another English restriction on Ulster, the Test Act of 1703, was designed to force compliance with the Church of England. Under the Act, Presbyterians, along with Irish Roman Catholics, were forbidden to hold a place in the Irish Parliament, or civil or military office. Presbyterian ministers were subjected to legal proceedings if they did not cease their actions, and Ulster children lost educations provided by the religious-based teachers. Historical scholars of the Church of England described the Test Act set forth by Queen Anne as unjustly bigoted.

The greatest cause of emigration however, was the practice termed "rack-renting." Most of the leases in Ulster were fairly long term, and had been renewed throughout the 1600's without much change. When they came due by the thousands in the early 1700's, landlords seized an opportunity to charge more for lands that had increased greatly in value, often giving leases to the highest bidder. The Scotsmen, who had brought about the increased value through their own enterprise, were reluctant to pay the higher rents. Often, the highest bidder was a group of native-Irish, who pooled their resources to acquire better lands, forcing the Scots from their homes. Once dispossessed, the Scots could either return to their native Scotland or make the crossing to America. When the first groups crossed the Atlantic—sometimes entire congregations at a time—word of their safe arrival and successes on the American shores opened the floodgates to a massive departure from the land of Ulster in Northern Ireland.

CHAPTER TWO

Across The Atlantic

FOR THOSE ULSTER FAMILIES WHO CHOSE to leave the North of Ireland for an uncertain future in the New World, there were similarities with those situations facing their grandfathers and great-grandfathers who departed Scotland for the Great Plantation of King James. One of the great differences was the financial condition of this second generation of emigrants. Where the lowland Scots were destitute and without significant possessions upon their arrival in Ireland, their descendants heading for America were faced with limitations on the amount baggage they could load upon the Atlantic bound ships. Having successfully brought themselves into an industrious economic situation, the Scots in Ireland were no longer penniless peasants struggling to survive. In some industries, such as the wool and linen trade, the Ulstermen had placed themselves among the contenders in the world market. Not all who departed Ireland for America were wealthy, but neither were they all struggling. There are accounts of entire congregations of Ulster Presbyterians who departed as a group for the colonies of America.

In most cases, each passenger was allowed to bring aboard a single trunk free of charge, and anything more was weighed to determine the appropriate surcharge. Some families disposed of their possessions by selling to their Ulster neighbors, assuming they could buy whatever replacement supplies and possessions as would be required, once arrived in America.

Accommodations for passage included payments by cash, and barter, as well as indentured servitude, in which the cost of passage was worked off in the service of those providing payment. Some indentures lasted years, but generally ended with some promise of payment at completion, in cash or land. They offered themselves as servants to those already in America, in exchange for their fare. Not all indentured servants lacked money for passage; some had simply chosen to save the fare and learn the ways of the new land under the protection and tutelage of a sponsor, intending to buy land with the money once their service was completed. Some who had neither money nor travel intentions found their way aboard the ships as well. Those ship captains lacking in scruples found an easy source of money by bringing to the American colonies a steady supply of indentured servants. The labor needs on some of the larger plantations were so great that landowners regularly met incoming ships, anticipating there would be men and women on board seeking to trade their services for the price of their passage. A young Scotsman watching the bustle of activity along the harbor might be offered a tour of the ship—a rare chance to see inside the hold of the mighty vessel, and sample the spirits in the sailor's flask. Once on board, the young man would be knocked out—either by the alcohol or the truncheon—then trussed, and tossed below. By the time he awakened, the ship was well at sea, the young man effectively kidnapped after being overcome by alcoholic spirits, a practice that coined the phrase "spirited away."

So great was the demand for passage to America, that some families hoped to avoid the delays at Belfast by traveling to Port Rush or Londonderry. There were ships to be boarded at Larne and Newry, as well. Those who would take their families through the South of Ireland might find passage at Dublin and Cork. Their destination was the same—the colonies of America, and more likely than not, Philadelphia.

Among the wills recorded in 1723 at Forseighan, in the Northern Ireland county of Armagh, was that of one William Houston, who in his dictation mentions his wife Jean, sons David, Hugh, John, William, and Richard, and daughters Mary and Jean. Those same names appear as early landholders in Pennsylvania and North Carolina in the Scot-Irish tracts, and are representative of those Scots, lately of Ireland, who departed for the chance at a new life.

———

In Philadelphia, the steadily arrival of so many ships and so many passengers had already caught the attention of colonists and the newspapers. The Pennsylvania Gazette carried word of the migration by way of a letter written by Robert Gambie of Londonderry and extracted from a London newspaper. Before the Great Migration ended around 1775, nearly a quarter of a million Ulster residents had arrived in America.

The voyage from Ulster took more than eight treacherous weeks, and the long cramped voyage was simply too much for some of the passengers. For most, it was simply another episode that served to firm their resolve, and toughen their spirits.

Packed into the holds of the sailing ships, there was plenty of time for the passengers to imagine their destination. The American colony had been opened to settlement just three years before the lands of Ulster were opened to Scots. King James had allowed a company of private investors to migrate to the lands that later became Virginia, a settlement founded in 1607 that was named Jamestown. To the north, the Massachusetts Bay Company had followed shortly after the arrival of Pilgrims in 1620, the first of numerous settlements along the northern coastlines of the new colony.

By 1717, when a fourth straight drought had ruined the crops in Ulster, colonists in America were avidly seeking others to join them. William Penn was among those who advertised and even journeyed abroad to find suitable residents for the province being settled. The majority of the eastern parts of the colonies had been settled for over one hundred years, primarily, but not exclusively, by the English. Both the British Crown and colonial land speculators were happy to accommodate those who could help fill the western lands and stem the expansion of the Spanish and French colonies in America. The Scots-Irish had been present in the colonies as early as 1649 and a Presbyterian church had been established in American as early as 1695, but the mass immigration of Ulstermen began in 1717.

Among those leaving Ulster in the early part of the eighteenth century were those most affected by the hard times. Others, who might have simply tightened their belts as a result of the diminished economy, left the North of Ireland as a matter of pride. Across the Atlantic, it was said, a man could own his home and his farmland, and not be subjected to the whims of a landlord.

Most of the Presbyterian Ulstermen hoped to establish small farms, and communities in which to establish new churches in the American colony. Since the Virginia and Carolina coastal settlements were already firmly established as Anglican slave-holding plantations, the first immigrants from Ulster landed primarily at destinations further north. Maryland and New York were both primarily plantation colonies as well, and not considered suitable destinations. A number of early Scots-Irish settlers wound up in parts of Maryland, but as more and more Scotch-Irish arrived in New England, the early welcome they had received eventually diminished to a point where ships bound from Ireland simply traveled up the Delaware River to Pennsylvania ports. There the Scots-Irish found a more sincere welcome.

In his advertisements, William Penn boasted of the wonderful climate of the province, the rich soil, its beneficial geographic location, and a religious tolerance. In 1681, Penn had advised those who were considering his invitation, to consider the expense involved:

> *"...they must either work themselves, or be able to imploy others. A Winter goes before a Summer, and the first work will be Countrey Labour, to clear Ground, and raise Provision..."*

There were specific costs listed in his prospectus, *A Brief Account of the Province of Pennsylvania.*

> *1st. The Passage for Men and Women is Five Pounds a head, for Children under Ten Years Fifty Shillings, Sucking Children Nothing. For Freight of Goods Forty Shillings per Tun; but one Chest to every Passenger Free.*

The advertisement suggested a list of items for the journey, such as tools, building supplies, and clothing.

> *Lastly. Being by the Mercy of God safely arrived; be it in October, Two Men may clear as much Ground for Corn as usually bring by the following Harvest about Twenty Quarters; In the mean time they must buy Corn, which they may have as aforesaid; and if they buy them two Cows, and two Breeding Sows; with what the Indians for a small matter will bring in, of Fowl, Fish, and Venison (which is incredibly Cheap, as a Fat Buck for Two Shillings) that and their industry will supply them. It is apprehended, that Fifteen Pounds stock for each Man (who is first well in Cloaths, and provided with fit working Tools for Himself) will (by the Blessing of God) carry him thither, and keep him, till his own Plantation will Accomodate him. But all are most seriously cautioned, how they proceed in the disposal of themselves.*

By the time of the first massive migration of Scots-Irish, the British colonies had a thirty-year history of success. When the Scots-Irish arrived in Philadelphia, they found colonists living in homes of brick and mortar, complete with windows and sashes. Some, like Penn's own home, were comfortably, if not elaborately, furnished. The streets of Philadelphia were well planned, and accommodated sturdy homes, merchant's stores, and office buildings. The areas outside Philadelphia, on the other hand, were much less refined.

Along with his Quaker settlers, Penn had successfully lured Germans from the Rhinish Palatinate who were still impoverished from the German Thirty Year's War. They had founded Germantown as an early settlement in 1683 and spread westward through what became Chester (later Lancaster) County. They borrowed building methods from those who had proceeded them, constructing homes out of logs, to which they attached an exterior siding of boards, making the cabin appear less rustic. As the Germans became more comfortable in the province, many began replacing their log homes with houses built from stone or brick.

The brick homes of Philadelphia and the well-constructed log houses of the Germans would both be passed by the Scotch-Irish in their travels to the western lands of the province.

Those new arrivals whose passage would be repaid by terms of indentured servitude might stay in Philadelphia, and the established towns of the English and Germans. The majority of the immigrants would be pushed on to western lands, a practice that generally pleased both groups. The passive Quakers and the reserved English historically viewed the incoming Ulstermen as a race of wild troublemakers, a group better suited to living on the frontier, between themselves and the "Northward" Indians. The Scots-Irish immigrants had no objections; the lands along the western frontier of the Province were everything an Ulsterman could have dreamed; there was plenty of fertile soil, endless timber for construction, and a seemingly boundless supply of wild game, which seemed to guarantee that no family would ever go hungry.

Germans continued to immigrate during the same period as the Scots-Irish migration, and the settlement of the remaining Pennsylvania lands, as well as the rich valleys of Virginia and the Carolinas, documents the movement of two groups.

While the Germans and Scots-Irish became neighbors along the frontier, socially, the two could not have been more different. When the Germans built a house, they squared the timbers and constructed well-designed homes that were intended to last, which suited their desire for permanence. They were industrious, orderly and dealt well with the native tribes. The Scots-Irish, on the other hand, were content to build homes from the trunks of felled trees, notching the ends of the logs and filling the resulting gaps with clay or mud chinking as a primitive insulation against the winds. The former Ulstermen, perhaps due to the tenuous nature of holding a home site, dating back as their days in the Scottish lowlands, appear to have had a need to press onward. It was said that the Scots-Irish were never content until they had moved families and possessions several times. Socially, they were viewed as quick-tempered, given to whim, and less efficient in their farming habits; some only tilled the sunlit strips between the shades of trees. For whatever reason, the early Scots-Irish viewed the various native tribes as a single people, with no distinctions between the various Nations, a fact that led to confrontations with otherwise peaceful tribes. One such incident clearly demonstrated the impetuousness of the Scots-Irish in dealing with America's native population.

In 1763, during a particularly savage period of hostilities between Indians and colonists, a group of Scots-Irish in Paxtang township in Dauphin County believed a circulating rumor concerning a tribe living in adjoining Lancaster County. The Conestoga Indians had long been at peace with both the Germans and Scots-Irish who shared the lands of Lancaster County. The "Paxton Boys," as they came to be called, believed that the Conestogas had given secret aid to hostile tribes, and as in retribution, the Scots-Irish farmers took measures into their own hands, without waiting to test the validity of the rumor. Their raid on the settlement resulted in the brutal murder of twenty unsuspecting members of the Conestoga tribe. Ben Franklin eventually served as an arbiter to end the hostilities.

There were occasional feuds between the Scots-Irish and the Germans as well, but generally, they cohabited the American frontier with a tolerance for the other's presence.

The first significant settlement that was predominately Scots-Irish was on the eastern shore of Maryland, beginning in 1649. By 1682, there were five Presbyterian meetinghouses in Somerset and Calvert counties of Maryland. The accounts of those early Scots-Irish settlers in Maryland encouraged many Ulster acquaintances and family members to make plans to emigrate from Ireland to the American colony.

It has been estimated that between 1717 and 1718 more than five thousand Scots-Irish made the move to America. There were four subsequent waves of migration: 1725–29, 1740–41, 1754–55, and 1771–75. The numbers are not exact, but as many as fifteen thousand may have immigrated between 1725 and 1729, and by 1790, an estimated 454,000 Americans were immigrants from Northern Ireland, comprising over 14 percent of the total population.

———

An Ulsterman himself, James Logan was Secretary of the Pennsylvania Province. He had met William Penn while engaged in trade in Northern Ireland, and accepted an offer to become Penn's secretary. He was among the first to extend an invitation to his Scots-Irish countrymen to move to the Pennsylvania province, but after a time, he became disenchanted with the idea of bringing more Irish. He was not alone in having a change of heart regarding the Ulstermen.

While the Quakers had little interest in local politics, the Scots-Irish were quick to take up the political cause, and by strength of their numbers alone were viewed as a threat to the status quo. Logan's perception of his Scots-Irish countrymen as men who had "bravely defended Londonderry," led him to believe that, as a group, they were well suited to live nearest the "Northern Indians." His perception eventually changed. Ten years after the Scots-Irish were given lands in Chester County, Logan noted his belief that five Scots-Irish could cause him more trouble than fifty other men. For a time after 1729, Logan refused to issue land patents to the Scots-Irish, but his denial of legal deeds only served to compound the problems.

Many of the Scots-Irish settlers viewed the land as free for the taking, a wilderness that could be rightfully claimed by the mere construction of a homestead on a piece of property. Some indentured servants who had fulfilled their obligation and were free to seek land of their own were not inclined to spend whatever money they had saved to buy land, when so many others were establishing claims through "squatters rights." Logan estimated in 1726 that those with no rightful claim had settled over one hundred thousand acres of the frontier.

There were attempts by officials in Philadelphia to enforce legal settlement of lands; cabins were sometimes burned as a show of force and to set an example. It had little effect; as their ancestors in Scotland had done, the squatters simply rebuilt. Some of the many British subjects in the colonies preferred allowing the Scots-Irish to remain on their illegally obtained lands, which would keep them from returning to Philadelphia and other settled communities. In the early days, many viewed the Scots-Irish as class that would make less than desirable neighbors, given their Presbyterianism religion and the unpredictable nature of their temperament.

Illegal squatters constituted only a portion of the Scots-Irish colonists. Donegal, the Pennsylvania settlement named for their home county in Northern Ireland, was filled with deeded Scots-Irish landowners. The area that constitutes present-day Lancaster County was divided ostensibly between Germans in the north, and the deeded Scots-Irish in the south. Provincial papers from Chester County list the sale of 200 acres of land to William Stephenson in 1734. Others in the Donegal region of present-day Lancaster County included a great many Scots-Irish who settled the area in the early part of the eighteenth century.

1716: Robert Middleton

1717: John Stewart and George Stewart

1718: Peter Allen, Robert Buchanan and William Buchanan, William Bryan, Thomas Bayley, Henry Bealey, James Galbraith and John Galbraith, John Gardner, James Mitchell, Samuel Smith, John Sterret, Robert, Thomas, William Wilkins and John Wilkins

1720: Patrick Campbell, James Cunningham, Joseph Cloud, James Couch, Daniel Clark, Widow Dunning, John Mitchell, Thomas Mitchell, Ephraim Moore, James Smith, and Joseph Work

1721: John Taylor

1722: Robert Allison, James Allison, John Allison, Gordon Howard, Thomas Howard, Alexander Hutchison, William Maybee, Richard McFarland, Robert Monday, John Maris, James Kyle, and Hugh White

1723: John Miller

1724: Thomas Black, William Beach, John Black, Robert Brown, John Davison, John Doaks, Christian Gardner, John Walker and Michael Wood

1725: Jeremiah Bringham, Matthias Blazer, James Brownlow, Abraham Inless, Hugh Scott

1726: Rev. James Anderson, Joseph Baston, James Harris, Alexander McKee, George Mayfort

1729: Lazarus Lowrey, James Lowrey, John Lowrey, Daniel Lowrey, and Alexander Lowrey

1730: James Buey, James Cook, Peter Hairston, James Hutchison, John Kelley, William Mitchell, Alexander Mitchell, Thomas Scott, and John Scott

On the east side of the Elk River, in Cecil County, in present-day Maryland, there were four deeded Alexander families near New Munster. By 1740, Alexanders in Cecil County included James, William, Moses, Nathaniel, John, Joseph, David, and Theophilus Alexander, many of whom moved to Lancaster County in Pennsylvania. The families of the Alexanders and the Stephensons contributed greatly to the number of people who pushed onward from the middle colonies into the Shenandoah Valley and the Carolinas.

William Stephenson, like many of the Scotch-Irish, had a large family, and there were few families that contributed a greater number of persons to the southward movement. William and his family were among the early Ulster emigrants; records of Cecil County, Maryland indicate they had settled on the eastern shore of that colony as early as 1672. Recalling that spellings of surnames were not standardized at the time, deeds were recorded by Scots-Irish settlers as Stevenson and Stephenson, and as Houston and Huston. The proximity of early land grants served to intertwine the lives of many Scots-Irish, as was the case with all colonists in areas of difficult geography. In many colonial era families, brothers and sisters of one family often found spouses in the homes of those living nearest.

The Houston families began arriving in America in 1729, about the time Lancaster County was formed from part of Chester County, Pennsylvania. David Houston was among those who took up residence first in Pennsylvania around 1929, who later migrated south to the Carolinas and Virginia. Another was John Houston, who arrived in 1735, and whose great-grandson Sam became President of the Republic of Texas, and the namesake of a city in that state. Accompanying John and his wife Margaret were six of their seven children, and John's widowed mother. James, their eldest child, had remained in Ulster to continue his studies. Other branches of the Houston family, among those originating in the Scottish lowlands, included Christopher and Samuel, who settled nearby in the Cumberland valley area, while William Huston settled in Connecticut around the same period.

Most of the Scots-Irish in Pennsylvania had been farmers in Ulster, and sought farmland when they arrived in Penn's province. In the earliest advertisements, colonists were offered five thousand acres for one hundred pounds. A renter could have fifty acres for a penny an acre. Prices escalated as the desirable lands became scarce.

There were those who took up new vocations. The Morrison family, including brothers William, Hugh, Andrew, and James, arrived in Pennsylvania with their father James in 1730. William and Hugh found homes in Nantmeal township in Chester County, and then later moved along with the other brothers, to Lancaster County. There, in Colerain township, William became prosperous serving as a tax collector.

The Cumberland Valley was one of the more attractive spots for the Scots-Irish settlers, and by 1734 so many had located there that Samuel Blunston of Wright's Ferry was given permission to sell land licenses to a limited number of pioneers. David Houston applied for a land grant in the Valley, and was awarded 320 acres in 1737. Although the land was fertile and the beautiful Cumberland

Valley made for attractive home sites, it was a difficult time for settlement. The Scots-Irish found themselves caught in a border disagreement between the provinces of Maryland and Pennsylvania, where the sheriff of Baltimore County at one point invaded Lancaster County with a force of two hundred men. The five-year dispute caused many of those living in the area to abandon their homesteads and move onward to the south and west.

The Blunston land grant awarded to David Houston is typical of those awarded the other settlers in the Cumberland Valley.

By the Proprietaries.

WHEREAS David Houston of the County of Lancaster hath requested that we would grant him to take up Three Hundred and twenty Acres of Land situated on the Western Sides of Clouds Creek Branch of the Conococheague opposite to the Lower Sides of John Black's Tract in Hopowell's Township in the said County of Lancaster for which He agrees to pay to our Use at the Rate of Fifteen Pounds Ten Shillings current money of this Province for one Hundred Acres, and the yearly Quit-rent of one Half-penny Sterling for every Acre thereof; THESE are therefore to authorize and require thee to survey or cause to be survey'd unto the said David Houston at the Place aforesaid, according to the method of Townships appointed, and said quantity of 370 Acres, if not already survey'd or appropriated, to make Return thereof unto the Secretary's Office, in order for further Confirmation; for which this shall be sufficient Warrant; which survey, in case the said David Houston fulfill the above Agreement within six Months from the Date hereof, shall be valid, otherwise void. GIVEN under my Hand, and the letter Seal of our Province, at Philadelphia, this 1st Day of March, Anno Dom. 1737.

David Houston settled on Conococheague Creek and erected a "dwelling-house" not far from the homesteads of John Beard, John Harris, and John Black. William McDowell was granted land on the northwest branch of the creek, and built his home there. On nearby Yellow Breeches Creek were settlements that included Francis Beatty, James Crawford, John Morgan, Morgan Morgan, John McWhorter, John Rankin, and William Robinson. James Cathey received a warrant for land on Conodoguinet Creek, as did William Cathey, Alexander Cathey, John Lawrence, Archibald Cathey, James Woods, Isaac Davenport, William Docharty, James Forster, John Potts, John Hunter, John Jones, William Ralston, and Reverend John Thompson.

David Houston and those settling on the Conococheague could attend Presbyterian services at the East Conococheague, or Rocky Spring Church, which was established along with five others in the Cumberland Valley between 1734 and 1740.

Before the end of the decade, the Scots-Irish farms were well established in the

Cumberland valley. Rough farmhouses would have gained some amenities and comforts over time, although situated as they were on the frontier, a man and his family had to be constantly alert, and ready to deal with whatever new situation might arise. The latest news of the day was generally passed along by those traveling south on what was called the Philadelphia Wagon Road or the Great Wagon Road.

By the time news of a war between England and France had reached the Cumberland valley, the French troops had already begun moving against some of the English settlements. Governor Shirley of Massachusetts requested help from England, and also issued pleas for support from the other colonies. The Scots-Irish in the Cumberland had large families depending on them for survival, and New England was a long way from their location on frontier farms. A treaty was signed between the French and English in 1748, ending King George's War, but the resulting peace lasted only a year.

Officials in Pennsylvania were constantly remaking deals with the resident native tribes in an effort to offset the encroachment of colonists onto lands conceded to be traditional grounds of various Nations. In 1749, the French began posting signs through the Ohio Valley, some near Pennsylvania, in attempt to establish their ownership.

France owned Canada and claimed the Ohio and Mississippi valleys, and viewed the expansion of English settlers as violations of their right of ownership. The British considered the French as a threat to increase their holdings on the continent. Meanwhile, the colonists were only concerned with the safety of their settlements, and the threat of attacks by Indians who were doing most of the French fighting.

By 1753, word was received that the French were using alliances with Indians and convinced them to attack English settlements beyond the Alleghenies. Later that year, there were several raids on settlements in Pennsylvania. It was the beginning of ten years of fighting in the colonies between the French and the British, both trying to establish colonial territory boundaries. The fighting between colonists and Indians, allied with the French, would eventually extend into the valleys of Virginia and the backcountry of North Carolina inhabited by the Scots-Irish

Among the early settlers of the Rowan County tract in the area that comprises south central portions of present-day North Carolina were both Scots-Irish and Germans, although the area was considered predominately Scots-Irish.

––––

Documented Early Settlers: Rowan Co. Scots-Irish Tract

Aaronhart, George	Arand, Jacob	Barkley, Henry
Aaronhart, John	Armstrong, Abel	Barkley, Robert
Adams, John	Armstrong, Mary	Barkley, Samuel
Agenda, John	Armstrong, Richard	Barr, Hugh
Agender, John	Armstrong, Robert	Barr, John
Agoner, Henry Sr	Armstrong, Samuel	Barr, Patrick
Agoner, Henry Jr	Armstrong, William	Barr, William
Ainsley, Alexander	Arndt, Godfrey	Barringer, J
Albright, John	Aron, Peter	Barringer, Paul
Albright, Michael	Aronhart, Phillip	Barringer, Peter
Alexander, Evan	Arrant, Conrad	Bartley, John
Alexander, James	Baker, A	Bashford, Thomas
Alexander, William	Baker, Absolom	Basinger, George
Allen, Bartley	Baker, Benjamin	Basinger, John
Allison, Andrew	Baker, Christopher	Beam, Jacob
Allison, James	Baker, Elizabeth	Beam, John
Allison, Mary	Baker, John,	Bear, Henry
Allison, Thomas	Baker, John Jr	Beard, John
Anderson, David	Baker, Joseph	Beard, John L.
Anderson, Isaac	Baley, Charles	Beard, Lewis
Anderson, James	Barne, John	Beard, M.A.
Anderson, Richard	Barbarick, Christian	Beard, Valentine
Anderson, Samuel	Barber, Elias	Beaty, Charles
Anderson, William	Barber, Jonathin	Beaty, Francis
Andrew, James	Barber, Luke	Beaty, Thomas
Andrews, James	Barber, William	Beaver, Daniel

Beaver, David
Beaver, Michael
Beaver, Nicholas
Beaver, Paul
Beaver, Peter
Beefle, Martin
Bell, Robert
Bell, Thomas
Bellah, Moses
Berger, George H.
Berger, Michael
Best, John
Betts, Andrew
Bettz, Andrew
Bettz, George,
Biles, Charles
Biles, Joseph
Biles, Thomas
Bird, John
Bird, Michael
Blackwelder, John
Blake, Hugh
Blake, John
Blue, Malcomb
Blythe, James
Blythe, Samuel
Bonachom, Michael
Boone, Jonathan
Bostian, Andrew
Bostian, Andrew Sr
Bostian, Jacob
Bostian, Jonas
Bostian, Methais
Boston, Michael
Bowman, James
Bowman, William
Brady, John
Braley, John
Braley, Thomas
Braley, William
Brandon, Alexander
Brandon, James
Brandon, John

Brandon, Richard
Brandon, Thomas
Brandon, William
Brazill, William
Brazle, William
Brem, Conrad
Bringle, Nicholas
Broner, Henry
Brougher, Jacob
Brown, Abraham
Brown, Andrew
Brown, Elisha
Brown, Henry
Brown, Jacob
Brown, John
Brown, Jonas
Brown, Leonard
Brown, Michael
Brown, Michael Sr
Brown, Peter
Brown, Samuel
Brown, Thomas
Brown, Timothy Sr
Brown, William
Bruner, George
Bruner, Phillip
Brunner, George
Bryan, John
Buck, Charles
Buckannon, James
Buis, Henry
Bullen, Conrad
Bullen, George
Bullen, John
Bullen, Phillip
Bullin, John
Buntin, James
Buntin, John
Buntin, Robert
Buntine, James
Buntine, John
Buntine, Robert
Buris, Edward

Burrage, John
Burns, John
Burrage, Edward
Burrage, George
Burroughs, Townsend
Butler, Adam
Butler, Harmon
Butner, David
Buyers, Richard
Caldwell, David
Callaway, Joseph
Campbell, John
Campbell, Joseph
Campbell, Matthew
Campbell, Patrick
Carlisle, Robert
Carn, Conrad
Carr, Andrew
Carruth, Adam
Carruth, James
Carruth, Robert
Carruth, Walter
Carson, Henry
Carson, James
Carson, John
Carson, Thomas
Carson, William L.
Carter, James
Casper, Adam
Casper, Peter
Caster, Jacob
Caster, John
Cathey, Alexander
Cathey, Andrew
Cathey, George
Cathey, Hugh
Cathey, James
Cathey, Jane
Cathey, John
Cathey, William
Cauble, Peter
Cever, Jacob
Chambers, David

Chambers, Henry
Chambers, Joseph
Chambers, Maxwell
Christman, John
Chunn, Thomas
Clary, Daniel
Clary, David
Clary, John
Clary, Sarah
Clingman, Alexander
Cluts, David
Clutz, Jacob
Clutz, Jacob, Sr.
Cobble, John
Coble, Adam
Coble, Michael
Coble, Peter
Cochran, Andrew
Cochran, James
Cochran, John
Cochran, Robert
Cohen, John
Coldiron, Conrad
Coldiron, George
Coleman, Jacob
Coles, WilliamT
Collins, James
Collins, Thomas
Cook, Alexander
Cook. Thomas
Cooke, Alexander
Cooke, James
Coon, Antony
Cooper, Samuel
Copple, Peter
Correll, Jacob
Correll, John
Correll, John A.
Correll, Peter
Correll, Phillip
Corriher, Daniel
Cosby, William
Coughenour, Christian

Coughenour, John
Coughman, Leonard
Cowan, Benjamin
Cowan, David
Cowan, Henry
Cowan, Isaac
Cowan, John
Cowan, Robert
Cowan, Thomas
Cowan, William
Cowan, William Jr.
Cowan, William Sr
Craig, David
Craig, James
Craig, John
Craiglow, William
Crawford, Jacob
Creglon, William
Criter, Leonard
Croos, Phillip
Crowell, Teater
Cruse, Phillip
Culbertson, John
Culbertson, Samuel
Culp, Adam
Culp, Henry
Cummings, Michael
Cunningham, Humphrey
Daniels, James
Darr, Valentine
Davenport, William
Davis, George
Davis, Edward
Davis, Jesse
Davis, Richard
Dawsey, Patience
Deacon, James
Deal, Jacob
Deal, Joseph
Derr, Valentine
Dickey, James
Dickey, James Jr.
Dickey, Thomas

Dickie, Elizabeth
Dickie, John
Dickie, Thomas
Dickson, Joseph
Dillon, Jacob
Dillon, Michael
Dillon, Peter
Dixon, Michael
Dobbin, Alexander
Dobbin, Hugh
Dobbin, James
Dobbin, John
Dobbins, Alexander
Dobbins, James
Dobbins, John
Donaldson, Alexander
Donaldson, Andrew
Donaldson, John
Douglas, Thomas
Duff, George
Duke, John
Dunn, Barnabus
Dunn, Charles
Dunn, John
Dunn, John Jr.
Durham, Benejh
Eagle, George Jr.
Eagle, George Sr.
Eagle, John
Eagle, Phillip
Earnhart, Elias
Earnhart, George
Earnhart, John
Earnhart, Moses
Earnhart, Phillip
Earonhart, George
Earry, Peter
Eary, Abraham
Eary, John
Eary, Zachariah
Eddleman, Peter Sr.
Eddleman, Peter
Eller, Christian

Eller, Jacob
Elliott, John
Ellis, Radford
Enos, William
Ervin, Arthur
Ervin, George
Ervin, Joseph
Ervin, William
Erwin, Thomas
Fanning, Edmond
Felhower, Nicholas
Fennell, Frederick
Fennell, John
Ferguson, Andrew
Ferguson, John
Ferrand, Stephen L.
Ferrned, S. L.
File, Jacob
Fillhower, Nicholas
Fisher, Charles
Fisher, Fred
Fisher, Frederick
Fisher, George
Fisher, Hannon
Fisher, Jacob
Fisher, John
Fisk, Methias
Fite, Peter
Fitspatrick, James
Fitspatrick, Edmond
Fleming, George
Fleming, Robert N.
Forster, Hugh
Fost, Peter
Foster, David
Foster, Joseph
Foster, Owen
Foster, Samuel
Fraley, David
Fraley, George
Fraley, Henry
Fraley, Jacob
Frazier, James

Frees, Adam
Freeze, Jacob
Freeze, John
Freeze, Peter
Frick, Henry
Frick, Jacob
Frisal, Lydia
Frock, Conrad
Frohock, Alexander
Frohock, John
Frohock, Thomas
Frohock, William
Fullenwider, Henry
Fullenwider, Jacob
Fullenwider, John
Fullerton, David
Fullerton, William
Fulton, John
Gaither, Nicholas
Galbreath, Samuel
Galbreath, Thomas
Gallagher, Hugh
Gardner, David
Gardner, Francis
Gardner, John
Gardner, Matthew
Gardner, Robert
Garner, John
Garner, Mathias
Gates, Edward
Gheen. Thomas
Gibson, George
Gibson, James
Gibson, John
Gibson, William
Giles, Henry
Giles, John
Gilihan, Abraham
Gillespie, Elizabeth
Gillespie, Isaac
Gillespie, James
Gillespie, John
Gillespie, Matthew

Gillespie, Robert
Gillespie, Thomas
Gillian, Abraham
Gillispie, Matthew
Goodman, Christopher
Goodman, George
Goodman, John
Goos, John
Gottle, Peter
Graham, Fergus
Graham, James
Graham, John
Graham, Joseph
Graham, Moses
Graham, Richard
Grant, William
Gray, James
Gray, Robert
Gray, William
Greenfield, Thomas
Greeson, Nicholas
Grimes, Richard
Grimminger, Frederick
Grubb, Conrad
Grubb, George
Grubb, Henry
Guffy, John
Haggins, John
Hair,Thomas
Hall, John
Hall, Joseph
Hamilton, Archibald
Hamilton, Malcolm
Hamilton, Sarah
Hampton, William
Hanley, Darby
Harden, Robert
Hardy, Robert
Hare, Daniel
Harkey, Jacob
Harkey, Reuben
Harris, James
Harris, Robert

Hart, James
Hart, Samuel
Hart, William
Hartline, George
Hartline, Peter
Hartman, Charles
Hartman, Harmon
Hartman, John
Hartman, Michael
Hartman, Harvey
Hartman, John
Hartman, Robert
Hayes, David
Hays, James
Hays, Joseph
Hearne, James
Heathman, Hezekiah
Heathman, James
Heathman, Jonathan
Heilig, Henry
Heilig, Michael
Heitman, George
Hellard, George
Hemphill, James
Hemphill, Samuel
Henderson, Archibald
Henderson, Thomas
Hendrix, James
Hess, John
Hickman, Joseph
Higgins, John
Hileman, John
Hill, Abraham
Hill, Edward
Hill, George Henry
Hill, James
Hill, Reuben
Hill, Seth
Hill, Thomas
Hillard, George
Hillis, Robert
Hillis, Samuel
Hinds, Ralph

Hodge, George
Hodge, Jesse
Hodge, John
Hodge, Joseph
Hoffman, Francis
Hoffner, George
Hoffner, Henry
Hoffner, John
Hoffner, Leonard
Hoffner, Martin
Holley, Zachariah
Hollobough, George
Holmes, Moses
Holmes, Moses L.
Holmes, Reuben
Holms, John
Holshouser, Andrew
Holshouser, Jacob
Holshouser, Michael
Honberger, Valentine
Horah, Henry
Horah, Hugh
Horah, Margaret
Houston, David
Houston, James
Howard, Benjamin
Howard, Gideon
Howard, John
Hudson, John
Hudson, Thomas
Huey, Henry
Huggins, James
Huggins, John
Huggins, Robert
Hughes, Alexander
Hughes, Joseph
Hughey, Henry
Hughey, Henry S.
Hughey, Isaac
Hughey, Samuel
Hughs, Alexander
Hughs, Hudson
Hughs, James

Hughs, Joseph
Huie, James
Hunt, James
Hunt, John
Huston, Agnes
Huston, David
Huston, John
Hyde, Benjamin
Hyde, James
Hyde, John
Isahower, John
Jacobs, Abraham
James, Vachall
Jamison, William
Jarrett, Phillip
Jenkins, Hugh
Jenkins, Samuel
Johnson, John
Johnson, Robert
Johnston, Francis
Johnston, John
Johnston, Joseph
Johnston, Nathaniel
Johnston, Thomas
Jones, Samuel
Josey, Frederick
Josey, John
Josie, Frederick
Josie, John
Josie, John, Jr.
Josie, William
Kaler, Lewis
Kaylor, Lewis
Kaylor, Lewis Jr.
Kearn, Conrad
Kearn, Keny
Kearn, John
Kennady, Andrew
Kennady, Jennet
Kernes, Caleb
Kern, Conrod
Kern, John
Kerns, Conrad

Kerntzer, George
Kerr, Andrew
Kerr, George
Kerr, John
Kerr, Stephen
Kerr, Wilson
Ketner, George
Kihor, Conrad
Killen, William
Kilpatrick, John
Kilpatrick, Joseph
Kincaid, Andrew
Kincaid, James
Kincaid, John
King, Richard
King, Robert
King, Thomas
Kirk, John
Klotz, Hans Leonard
Kluttz, David
Kluttz, Leonard
Klutz, Jacob
Klutz, Martin
Klutz, Windle
Knight, Michael
Knop, John
Knox, Abraham
Knox, Andrew
Knox, Benjamin
Knox, James
Knox, John
Knox, Robert
Knup, Jacob
Knup, John
Knup, William
Krider, Jacob
Krite, Michael
Krotzer, Phillip
Krowell, William
Lamb, James
Lamb, John
Lambert, Thomas
Lambeth, John

Lance, Boston
Lance, John
Lathran, Aaron
Law, William
Lemley, George
Lemley. John
Lemley, Joseph
Lence, John
Lence, Peter
Lentz, Bastian
Lentz, Davalt
Lentz, Jacob
Lentz, Peter
Leonard, Elizabeth
Leopard, Henry
Lewis, James
Lewis, Peter
Lewis, William
Lightell, Benjamin
Lin, John
Linbarrier, Nicholas
Lingle, Casper
Lingle, Francis
Lingle, Lawrence
Link, Jacob
Linn, Hugh
Linn, James
Linn, Joseph
Linn, Robert
Linster, Moses
Litaker, John
Little, Daniel
Little, John
Little, Peter
Little, Thomas
Locke, Elizabeth
Locke, Esther
Locke, Francis
Locke, George
Locke, John
Locke, John B.
Locke, M. A.
Locke, Mathew

Locke, Moses A.
Locke, Richard
Locke, Robert
Logan, John
Long, Alexander
Long, Frederick
Long, John
Long, Joseph
Louchran, Lawrence
Love, Robert
Lovewasser, Jacob
Lowery, John
Lowery, Robert
Lowery, Thomas
Lowery, William
Lowrance, Abraham
Lowrance, Alexander
Lowrance, Andrew
Lowrance, David
Lowrance, Jacob
Lowrance, John
Lowrance, John Jr.
Lowrance, William
Lowry, Charles
Lowry, James
Lowry, John
Lowry, Samuel
Luckey, John
Luckey, Samuel Jr.
Luckey, Samuel Sr.
Luckie, James
Luckie, John
Luckie, Joseph
Luckie, Mary
Luckie, Richard
Luckie, Robert
Luckie, Samuel
Luckie, William
Lyall, Margaret
Lyall, Thomas
Lyerly, Christopher
Lyerly, Peter
Mack, Thomas

Mahon, Dennis
Marlin, Elijah
Marlin, James
Marlin, Joseph
Martin. Alexander
Martin, James
Martin, Robert
Martin, Samuel
Masters, George
Mauney, E.
Mauney, Valentine
Maurer, Fred
Maurer, Rudolph
Mawra, Peter Jr.
McBride, Hugh
McBride, Robert
McBride, William
McBroom, Abel
McBroom, John
McCaughey, Archibald
McCay, Spruce
McClain, Andrew
McConnaughy, Samuel
McConnel, William
McConnell, Daniel
McConnell, John
McConnell, Montgomery
McConnell, Samuel
McConoughey, Joseph
McCorkle, Alexander
McCorkle, Joel
McCorkle, John
McCorkle, Samuel
McCraken, James
McCraken, John
McCulloch, Henry
McCulloch, James
McCulloh, Alexander
McColloh, George
McColloh, James
McCullom, Andrew
McCullon, George
McEllwrieth, John

McElwaith, John
McElwaith, Joseph
McElwaith, Robert
McElwaith, Thomas
McFeeters, Daniel
McGee, William
McGinnis, John
McGloughlan, James
McHenry, Archibald
McHenry, Henry
McKinzie, Charles
McKnight, James
McKnight, John
McKnight, William
McLain, William
McLaughlin, James
McLaughlin, John
McLean, John
McLung, John
McManus, James
McManus, Thomas
McNeely, Adam
McNeely, Archibald
McNeely, David
McNeely, Isaac
McNeely, John
McPherson, Joseph
McPherson, Robert
McQuon, Hugh
Mendenhall, George C.
Michael, Conrad
Milford, Thomas
Miller, Benedick
Miller, Casper
Miller, Christian
Miller, Christopher
Miller, David
Miller, Frederick
Miller, George
Miller, Henry
Miller, Jacob
Miller, James
Miller, John

Miller, Martin
Miller, Michael
Miller, Peter
Miller, Samuel
Miller, Thomas
Miller, Tobias
Miller, William
Miller, Windle
Misenheimer, Daniel
Misenheimer, Peter
Mitchell, John
Moler, Valentine
Montgomery, Hugh
Montgomery, Humphrey
Moore, Audline
Moore, John
Moose, Henry
Morehead, John M.
Morgan, John
Morgan, Nathan
Morgan, Robert
Morgan, Wiley
Morr, Michael
Morrison, Andrew
Morrison, Archibald
Morrison, David
Morrison, Robert
Morrow, Allan
Morrow, James
Mowery, Jacob
Mowery. John
Mowry, A.
Moyer, Nicholas
Moyer, Simon
Mulhollan, James
Mull, John
Nealy, James
Neasbit, John
Neely, Francis
Nesbit, David
Nesbit, John
Nesbit, William
Newnan, Anthony

Newnan, Hugh
Newnan, John
Niblock, George
Niblock, William
Nichols, Jacob
Nichols, Joshua
Nivens, James
Nivens, Robert
Nixon, James
Obercash, Franz
Orton, John
Osborne, Adlai
Otten, Richard
Overcash, Jacob
Overcash, Michael
Park, Ebenezer
Noah, Noah
Parker, Drury
Parker, Richard
Parker, Richard Jr.
Parks, Ebenezer
Parks, Hugh
Parks, Noah
Partee, Charles L
Partee, Noah
Patterson, James
Patterson.,James Jr.
Patterson, John
Patton, John
Payne, Alpheus
Pearson, Richmond
Peeler, Anthony
Peeler, Michael
Pence, Valentine
Pendry, Agnes
Pendry, James
Peniston, Anthony
Penny, Alexander
Peteet, Richard
Peterson, William
Phifer, Caleb
Phifer, Margaret
Phifer, Martin

Phifer, Paul
Phillips, Enoch
Phillips, Jessie
Phillips, John
Phillips, Reuben
Phillips, Reuben Jr.
Phillips, Thomas
Phillips, William
Phipps, Isaah
Pinchback, John
Pinkston, John
Pinkston, Meshack
Pinkston, Nelly
Pinkston, Peter
Pinkston, Turner
Pinkston, William
Pinkston, Wm. Turner
Pitman, Micajah
Pless, Henry
Pless, Joseph
Plummner, William
Poole, Henry
Porter, Edmond
Porter, James
Porter, Robert
Porter, Thomas
Poston, Benjamin
Powlas, John Adam
Randleman, John
Randleman, John Jr.
Rankin, Samuel
Reaves, James
Redwine, John
Reed, Hugh
Reed, John
Reed, John Jr.
Reed, Moses
Reed, Robert
Reeves, Samuel
Rendleman. Jacob
Rendleman, John
Rendleman, John Jr.
Rendleman, Martin

Renshaw, William
Ribelin, Isaac
Ribelin, Peter
Riblin, Martin
Rice, E. B.
Rice, Isam
Rice, Johan
Rice, Phillip
Rice, William
Richause, Henry
Rimer, Nicholas
Rinehart, Jacob
Rintleman, Christopher
Rintleman, Martin
Roan. Henry
Roan, Henry Jr.
Robbley, John
Robertson, Moses
Robinson, Benjamin
Robinson, Henry
Robison, George
Robison, Henry
Robison, Hugh
Robison, Moses
Robison, Richard
Robison, William
Rodgers, John
Rogers, Allen
Rogers, Robert
Roseman, Adam
Roseman, George
Ross, Francis
Ross, John
Ross, Joseph
Rough, Daniel
Rough, John
Rounsecal, Benjamin
Rumple, Jacob
Rusher, Jacob
Rutherford, David
Rutherford, Griffith
Rutherford, Henry
Saltz, Anthony

Sammons, Grove
Sanders, Robert
Sanderson, Joseph
Satterwhite, Horace
Savitz, George
Schiles, Henry
Schiles, Jacob
Scools, John
Scott, John
Sechler, Abraham
Setzer, John
Sewell, Greenbury
Sewell, Moses
Shafer, John
Shaffer, Richard
Shaver, Abraham
Shaver, Andrew
Shaver, Jacob
Shaver, John
Shepherd, Edward
Shields, Andrew
Shields, Joseph
Shiman, John
Shinn, Benjamin
Shireman, George
Shiver, Andrew
Shooping, John Nicholas
Short, Peter
Shrock, Henry
Shulenburger, David
Shulenburger, Frederick
Shuping, Jacob
Shupink, Michael
Sifford, Lewis
Simmons, Phillip
Skiles, Henry
Skiles, James
Skiles, John
Slavin, William
Sloan, Henry
Sloop, Conrad
Slough, Phillip
Smart, William

Smather, Henry
Smather, Jacob
Smether, William
Smith, Eberhart
Smith, George
Smith, James
Smith, John
Smith, Joseph
Smith, Lewis
Smith, Peter
Smith, Samuel
Smith, William
Smoot, Alexander
Smother, William
Snap, Lawrence
Steele, Andrew
Steele, James
Steele, John
Steele, Robert
Steele, Samuel
Stewart, David
Stewart, James
Stirewalt, Frederick
Stirewalt, John
Stirewalt, John Jr.
Stirewalt, Michael
Stirewalt, Peter
Stokes, Christopher
Stokes, Littlebery
Stokes, Montford
Stoner, Charles
Stoner, Michael
Stories, James
Stork, Charles
Sulfin, Jacob
Swan, Charles
Swann, John D.
Swink, John
Swink, Leonard
Swink, Michael
Tate, John
Tate, Robert
Taylor, Abslom

Thomas, John
Thompson, Alexander
Thompson, Anne
Thompson, Claus
Thompson, John
Thompson, Joseph
Thompson, Moses
Thompson, Thomas
Thompson, William
Tiel, Jacob
Todd, John
Todd, John B
Todd, John Jr.
Todd, Thomas
Trease, Jacob
Trexler, John
Trexler, Peter
Tries, Adam
Trott, Absalom
Trott, Henry,
Trott, James
Trott, John
Trott, Samuel
Trott, Sarah
Troutman, Adam
Troutman, Andrew
Troutman, Michael
Troutman, Peter
Troy, John
Troy, Matthew
Turner, William
Utzman, John
Van Pool, David
Van Pool, John
Verble, Charles
Verble, John
Verrel, John
Vickers, Thomas
Virble, Charles
Voiles, James
Waddell, Hugh
Wails, John
Walker, Henry

Walker, Robert
Wallace, Samuel
Walton, Richard
Walton, William A.
Warmington, John
Wasson, Archibald
Wasson, John
Weakley, Robert
Weakly, Robert
Weant, John
Weathrow, Awalt
Webb, Caleb
Webb, Mary
Webb, Mary A.
West, William
White, Henry
White, Joseph
Wiatt, Brantley
Wiatt, Thomas

Wiley, Benjamin
Williams, Thomas
Williamson, William
Wilson, Joseph
Wilson, Samuel
Wilson, William
Winsel, Henry
Witherow, James
Witherow, John
Withrow, John
Wolfogill, Joseph
Wood, Charles
Wood, Daniel
Woods, Andrew
Woods, David
Woods, Joseph
Woods, Matthew
Woods, Robert
Woods, Samuel

Woods, William
Woodside, Archibald
Woodson, David
Woodson, David Jr.
Wray, William
Yarbough. Edward
Yoast, Jacob
Yoss, Phillip
Yost, Jacob
Yost, Phillip
Young, John
Young, Jonathan
Young, Samuel
Zively, Henry

CHAPTER THREE

The Shenandoah Valley

JUST BEYOND SWIFT RUN GAP in the Blue Ridge Mountains is a magnificent and fertile valley, nestled in between the Appalachians and the Blue Ridge. An explorer who was trekking through the backcountries of America passed through the Swift Run Gap and was overwhelmed by the sheer beauty of the valley beyond. He called the region the Euphrates, but his romantic term became forgotten in favor of an Indian term meaning "Daughter of the Stars." The "Shenandoah" valley, with its rich soil, grassy plains, and forested hills, became an important destination for a great number of Scots-Irish immigrants.

When the rich lands became available beginning in the first half of the 1700's, many Scots-Irish were quick to undertake the journey, and the majority of those comprised a third wave of Ulster emigrants to America. They barely hesitated in Pennsylvania before heading for the lands of "Shenando." Others who headed for the Virginia frontier were established Scots-Irish families with younger members who were ready to start their own households and found land prices had become too expensive in Pennsylvania.

In 1730, Governor William Gooch granted forty thousand acres of choice Virginia land to John and Isaac Van Meter of Pennsylvania. The Van Meters almost immediately sold the extensive tract to Joist Hite, who built an estate and brought in a number of families to join him. The first settlers made homesteads two miles south of present-day Staunton in Augusta County, in 1732.

Two later grants added additional lands for settlement, attracting a large number of primarily Scots-Irish families to the province. William Beverley was given 118,491 acres in Orange County for the "Manor of Beverley," a tract that extended into what is now Augusta County, Virginia, which developed into one of the most predominately Scots-Irish settlements in America. Benjamin Borden of New Jersey was given a land patent in 1739 for 92,100 acres that included the southern part of present Augusta County and nearly all the present Rockbridge County lands. Borden was required to have one hundred settlers on his tract before he could receive title, a feat he accomplished within two years. He attracted so many Scots-Irish settlers in the process that the land grant came to be called the "Irish Tract."

Borden was able to quickly settle the area, in part, due to his friendly dealings with squatters who had already established themselves in the new territory. Since authorities over the region were nearly two hundred miles away, men on the frontier had to apply their own brand of legal practice; a "corn right" entitled a man to a hundred acres for each acre he planted, a "tomahawk right" declared that trees felled and marked with indicated property lines, and a "cabin right" was understood to declare ownership of surrounding land for the builder of a cabin. Until the administrators of the land grants arrived to oversee the allotment of farms, the frontier "rights" provided for a way to settle disputes among the earliest settlers in the Shenandoah Valley of Virginia. Augusta County was formed in 1738, but it wasn't until 1745 when the organization meant anything, since previous to that there was no courthouse, no records, no sheriff, and no justices of the peace.

John Stephenson and his brothers Thomas, David, and William, were among the early settlers of the Shenandoah, arriving in the northern area in 1740. They along with others who were looking for an area that would better accommodate their Presbyterian faith, found rich farmland in the Shenandoah Valley. John Houston and his family left their home in Pennsylvania in 1742, also bound for the Shenandoah Valley. Archibald, the eldest son of David Houston of what was then called New Providence, North Carolina, joined other Houston families who were following the primitive road leading to the southwestern frontier.

William Stephenson was the head of a large family taking the "Great Philadelphia Wagon Road" to Virginia. He and his wife Sarah, along with their eight children, Adam, John, David, Matthew, James, William, Elizabeth, and young Sarah, had recently arrived from Ulster by way of Pennsylvania. Not surprisingly, several of William's sons would later find involvement in the frontier militia companies during the years of the American Revolution.

In the 1720's, the Great Wagon Road originally reached only from Philadelphia to the settlements in Lancaster County, and at its frontier end, where the trees and undergrowth were thickest, it would hardly accommodate a wagon. As the frontier extended, the Pennsylvania end of the trail was beaten down into a colonial highway of sorts. As the country's primary road heading south, the Wagon Road crossed through York and Gettysburg and by 1760 extended all the way to Salisbury, North Carolina—a distance of more than four hundred miles. The village of Lancaster, Pennsylvania became the starting point for many colonists, and eventually, traffic was so great that the settlement became an important trade center and one of the "last-stops" before the long haul toward Virginia.

The lands along the Wagon Road were as beautiful as they were rugged. Travel for the Scots-Irish heading for the frontier was usually in groups consisting of several families, since safety was better insured in larger numbers. Attacks from native tribes were still a genuine threat; it wasn't until 1744 that a temporary peace was achieved through the signing of the Treaty of Lancaster. In that agreement, the British purchased lands in the Ohio Valley that were claimed by the Iroquois by right of conquest, and Nations in the Virginias agreed to move west. Ironically, the French also claimed the Ohio Valley, and another colonial war would result from the rush to settle the colony, and thereby establish ownership.

The Shenandoah Valley had long been an Indian hunting ground and consisted primarily of lush prairie, due to the Indian's burning of grasslands at the end of the hunting season. The annual prairie fires promoted the heavy growth of new grass the following season, and the resulting stands attracted large herds of buffalo. The forests were diminished annually as the range fires consumed the trees edging the prairie.

The forest at the edge of the valley was thick with brush and grasses that allowed Indians to easily escape detection. At times, the quiet in those woods was said to have been like the still of a calm sea. Other times, the silence could give way instantly to the ferocious inhabitants of the forests fleeing before the advancing settlers. Wildlife was not confined to squirrels and birds; the heavy hooves of buffalo had stamped out the first traces and deer were plentiful; it was not unusual for travelers along the frontier to see twenty or more near the trail before they darted warily into the safety of the trees. Other animals had no cause to dart away. Panthers still roamed the southeastern forests and could pose a threat to frontier families, along with bears, bobcats, and poisonous snakes. The wolves, most of which had never encountered a man, had not yet learned a need for fear, and were so brazen that they were initially undeterred by the sound of a gunshot.

A gun was required for travel. The Scots-Irish called the tool a rifle-gun, and most preferred the long-barreled weapon called the Pennsylvania Rifle. It was just one of the many items each traveling party could find at the village of Lancaster before taking up the Wagon Road. The flintlock was a modified European gun with a barrel over forty inches long, and was treasured as one of the primary tools of the colonists on the frontier. Even with its primitive firing mechanism, it served both as a source of protection and a provider of food and clothing. Equipped with the long rifle, an ax, salt, seed, and sewing items, a family could draw from the land all the things needed to make a home. It was not uncommon to have a colonist's "rifle-gun" mentioned in a prominent fashion in his last will and testament.

The early settlement of the Shenandoah Valley occurred at a time when quick thinking, horse sense and a little ingenuity were not only admirable, but also required, for survival. Anything that needed to be done had to be done by the family. When the Scots-Irish settlers reached the Virginia valley, there was no hotel to accommodate them while their homes were built, no warm bath in which to soak after the long trip. There were no workmen waiting to take up the hammer. It would take days, cutting the trees, notching their ends and stacking them, to achieve the barest of shelters. Those arriving later might be afforded some shelter by neighbors with completed houses; lacking neighbors, the family would have to sleep under the stars, if at all. A number of the early settlers complained that the howling of the wolves was so distracting they were unable to sleep.

John Stephenson was the earliest settler in the Mill Creek Valley of the Shenandoah, receiving a patent in 1741 for 760 acres of land located just south of present-day Harrisonburg in Rockingham County. He had presented himself before the court; "*22nd. May, 1740, John Stephenson came into court and made oath that he imported himself Sarah and Mary Stephenson from Ireland to Philadelphia, and thence to this colony.*" His brother Thomas declared importation the same day for he and his wife Rachel. The Mill Valley they chose for their settlement was a fertile creek bottom with a breathtaking view; at the base of the Peaked Mountain in the Massanutten Range, three creeks wound their way toward the Shenandoah River. Cub Run, Mill Creek, and Stony Lick Branch (later called William's Run) all provided impressive settings for the valley pioneers, most of whom desired that the neighbors be friendly—but located a fair distance down the road. The western slope of the Massanutten is drained by the North Fork of the Shenandoah, with the mountain rising between the north and south forks. The settlement chosen by the John Stephenson was about midway between the lands of William Beverly and Jost Hite, to the south and north, respectively. John and his wife Sarah lived about fifteen miles east of the land homesteaded by John's brothers. Thomas, David, and William patented land in the Mossy Creek-Mount Solon area of Augusta County, some fifteen miles southwest of present-day Harrisonburg. Five brothers moved from Delaware to settle the region around present day Harrisonburg—John, Daniel, Thomas, Jeremiah, and Samuel Harrison. Daniel Harrison received a patent August 20, 1741 for a tract of 400 acres on Dry Fork of Smiths Creek (about two miles north of present-day Harrisonburg). The holdings of the Harrison brothers constituted a huge percentage of the land in what later became Rockingham County. Although the land patents issued to both Daniel Harrison and John Stephenson were dated 1741, both men were in the Shenandoah Valley along with several others, several years previous to the official deeding of the land.

Germans emigrating from the economically depressed Rhinish Palatinate in Europe made up a sizable percentage of the settlers in the northern region of the Shenandoah, but the Cross Keys area (south of present-day Harrisonburg, and the site of a Civil War battle) was a settlement primarily populated by the Scots-Irish. John Craig and his wife Sarah took up land on lower Cub Run. William and Janet Craig, and their son John, homesteaded some two miles south of Cross Keys near Robert and Jean Hook. Near Good's Mill on the same creek was William Williams. Robert Scott built on the North River near present-day Port Republic. Patrick Frazier bought land on Stony Lick Branch, as did Robert Shanklin. The Mathew Thompson Senior and his son Mathew Junior made homes on Stony Lick Branch near the North River. James Laird, who later led a militia company from the area, built a home for his wife and three children at the headwaters of Cub Run, near the base of Peaked Mountain. Nearby were William and Mary Beard, and the home of Samuel Scott.

There were three families with homes on the headwaters of Mill Creek, those of John Stephenson, Archibald Huston, and James and Catherine Waite. The families eventually comprised two sets of "in-laws" who located in close proximity near Cross Keys, and exemplify the frontier patterns regarding marriages based on need and proximity. Archibald Huston wed Stephenson's daughter Mary, and John Stephenson was married to Sarah Waite, the daughter of James and Catherine. After the death of Sarah, John Stevenson married her sister Esther, who was the widow of John Taylor. Times required that a woman have a husband, and it was nearly equally necessary for a man, particularly with children, to have a wife. Marriages between widows and widowers were fairly common.

In addition to his 1741 patent, John Stephenson bought additional land from Benjamin Borden two years later and recorded the deed in Orange County. Between 1740 and 1745, Andrew, David, Thomas, James, John, and William Stephenson were all present in the Virginia valley. William's 200-acre purchase in

1747 for eight pounds "current money Virginia" added to the Stephenson family holdings. William's land was on the southernmost Fork of the South Branch of the Potomac, in what is now Pendleton County, West Virginia, and just over the mountain from the rest of the family.

When John Stephenson completed construction of his plantation house on Mill Creek, he called it "Meadow View"—a name that would endure for more than 250 years. As more travelers passed Meadow View, the trace became a road—first called the Indian Road, for the nearly constant moving of native tribes along the path during the signing of the Treaty of Albany in 1740. It was later called the Courthouse Road, and finally named the Keezletown Road. Shortly after the Revolution, a Scotsman named John Loudon McAdam invented a process using tar and asphalt to bind small stones together for the surfacing of roads. The Keezletown Road was the first in Rockingham County to be given a macadam surface, and in the early years of western Virginia settlement, the road served as the main route of north-south travel through the valley.

The first homes, particularly those far from the towns and stores, were simple structures intended as immediate shelter. Tables and three-legged stools were pieced together from branches and pieces of wood; pegs were driven into the interior walls to hang the few articles of clothing and the flintlock. Spoons for cooking and eating had to be carved, as did the serving bowls and ladles, unless a gourd or hard squash was to be found. It was only much later that dishes and drinking mugs began to appear, bartered for from wandering merchants; any guest served a meal on pewter or china would leave for home much impressed at the affluence of his host and hostess.

The majority of those moving into the Virginia valley had just crossed the Atlantic, leaving most of their possessions behind in Ulster. Other Scots-Irish migrants like the Stephenson, Houston, Harrison, and Morrison families, had been in the provinces long enough that some had even grown relatively prosperous. They were able to bring with them a fair amount of their household goods.

John Stephenson's Meadow View quickly became one of the largest farms in the valley, containing over 1400 acres. The road that cut in a westerly direction across the hill—The Old Mill Road—was the scene of constant activity as the valley filled with settlers. Mill Creek was appropriately named, accommodating a sawmill, a gristmill, and a flourmill—all located in the immediate vicinity of the Stephenson property. Just upstream, the Huston family operated a powder mill at the headwaters of Mill Creek.

Even while the Stephenson brothers were still patenting land in the valley, John devoted a portion of his property to one of the Scots-Irish pastimes—horse racing. The racetrack across the road from the Meadow View plantation house was built by John Stephenson around 1746, and is believed to be the first track to be built in America west of the Blue Ridge Mountains. While many of the early settlers enjoyed their horses, it was a sticking point among the hard-liners of the Presbyterian Church.

Augusta Church was the first Presbyterian Church in the valley and was founded in 1740; the church house served as headquarters for the community of people, a gathering place for social and spiritual events. John Houston bought land not far from the Old Providence Church in 1742. His 228 acres in the

Borden tract were located in what would later become Rockbridge County, and was situated near present-day Brownsburg. After a disagreement with the Presbyterian traditionalists of Augusta Church, John Houston donated land and founded the New Providence Church near Timber Ridge, the name he had given his plantation. Mill Creek Valley settlers were between sixteen and twenty-five miles from the Augusta Church, which was closer than New Providence Church, which prompted the holding of church meetings at the various homes in the valley. Meadow View frequently served as a meetinghouse for visiting preachers until a regular church building was constructed at Cross Keys, an area seven miles south of present-day Harrisonburg, and a mile and a half south of Meadow View. Massanutten Cross Keys is located on the old Keezletown Road just south of the old Port Republic Road. At the time the meeting house was constructed, Henry Downs, Jr. lived at the location of present-day Port Republic, and on May 29, 1751, Henry was appointed Surveyor of the Highway from his house to the "Stone Meeting House." When the old Port Republic Road was established from "Henry Downs' Mill to ye Meeting House," Thomas Stephenson was appointed as overseer for its upkeep.

Later, many of the members of the Peaked Mountain congregation petitioned the court for a new road running from just west of Swift Run Gap (near present-day Elkton, Virginia) "in a westerly direction joining the court house road at the New Stone Meeting House." John Stephenson signed the petition, as did John and William Craig, Robert Hook, William Williams, David Chambers, Robert Scott, Mathew Thompson Sr., and Mathew Thompson Jr.

One of the earliest preachers in the Valley became fast friends with the settlers, literally as well as figuratively. His name was John Hindman and he came from County Londonderry in Ulster to serve as a missionary among the newly planted Scots-Irish. He was preaching in the Shenandoah Valley as early as 1742, and records of the Donegal Presbytery indicate Hindman was preaching "at the head of the Shenandoah" (near present-day Port Republic) in 1745. The Presbyterians had no church in the area other than the Peaked Mountain Church at Cross Keys (later called the Massanutten Church), and Hindman is believed to have been its first preacher.

The Reverend Hindman was comfortable not only in the pulpit, but in the saddle as well. An avid horse racing fan, he owned a large stable of his own horses and jockeyed the mounts at Stephenson's track. When the Presbytery objected to Hindman's participation and he declined to give up the sport, the church excommunicated him in 1747. Rather than see his friend and fellow horse-enthusiast be forced from the pulpit in disgrace, John Stephenson loaned Hindman the money to travel to Europe to be ordained as an Episcopalian minister. On his return, Hindman was elected the first rector of the Augusta Parish, giving some of the more moderate Presbyterians in the valley an option in their church affiliation. Hindman maintained his affection for the Mill Valley settlers of the Cross Keys area, and when he was taken gravely ill less than a year after his return from England, Hindman returned to Meadow View, and stayed there I the care of John Stephenson and his wife until his death, some five weeks later.

The Reverend Hindman named Stephenson as administrator of his estate, which included a collection of wigs and gowns, divinity books, twenty-three horses and a "jockey coat and cap." John Hindman was buried at the Cross Keys cemetery, the burying ground for the Scots-Irish congregation of the Massanutten Presbyterian Church—the parish where he had formerly preached.

These excerpts from the Peaked Mountain Session book are copied as found, with original abbreviations and parenthetical notations as found in the transcription.

From: The Session Book of Peaked Mountain Church, 1759
Alexander Miller, Minister

Baptized in 1759

Jany.	Margaret Irwin	Jean Snodon
	Nathan Huston	Susanna Berry
Feby.	Anne Harrison	Eleanor Semple
	Betty Semple	Margt. Johnston
	Hugh Brewster	John Curry
	Alexr. Wilson	Margery Thomson
March	George Malcom	William Poague
	Helen Ralston	William Woodhall

Married in 1759

Febry. ye 20th	John Crevens	Margaret Dyre
March 6th	Isaiah Shipman	Eliz. Hodge
March 13th	Michael Carn	Eliz. Persinger
April 3rd	John Kengere	Eliz. Sargant
April 17th	Saml. Hemphill	Mary Crevens
April 17th	Christopher Huffman	Barbara Evighly
Sept. 19th	John Pharis	Elizabeth Hill
Sept. 26	Thos. Spencer	Anne Duncan
9br. 19th	John Jackson	Martha Claypool
10br. 11th	Andrew Ewen	Susanna Shannon
10br. 12th	John Hopkins	Jean Gordon

Baptized 1760

Jany.	John Magil	June	John Hemphill
	Jonathan Shipman		Wm Stuart
	Henry Smith	7br.	Jas. Magil
Feby.	Walter Davies	8br.	William McClure
	Mary Crevens		Dan'l Harrison
March	Sarah Craig		Jean Ewen
April	James Brewster		Sarah Frazier
	Wm. Elliot	9br.	Sarah Guin
	Thos. Lewis		William Smith
May	Robert Grey		Mary McClure
May	Jean Semple	9br.	Mary Hopkins
			David Ralson

Married 1760

Jany. First	John Pickens (Picken)	Anne Oliver
Jany. 17th	John McCay	Sarah Oliver
Jany. 24th	Saml. Briggs	Mary Logan
June 28th	Joseph Dictum	Rachel Love
July 15th	Henry Armintroute	Mary Wagonier
July 29th	Henry Henry	Mary Chesnuts
Septr. 15th	Christopher Ermintrout	Susanna Bower
8br. 21	William Glasgow	Eliz. Colley
8br. 26	Wm. Gregg	Margt. Johnston
Decembr. 25th	Thomas Stinson (Stephenson)	Eliz. Logan

Baptized 1761

Jany.	Joanna Berry	June	Ephraim Wilson
	John Virdon		Martin Turpine
	Jas. Virdon		Wm. Sholl
	Lydia Virdon	July	Margt. McClure
	Eliz. Ralston		Mary Irwin
Febry.	Eliz. Poague		Jean Briggs
	G--n Henderson		Mary Shannon
	Sarah Duglass		John Woodal
	Wm. Curry	August	Wm. Gregg
March	John Brewster		Eliz. Carlile
	Eliz. Brewster		Wm. Stuart
	Sarah Lawrence	7br.	George Stringer
April	Sarah Smith		Ruth Stringer
	Jenat Brewster		Sarah Hopkins
May	John Hopkins	8br.	Sarah Smith
	Jos. Ramsey		Abraham Pickens
		9br.	Davd. Magary

Married 1761

March 5th	Rob t Crevens	Esther Harrison
March 31	Saml. Peterson	Martha Ledgerwood
April 16	Skidmore Monsy	Mary Scot
April 20th	Henry Long	Catrina Pence
May 26th	Saml. Semple	Hannah Copeland
Septr. first	Jas. Bell	Margt. McBride
9br. 11th	Saml. Hyrons	Christian Wilson
10br. 11th	Wm. Shannon	Catrine Thaim
10br. 24th	Thos. Peterson	Margt (Harrison?)

Baptized in 1762

Feby.	Agnes Peterson	June	Mattw. Semple
	John McClure		Anne Black
	Jean Rubertson	July	Jesse Harrison
	Eliz. McKnoughtan	Septr.	Gideon Harrison
	Saml. Irwin		Joseph Hyrons
March	David Magil		Gideon Harrison [2x]
	Eliz. Snodon		Wm. Ralston
	Anne Greg	Octbr.	fin. Lusk (Tim?)
	Margt. McMullen		John Lusk
April	Benj. Semple		Mary Malcom
	Robt. M'Cay	Novbr.	Eliz. Hopkins
	Hannah Crevens		Sarah Henderson
	Eliz. Crevens		Ephraim Hopkins
May	Eliz. Ewen		Joseph Crevens

Married 1762

Jany. 7th	Matthew Black	Margt. Ponder
Jany. 9th	John Peartree	Rebeckah Lovegrove
Jany. 16th	Thomas Wilmoth	Agnes Wait
Feb. 24th	Edwd. Irwin	Eliz. Curry
Feb 25th	Robert Cunningham	Margt. Kilpatrick
March 2d	John Skidmore	Magdalene Hindoll (Kinnoll)
April 1st	David Smith	Elenor Esom
April 5th	Martin Humble	Anna Delay
April 16th	Jas. Belshaw	Esther Hook
June 24	Isaac McDonald	Jean Scot
July 28	Wm. Chesnut	Catrine Callachan
August 26	Isaiah Curry	Margt. Irwin
Octbr. 28	Hugh Dickson	Mary Londey
9br. 22	Robt. Rutherford	Mary Sevier
9br. 30	Amos Bird	Sarah Bedhill
10br. 9th	Wm. Semple	Sarah Coplin
10br. 15th	Patrick Savage	Judith McThoron
10br. 27	Leonard Propst	Catrine Capliner

Married 1763

Jany. 20th	Robert McKemmy	Sarah Cunningham
March 17th 1763	Adam Stinson	Rebeckah Peterson (Patterson)
March 31	Jas. Wallace	Jean Baird
May 10th	Benjn. Thos.	Susanna Lewis
May 24	Geor. Bedhill	Magdalen Birde
August 10th	Benj. Harrison	Mary McClure
August 17th	John Johnston	Mary Shelpman
	Benjn. Harrison	Mary McClure
8br. 15th	Wm. Davies	Rachel Guin
8br. 20th	John Logan	Mary McClure
9br. 8th	Robt. Davies	Sarah Morse
10br 29	George Brewster	Mary Love

Baptized 1763 *The War prevents ye compleating ye list this year.*

Jany.	Agnes Marshal	---- Green
	Arnold Custard	---- Smith
	Bridget Custard	---- Davies
Feby. at Henry Smith's		
March	John Irwin	---- Williams

Baptized 1764 *The War prevents ye compleating ye list this year.*

Janry.	William Laurence	April	Mary Hemphill
	Anne Semple		Jeremiah Crevens
March	John McKemmy		Jenat Brown
			Wm. McMullan

Married in 1764

Jany. 19th	Robert Caldwell	Sarah Duglass
Febry. 27th	Charles Hedrigh	Barbara Conrode
March 19th	Cornelius Boman	Susanna Painter
April 10th	John Munger	Agnes Pirke
April 26th	Kelham Price	Elizth. Null
June 26th	John Harman	Mary Van Gummundie
July 9th	Saml. Curry	Jean Irwin
Novr. 6th	Obadiah Monsey	Anne McBride

Archd. Huston to Settle ye State of Pyked Mountain Congn. which is as followeth to wit of a bond from Patrick Frazier John Davison John Stephenson & James Brewster Eight pounds twelve & two pence halfpenny

Augusta County Militia, 1742
Captain John Buchanan's Company

Lieutenant William Evans	John Edmoston	William Mitchell
Ensign Joseph Cotton	Nathaniel Evans	Solomon Moffot
Sergeant John Mitchell	John Gray	Alexander Moore
Jacob Anderson	Samuel Gray	Andrew Moore
John Anderson	James Greenlee	John Moore
James Anderson	William Hall	William Moore
Isaac Anderson	Andrew Hayes	Michael O'Docherty
William Armstrong	Charles Hayes	John Paul
William Buchanan	Robert Huddon	John Philipmaver
Edward Boyle	William Humphery	William Quinn
Charles Campbell	Joseph Kanada	James Robinson
James Cooke	William Louchrage	William Sayers
Robert Cotton	Mathew Lyle	John Stephenson
Richard Courser	Andrew Martin	James Sunderlin
Charles Donooho	John Mathews	Isaac Taylor
Thomas Duchart	Nathaniel McClewer	Alexander Walker
Robert Dunlap	Samuel McClewer	John Walker
Samuel Dunlap	William McCoutes	Joseph Walker
John Dyche	John McCrosseree	Samuel Walker
James Ecken	Thomas McSpedan	Thomas Williams

David Stephenson served in Captain James Cathey's militia company, and would later serve in the Continental Army regulars. Other companies from Augusta County that year were commanded by John Christian, Peter Scholl, John Smith, Charles Campbell, John McDowell, Andrew Lewis, John Willson, and John Buchanan.

There were "foot" and "horse" companies and accounts were kept and paid to those men in service, as well as those involved in "waggoning" and patrolling. In 1747, John Stephenson was given the rank of Lieutenant of Foot, and some years later, he, along with a great many of the Scots-Irish planters found themselves caught in the midst of the French and Indian War.

By 1747, John Houston had become one of the prominent men among those in the Scotch-Irish tract, in the area that later became Rockbridge County. His plantation did well, and he and Margaret were able to assist their son Robert and his wife Mary Davidson, in setting up a household. Children Isabella, Esther, and John had already taken spouses, and they, along with brothers Samuel, James, and Matthew, all shared in the chores of the Virginia plantation. The men of the time were expected to provide food and shelter for the family, keeping the house in good repair and tending to the farm, as required. To acquire those things that could not be grown or made, the men would have to barter or sell something to raise the money.

The women of the time had little legal standing. Those who found themselves widowed on the frontier, who were not adequately provided for, were completely dependent on relatives. Few widows managed farms on their own, although there are accounts of frontier women who proved to be shrewd businesswomen following the deaths of their husbands. More often than not, widowed women hoped to remarry before their inheritance was expended, which assumed that provisions were made in that regard. Many frontiersmen died without making a will, although the early legal books are filled with the last intentions of the more conscientious. Most were respectful and caring, and many were quite meticulous in providing for their widows and "orphans" as the children were termed—regardless of whether the mother was still living. Others were not as kind. John Hood Sr. willed that his several thousand dollar estate be generously divided among his children. His spelling was lacking, but his intentions were clearly spelled out. His daughter "Sophiah" received $153 dollars worth of property in addition to "a negro girl Dabney valued at $700," but the said "property" was to be "in nowise the property of Moses Moore her husband." Daughter "Saselia" (likely Cecilia) received a similar inheritance, as did Elizabeth, Mary, "Illuise" (Eloise?), "Sarahann," and "Narcisa." Their mother may have had an inkling of what was in store for her, or it may have been quite a shock when the will was probated. To his widow Mary, John Hood left "one silver dollar as she as Bin so stubron with Me so carless of Me & so neglet full of mine." Presumably, sons John and Thomas, who were also left out of the will, were allowed some leeway as executors, to provide for the well being of their mother.

The women were expected to raise the children, make the clothing, and prepare the meals. Naturally, cooking was done over the fire, but the type of cooking depended on the utensils available to the family. An iron spit was used to roast meat over the flames, and since the side of the cut nearest the flame tended to overheat, a member of the family—usually one of the younger children—was required to sit at the fire and turn the spit. The resulting meal, not unlike modern cookouts, probably would have surpassed many modern efforts.

Not surprisingly, there were settlers who lacked even the most basic of cooking utensils. There were others who had the basics, but not much else. John McClure worked as a tailor, but the income was limited and his life's accumulation resulted in a rather thrifty inheritance for the family. To his son James, he left "the Bible and the big pot." Son Samuel McClure received "the next biggest pot." John realized his family had to eat, and not wanting to overlook his widow, declared "wife Agness to have use of both pots." Sons John and Andrew, along with daughters Eleanor, Jean and Esther were left—without a pot, or the use of one.

Those who were fortunate enough to own an iron pot or two could boil meat and vegetables to provide a variety of meals for the family. The practice of baking was limited to those who could improvise or those who owned a bake kettle. The heavy covered pans came in a variety of sizes and shapes, but were usually equipped with legs to allow the pan to be placed directly among the embers. Red-hot coals were piled on top of the kettle, which allowed food inside to be baked.

The wife and daughters were expected to serve the men their meals, and many preferred to eat alone afterward, rather than trying to serve and eat at the same time.

Beyond the church and the family, social activities were fairly limited for the Scots-Irish in Virginia. Part of the reason was the strict Presbyterian discipline, in which dancing and other frivolities were strictly forbidden. Even the serving of hot coffee on Sunday was frowned upon by the strictest Presbyterians. There was much to keep the colonists occupied without a busy social calendar, but like any other community, there were those who weren't as skilled at putting time to good use. James Houston found himself in a scrape, along with his friends David Bryans, Israel Robinson, and James Bullock, when their hunting trip ended with a woodland blaze. Although the hunt was successful, the outcome was less than desirable; James was charged with killing a deer, setting the woods on fire, and with swearing in public.

There was little tolerance among the Presbyterians of Augusta County for rough language. Swearing in public was an offense punishable by fine—the amount dependent on the severity of the curse. Fines and fees declared by the county were used to subsidize the cost of county salaries and supplies.

Since the Scots-Irish preferred the civilized social amenities of church and community, there were positions such as Constable and jailer to be filled. As residents of a new county, Augusta citizens found themselves with a list of tasks required for the good of the community, many of which required funding. The colonists appear to have shouldered their financial obligations with an understanding as to the need. The court appointed overseers and those "tithables" within their districts were required to perform civic work, or pay an equivalent amount of "Current Money." The designation of currency was due to the variety of payment methods available; most of the provinces issued their own currency, and even those were subject to change.

When Staunton became the county seat, the courthouse became a center of activity during the monthly sessions. Construction began on a jail in late 1746,

Larry J. Hoefling • 49

and a guard was hired to secure the "prison" until it was finished. Robert McClenahan was obliged to find candles and small beer, and to keep the court house in order, besides finding stables for the horses of the Justices, attorneys, and the Officers. John Stephenson became respected as a man who could fairly represent the interests of those around him, and was called on frequently to appraise estates and administrate the last wills of his neighbors. Some years later, John Stephenson made appraisals along with his son-in-law Archibald Huston, who learned the value of both property and respect, and was eventually called upon to perform similar duties.

Colonial times were not without scandal. In 1746, Humberston Lyon and Susan Mires, the wife of William Mires, were suspected of conducting an illicit love affair, and both faced adultery charges in court. That trial paled in comparison to the Buchanan scandal, beginning in the early part of the following year. Much of the county was swept up in a murder trial beginning in April and those who were not called to take the stand filled the courthouse to watch as Rebecca Buchanan faced murder charges. Her mother Rebecca (referred to as Rebecca Senior), along with Ruth Buchanan Carmichael, and Mary Ann Campbell were charged on "suspicion of being accessories," and many of the county wives apparently knew something about the death and the purported conspiracy. More than a dozen persons took the stand to testify against the four "criminals," as they are referred to in the court records. The younger Rebecca was bound over for trial at Williamsburg, while the three accused accessories were all acquitted on May 20.

A good amount of the county activity was the direct result of the monthly court sessions, and landowners were required to petition for the establishment of new roads and improvements. If the court agreed to the need, men would then be obliged to assist in the clearing and maintenance. William Stephenson and son John successfully petitioned for a road from Caleb Jones' mill to the County line, and more than two dozen Scots-Irish settlers were ordered to maintain it. The court even made decisions on such things as road direction signs that were set up along the county roads.

In the early years of Augusta County, the focus of activity was on farming the land and furnishing the needs of the colonists, although farming was not the only livelihood in August County. Entrepreneurs were quick to spot the need for enterprises such as grain mills. If the gristmill was to be run by water, and the miller had none on his property, he could petition the court to condemn a suitable piece of land. The court appointed a jury of men to survey the value of the land and return with an appropriate amount of compensation for the landowner.

The court appointed men to serve as appraisers, as estate sales were a common practice following a death. Neighbors were asked to witness the sale of land and the filing of wills at the courthouse. During monthly sessions, men were called to serve on juries, although serious offenses were sent for trial at Williamsburg. Not all the jurymen were practiced in the art. Walter Davis and Malcolm Campbell had their fill of the trial in which they had been assigned a seat on the jury. Suddenly, Walter bolted out the door and Malcolm leaped out the courthouse window. The court noted it was forced to stay a verdict, since the two "separated themselves from their fellows and talked with other persons."

Henry Witherington was an indentured servant working in the employ of John Stephenson in 1751. Many of those in indentured service worked out their time to repay their passage fees, but others, perhaps daunted by the conditions or the work—slipped away in attempts to escape their obligations. Others, like those bound to John Stephenson and Thomas Dansie, were noted in court records as having attempted escapes, only to be later recaptured and held in the jail until their disputes were resolved.

Marriages on the frontier were occasions for great celebrations. On June 20, 1749, Archibald Huston wed Mary Stephenson. A home was built next to her parents and grandparents on a 367-acre gift of land from John Stephenson, but as with many of the Scots-Irish, the land would later be sold as families followed the frontier into Kentucky.

CHAPTER FOUR

The Carolina Country

WHATEVER ARGUMENTS THE EARLY settlers might have had among themselves, they were in agreement about the beauty of the frontier's rugged geography. Beyond the Shenandoah Valley, heading southward along the Blue Ridge Mountains and crossing at the Manassas Gap, travelers on horseback saw wide valleys that were thickly carpeted with grasslands and colorful flowers. Where the Yadkin River and the Catawba River basins coursed through the western part of North Carolina, herds of deer roamed through grasses that grew so tall that a rider on horseback could tie handfuls of it together across the top of his saddle. They were Granville's lands.

Of the eight Lords Proprietor of Carolina, all but one sold their holdings to the crown in 1728. John Carteret, Earl of Granville, retained his share, stretching from the Virginia border to fourteen miles southwest of present-day Salisbury, North Carolina. John Lawson, an early day trader who traveled extensively through the Granville district, reflected on the beauty of the Carolinas that would serve to draw settlers to its fertile meadows.

51

A man…may more easily clear ten acres of ground than in some places he can one; there being much loose stone upon the land, being very convenient for making of dry walls or other sort of durable fence…we passed through a delicious county—none that I ever saw exceeds it. We saw fine bladed grass six feet high along the banks of these pleasant rivulets…This most pleasant river is beautified with a numerous train of swans and other sorts of river fowl, not common though extraordinary to the eye.

Between 1732 and 1737, many of the colonists living along the boundary between Maryland and Pennsylvania had grown so weary of the provincial border disputes they began to move away. Many sought lands in the Shenandoah Valley, others settled in the Cumberland, and still others pressed onward, eventually reaching the Carolina frontier. Recent immigrants and those unable to afford the farms in Pennsylvania joined them on the journey along the Great Wagon Road. A fifty-acre farm in Lancaster County of present-day Pennsylvania sold for an average of seven pounds ten shillings, while one hundred acres in the Granville district could be had for a mere five shillings. The North Carolina frontier also had an appeal to colonists from New Jersey and Pennsylvania in 1744, who were under threat of attack from the Indians allied with the French during King George's War.

By 1749, much of the choice land in the Shenandoah Valley had already been claimed as well, and the frontier was pushed into the Yadkin River Valley of North Carolina. That same year, Anson County was formed in western North Carolina, and the provincial council considered eighty petitions from settlers seeking land in the new county. Most of the earliest settlers headed large Scots-Irish families. They joined—however tenuously—the established inhabitants of the region; the Keyauwee, Saponi, and Tutelo Indians lived in the valley between the Yadkin and Catawba Rivers, and the Catawba and Waxhaw Tribes lived west of the Catawba, to the south of the other tribes.

Grants for land parcels to the Scots-Irish and other settlers within Granville's tract are typified by that recorded for David Huston.

George the Second, by the Grace of God, of Great-Britain, France, and Ireland, King, Defender of the Faith, &c: To all to whom these presents shall come, Greeting. Know ye, That We, for and in Consideration of the Rents and Duties herein reserved have Given and Granted, and by these Present for Us, Our Heirs and Successors, to Give and Grant unto David Huston a Tract of

Land, containing Four Hundred Ninety Five Acres, lying and being in the County of Anson in our Province of North Carolina.

On the N side of the Cataba River On the N side of McColloh's Line on both sides of Bufflow Creek Beginning at Hickory runs E. 220 poles to a white Oak then N 220 Poles to a Hickory then E 74 Poles to a pine then N 12 poles to a Black Oak then W 294 poles to Pine then S 320 poles to Beginning. signed Mathew Rowan, President and Commander in Chief...31 day of March in the XXVI Year of our Reign, Anno Domini, One Thousand Seven Hundred and Fifty Three.

———

In colonial days, when the science of surveying land was still in development, measurements for Royal Land Grants were taken based on landmarks such as trees, streams, tree stumps, or even man-made structures. It soon became apparent that using rope or cloth for taking measurements gave varying results, since the length of the rope was dependent on its age and condition. An old wet rope might give a settler a significantly larger piece of land, once stretched. To offset that possibility, surveyors carried metal poles, sometimes called chains, of a determined length, that fastened together at the ends similar to the links of a chain. The poles could be neatly folded at their links, stashed in a long pouch or saddlebag, and easily carried through the wilderness.

The Catawba River is in the western part of the state, running east from present day Pisgah National Forest near the Tennessee line to a point just northwest of present day Charlotte, where it turns south. In David Houston's day, there was no dam at Cowans Ford and no Catawba Dam near South Carolina. The county was called Anson, and its presumed western boundary was the Mississippi River, or beyond. Later, a more reasonable western line was set, and over the years, Anson County was carved into a number of smaller counties. Almost immediately after settling the land, due to redrawn lines, David and Mary Houston found themselves residents of Rowan County. Eventually, 26 counties were formed from Rowan County's original boundaries. Years later, due to redrawn county lines, many of David's children found themselves in Iredell County and Mecklenburg County, the site of present day Charlotte. The land described in the deed to David Huston by current day surveys is situated at Kannapolis, straddling the line between Rowan and Cabarrus counties.

The changes in county lines were often at the request of colonists, who were forced to travel great distances to conduct business, and often petitioned the government to establish closer legal centers. The Yadkin-Catawba River valley constituted one of the largest primarily Scots-Irish settlements in America.

There were several major areas of settlement when the first wave of Scots-Irish moved onto lands originally claimed by Sapona and Catawba tribes. The Fourth Creek Settlement comprised fertile lands east of the Catawba River, on the upper reaches of Third Creek and Fourth Creek. The Davidson's Creek Settlement was established as colonists made homes along the branches of Davidson's Creek, east to Coddle Creek. The Irish Settlement and the Trading Camp Settlement were found between the Yadkin River and Lord Granville's Line.

David Houston and his family were among the earliest of settlers in the area of present day Rowan County. In 1751, David and his sons cleared land on their 640-acre tract west of what would become the Irish Settlement. At the time, he was one of just over three-dozen landowners present in the Yadkin River area.

Early Settlers of Present-Day Rowan County

James Alexander	1750
William Alexander, son of James	1750
James and Mary Allison	1750
Andrew Allison, brother of James	1750
Peter Arndt	1750
Charles Burnett	1751
John Burnett	1751
Samuel Burnett	1751
William Burnett	1751
George Cowan	1750
John Cowan	1750
James Deacon	1751
Alexander Dobbin	1750
David Fullerton	1751
Archibald Hamilton	1750
Robert Harris	1751
David Houston	1751
George Henry	1751
John Lynn	1751
Robert MacPherson	1751
John Nisbet	1750
Arthur Patton	1750
Lorentz Schnepp	1750
Robert Tate	1750
Samuel Young	1751

William Morrison called himself the "first Inhabiter of the country," although there were others who might take issue with his claim. The Morrisons were certainly among the early residents of the Carolina backcountry, and settled near John McConnell in the Davidson Creek settlement. William Morrison had a mill in operation by 1752 and built a house on Third Creek, on land he bought in November of 1753 in present-day Iredell County.

As had been the case in Pennsylvania, not all of the settlers taking up land on the frontier of North Carolina had established a valid title to the land.

On the first day of April, a meeting of the Governor's Council was held, and it was pointed out that a number of those who had petitioned for land had never taken out a warrant to have it surveyed, and others who had completed a survey, had never returned with the information to complete the land patent. Whether it was a matter of purposely avoiding the payment of fees, or simply an oversight on the part of colonists, they found their names listed at the Council Chamber, along with a notice requiring that the patent application be completed within eight months time, or rights to the land would be forfeited. In light of the fact that people were pouring into the area, legal rights to property were becoming increasingly important. Many of the settlers had been living for up to four years on the Granville tract without legal claim, and the Council notice set in motion a rush to establish rights.

48 individual grants for land in North Carolina were made on a single day—March 25, 1752. It may have been because it was New Year's Day, the last time it would be celebrated in March. Unlike the Roman Catholic countries, England and its colonies had retained the Julian calendar, in which the New Year was marked on March 25th. On September 2, 1752, the colonists lost nearly two weeks—on the calendar, at least—when the Gregorian calendar was adopted. September 14 was the day that followed September 2.

While most who applied for land were seeking a place to settle, there were a number of known land speculators, some of whom grew prosperous dealing in the sale of land. Not all the deals were honest. There are accounts of lands being sold more than once, and of failures to properly record deeds on behalf of new owners. Either way, land went quickly in Rowan County, and mostly went to "transfers"—colonists who had already established a previous home in Pennsylvania or Virginia, and were removing to the Carolinas.

The rich bottomland of the Yadkin and Catawba Rivers was advertised to the Scots-Irish, much in the way the Virginia valley was marketed years earlier. North Carolina Governor Gabriel Johnston had come from Dumfrieshire, Scotland, and the man who took the seat in 1754, Arthur Dobbs, originated in Ulster.

Between the years of 1752 and 1755, the Centre Presbyterian Congregation was established in the Davidson's Creek settlement area, placing the Scots-Irish at the edge of the Carolina frontier, and establishing the earliest organized settlement to be found as far west as the Catawba River.

By the time Governor Dobbs visited the area in 1755, seventy-five families had already settled. Dobbs owned several large tracts of land nearby, and was pleased at the progress made by the frontier families. He reported that most contained eight or ten children each, and that some "Scotch-Irish Presbyterians" had banded together to have a preacher and a schoolteacher of their own. The family of David Houston was typical of those visited by Governor Dobbs; David's wife Mary had given birth to sons William, David Jr., Archibald, Aaron, and John, and daughters, Ann, Mary, Jane, Agness, Hannah, Margaret, and Elizabeth.

Third Creek Church, Rowan County NC

Acting Governor Mathew Rowan wrote in 1753 that, only seven years earlier, there were not more than "one hundred fighting men," a number "now at least three thousand." The number of fighting men was a general concern, since colonists were still under the threat of attack. The so-called French and Indian War had several phases, and there were almost constant reports of incidents in North Carolina from 1753 to 1760. During that period, skirmishes were often close to home for the Scots-Irish; a raiding party of French and "Northward" Indians was met by a contingent of Catawbas less than two miles from the Rowan Courthouse, resulting in a battle in which more than half of the French and Indian group was killed.

The Catawba Tribe had been on good terms with colonists until the middle part of the 1700's. Perhaps frustrated by the influx of white settlers into their traditional territories, they began to take up the ways of the more hostile Nations such as the Cherokees, and staged raids on colonists. Assaults on colonists were semi-regular occurrences, although not as frequent as the surreptitious thefts of food and clothing. Occasionally, actions included the kidnapping of women or children. Governor Dobbs decided the threat to settlers was real enough to require protection, and ordered the construction of a fort, to be located west of Salisbury. By January of 1757, the three-story fort was under the command of Captain Hugh Waddell, whose company of forty-six soldiers was enough to convince the Cherokees to end their hostilities—at least temporarily. The Catawbas continued their attacks, but Governor Dobbs suspected there was an ulterior motive. The border between North and South Carolina was under dispute, and Dobbs believed South Carolina settlers were goading the Catawbas into attacking colonists in North Carolina.

Casualties were not as severe for North Carolina colonists as they were during the same period in Virginia's Shenandoah Valley, where some 68 persons died during attacks over the course of two years. In those early years, before officials addressed the safety of the colonists, the Scot-Irish had to depend on their own wits and the aid of their neighbors, just to stay alive. Many others determined it wasn't worth the risk, and moved to lands east of the Yadkin River. The population of Rowan County dropped nearly half between 1756 and 1759, when only 800 taxable persons were counted.

While Rowan County settlers were considering whether to flee to safer areas to the east, a number of Virginia residents were moving into the Carolinas, seeking safety from hostilities in Augusta County. In 1758, Martha Mitchell wrote out her last will and testament, fearing the worst, noting that "son David Mitchell, through the necessity of the times, hath been forced to leave his own habitation, he is to live with James until it pleases God to restore peace to the land."

Two major roads eventually passed near Salisbury, which began as a tiny settlement and after a short time became a major trading center for colonists in the backcountry of North Carolina. From the eastern parts of the province, travelers could take the Trading Path west to Salisbury, or if heading southward from Pennsylvania and Virginia, the Great Pennsylvania Wagon Road, which extended through Salisbury, and eventually south to Charlotte and beyond. The earliest residents of Anson County had to create their own roads.

Many of the Scots-Irish farmers preferred living at the frontier, where a good days hunting could provide much more for the family than tending a garden. Many persisted in the belief that areas of land on which no trees grew represented barren soil, and as a result, declined to plant in the meadows. Planting among the trees forced the clearing of land to allow sunlight to penetrate. The Scots-Irish farmers were often content to chop down as few trees as possible and then girdle the rest at the trunk. When the trees eventually died, the trunks were hauled away, but the rows of corn were forced to detour around the numerous tree stumps dotting the gardens. A tree stump near enough to the house could serve a practical purpose. The center was hollowed out until a hard depression was formed in the trunk. In the bowl of the trunk, corn could be pounded into meal.

Although there were others, corn, tobacco, and flax were among the primary crops grown by the Scots-Irish. When flax was grown, it could be made into coarse linen that was tailored by the women into clothing.

Even during the summer months, it was a common sight to see long trails of smoke rising from the rock chimneys of the homes throughout the country. The fireplace on the frontier burned constantly, for cooking and for the warmth it provided. There were no panes in most of the settler's windows, which were covered with cloth or hides. As a result, to allow sunlight into the cabin in winter also brought in gusts of cold air.

Isolated as they were, the Scots-Irish quickly discovered that when the corn crop was brought in, haste was essential in preserving the harvest. Corn was used in the feeding of livestock; it was ground into meal, and was served at the table—but what was not immediately used quickly rotted where it was stacked. Markets were too distant to allow the practical hauling of produce, and as perishables, the crop was of limited value in bartering with others. Rather than let the corn go to waste, most farmers found that a simple process would preserve the harvest through an entire winter. In addition, processing the corn insured a constant value and allowed the harvest to be easily transported. That process was distillation, and in the days before temperance became a social agenda, whiskey from the "still" was considered "God's Gift." Not only was it viewed as a remedy for aches and pains and an aid to good health, distilling the corn mash purified it of the bacteria that perpetrated the "summer discomfort" brought on by spoiled milk and the water of many wells and streams. There was drinking to excess among some, but most residents of the colonies simply took a quick nip or two at various times throughout the day. Even the strict Presbyterians had little problem with the practical use of whiskey. A traveling preacher could not carry corn or a chicken as payment for his rousing sermons and wedding pronouncements, but could easily pocket a flask of "God's Gift." Taking a pull on the bottle was so commonplace an event that even courtroom activities might be halted to allow everyone—including the judge and the defendant—a quick nip from the same bottle.

Normally, drinking in moderation was the standard practice among the majority of the Scots-Irish, but weddings and funerals were another matter. For a wedding, the bride's father was expected to provide gallons for the ceremony, which usually lasted throughout the day. Before the dancing and merry-making got into full swing, two of the younger men would race to the bride's cabin to fetch the jug of "Black Betty." The winner of the foot race got to carry back the prize, and he, along with his defeated opponent, would run—leaping and yelling like madmen—back to the ceremony. Once returned, the winner was allowed the first kiss of the new bride, and—with great ritual—the groom was handed the jug of whiskey. After his quick swig, the container would then be passed around the room. It was a semi-formal ceremony of calling the toast, and as each was handed the jug he called to the crowd, "Health to the groom!...not forgetting myself!"

In the community of Carolina plantations, weddings were among the few diversions. The shivaree, as it was called, was the wedding party that extended well into the evening, and included escorting the bride and groom to their bed, with much joking and laughing. Once the newlyweds were sufficiently attended, the crowd returned outside and began a tremendous ruckus, beating together anything that made a decent noise, and calling out taunts to the newlyweds. Often, the bride could end the celebration by promising a meal or party the next day. It was the unfortunate bride who attempted to silence the crowd, which would only clamor all the longer and all the louder at her pleadings.

Horseracing was another popular diversion, and many times betting occurred, even among the Scots-Irish Presbyterians, although swearing at the losing horse was strictly forbidden. Another popular pastime was a game called "long bullets," in which a large iron ball was moved by one team toward a goal, defended by the other team, a sort of cannonball soccer. Later, many communities outlawed the game, citing its disruptive nature along the streets and roads.

Among the frontiersmen in western North Carolina life gradually became less about solitary struggles in the wilderness, and more about co-existing with the ever more numerous residents, in addition to the rigors of life on a farm. Crops had to be planted and harvested. Livestock required tending. Meat had to be cured for storage. Cloth was woven, shoes were made and tools repaired. When families began moving into areas that became Charleston and Salisbury, cattle and other livestock were sold or bartered with merchants who had opened shops. Bounties for wolves were paid at Salisbury, and it was there colonists who preferred the hunt could find a ready market for deerskins.

Settlers of Rowan County By 1762
Irish Settlement

James Andrews	John Braly	Michael Dickson
James Armstrong	Thomas Braly	James Dobbin
Mary Armstrong	John Bunting	John Dobbin
William Armstrong	Charles Burnett	James Docharty
William Bailey	Patrick Campbell	Alexander Douglass
Henry Barclay	James Carson	Thomas Douglas
Robert Barclay	James Cathey	Samuel Galbraith
John Beard	Henry Chambers	John Gillespie
William Beard	Samuel Cochran	Matthew Gillespie
James Best	Jacob Crawford	Thomas Gillespie
John Best	William Crawford	James Graham
John Biggs	Humphry Cun'ghm	William Grant
Samuel Blythe	John Cunningham	Robert Gray
William Boggan	William Cowan	Malcom Hamilton

Robert Hardin
James Hemphill
John Hickey
Samuel Hillis
James Hynds
Francis Johnston
Robert Johnston
John Kerr
John Kilpatrick
James King
Richard King
Robert King
John Kirkpatrick
John Knox
Dennis Lafferty
Alexander Lawrence
John Lawrence
John Little
Thomas Little
Francis Lock
John Luckie
John Luckie, Jr
Joseph Luckie
Robert Luckie
Samuel Luckie
William Luckie
William Mackey
James Martin

Samuel Martin
Hugh Mathews
Alexander McCorkle
David McDowell
John McElwrath
Henry McHenry
William McKnight
Humphry Mntgomry
Mary Murray
William Niblock
Joshua Nichols
Alpheus Paine
James Patterson
John Patterson
James Patton
John Patton
Robert Patton
Alexander Pendry
John Poston
Hugh Reed
Robert Reed
James Porter
William Porter
Robert Rankin
Samuel Rankin
George Robinson
John Robinson
Richard Robinson

William Robinson
John Russell
Griffith Rutherford
Henry Schiles
James Scott
John Scott
John Scott, Jr
William Sleven
John Smith
Robert Steel
David Stewart
James Stewart
James Storey
David Strain
Robert Tate
John Thompson
Joseph Thompson
John Todd
Archibald Wasson
Francis Wilson
John Wilson
John Witherspoon
Matthew Woods
Robert Woods
Samuel Woods
Samuel Young

Fourth Creek Settlement

Allen Alexander
Adam Allison
Andrew Allison
Robert Allison
Thomas Allison
David Andrew
John Archibald
Andrew Barry
David Black
Hugh Bowman
William Bowman
Robert Carson

William Carson
Robert Cavin
Samuel Cavin
George Davidson
Joseph Davis
Patrick Duffie
John Edwards
George Elliott
Christopher Erwin
George Erwin
William Erwin
John Fleming

Peter Fleming
George Hall
Hugh Hall
James Hall
Thomas Hall
Samuel Harriss
David Houston
John Ireland
William Ireland
John Jack
Roger Lawson
John Leech

Richard Lewis
Walter Lindsay
George McDonald
James McIlwaine
John McKee
James Miller
James Mordah
John Mordah
Andrew Morrison
James Morrison
William Morrison

John Oliphant
James Potts
John Potts
William Rea
Andrew Reed
George Reed
Robert Reed
Samuel Reed
Michael Robinson
Richard Robinson
James Roseborough

Robert Simonton
William Simonton
Fergus Sloan
William Stevenson
Jacob Thomas
Samuel Thornton
Hugh Waddell
James Watt
William Watt

Davidson's Creek Settlement

Robert Adams
Andrew Allison
Samuel Allison
Catherine Barry
Francis Beatty
James Crawford
William Denny
John Dickey
Joseph Gillespie
John Gullick
David Hall
John Hall

William Hall
Patrick Hamilton
Abraham Jetton
Robert Johnston
James Lambert
Hugh Lawson
Alex McCulloch
James McCulloch
John McCulloch
John McDowell
Thomas McQuown
William McRae

Hanse McWhorter
William Morrison
Andrew Neill
James Neill
William Neill
John Parks
John Sloan
Gilbert Strayhorn
Jeremiah Streater
James Tennant
Moses White
Benjamin Winsley

Hugh Parks and James Huggen bought property on the Catawba River, and near the forks of Dutchman, Cedar, and Cubb Creeks, Squire Boone settled with his wife Sarah. The Pennsylvania Quakers had disowned Squire Boone when his son Israel and his daughter Sarah were married outside the church. Rather than submit to the Quaker scorn, Squire Boone sold his Buck's County land to Edward Milnor in 1730, and moved his family to Philadelphia County. In 1750, after a brief time in the Shenandoah Valley, the Boones settled in the Yadkin river area of western North Carolina, establishing a home on Bear Creek.

At fifteen, young Daniel Boone was already an accomplished woodsman. He was a frequent sight, carrying hides by packhorse to Salisbury, where he could make a quick sale. The hide of a buck was worth a dollar, and the term buckskin, or buck, to represent a dollar, is a remnant of colonial times. In the summer of 1755, Daniel Boone married Rebecca Bryan. A few years later, Squire Boone sold 640 acres near Bear Creek to his son for 50 pounds. Record of the transaction in

October of 1759 is recorded in Deed Book No. 1 for Rowan County, and imme-diately follows an entry for the sale of a tract of land in which David Houston served as a witness. It was not only in the legal records and the wagon trails of North Carolina that the two families would encounter one another. The grand-sons of Carolina Boones and Carolina Houstons would meet again in the wilds of Kentucky, along with a good many other Scots-Irish, chasing the frontier beyond the Cumberland Gap.

CHAPTER FIVE

Scots-Irish and the
Frontier Wars

SCOTS-IRISH SETTLEMENT was well underway in the Shenandoah Valley and in the backcountry of the Carolinas when the Ohio River Valley became the center of attention on two continents. At the time, that region was considered by colonists to be part of the Province of Virginia, although the area nearest the headwaters of the Ohio is that lying in present-day western Pennsylvania.

Virginia land speculators, already successful in luring settlers to the South, began eyeing the American interior, lands which were claimed by the French, the English, the Iroquois, and the Province of Virginia. Some English colonial charters claimed ownership rights from coast to coast, while the Iroquois staked their claim by right of conquest. The French, while allowing that the Iroquois were claimed by the British to be their subjects, argued that La Salle had asserted ownership of the land for France when he reached the area in 1679. Britain made additional motions to establish their rights by signing the Treaty of Lancaster with the Iroquois in 1744, which had the effect—at least in the eyes of the

British—of transferring title from the Indian Nation to England. It was confusing, to say the least.

The Ohio Land Company of Virginia was formed in 1749 and obtained two hundred thousand acres south of the Ohio River, with the promise of additional land as soon as one hundred families moved into the area. Eight hundred thousand acres were allotted to the Loyal Land Company to the west, in the area historically recognized as Indian lands.

With strong settlements in Canada and Louisiana, the French intended to span the distance in between with forts and missions along the Mississippi River and through the Ohio Valley. Lacking the colonists to establish settlements, the French governor of Canada dispatched Captain Pierre Joseph Céleron de Blainville to stake claims of ownership through the area. Leaving Montreal in June of 1749, Céleron lead a party of eight officers, six cadets, two hundred soldiers, thirty tribal mercenaries, and a chaplain through New York to the east end of Lake Erie. By July, they entered the Allegheny River, the place considered at the time as the headwaters of the Ohio. At present-day Warren, Pennsylvania, Céleron erected a metal sign bearing a coat of arms, and buried a metal plate that declared "…the renewal of possession which we have taken of the said river Ohio, and of all those which fall into it, and of all the territories on both sides as far as the source of the said rivers…" The party continued its expedition southward, advising the few British subjects they encountered that they were trespassing, and eventually passed the site of modern-day Pittsburgh.

Although the area was considered frontier, and officially reserved for the Indian Nations, there were colonial trappers and traders living beyond the Blue Ridge. Word of the French expedition quickly traveled through the frontier. The Scots-Irish were well established in the Shenandoah Valley at the time the French began moving closer to the boundaries of Virginia. Scots-Irish landowners living in the Cumberland Valley at the time were relieved when news arrived that the French traveling party had turned to the west. There was anticipation that trouble was ahead, and families considered the brewing showdown between the French and the British, along with the continued border disputes between Maryland and Pennsylvania, in making decisions about continuing their settlements or moving on to the south. It was about the same time that David Houston and others in the Blunston tract began to move south to acquire a land in the Carolina back country, and just shortly before the French constructed a fort on the Ohio.

By 1753, the French, under Governor Marquis Duquesne, had established posts at the present-day cities of Erie, Waterford, and Franklin, Pennsylvania. Although colonists and the English were alarmed by the French activity, the expansion ended without interdiction by either colonists or the English. By fall of that year, the two thousand men involved in the French expansion had been reduced to eight hundred, mostly due to sickness and exhaustion. Rather than continuing south in the face of the approaching winter, most of the force was ordered back to Montreal.

Colonists were concerned about the French intentions, particularly those living at the edge of the frontier in Virginia, and Lieutenant Governor Robert Dinwiddie of Virginia saw an opportunity to protect both the colonists and his personal interests in the Ohio Company. He secured royal approval to build forts along the Ohio, and in October sent a twenty-one-year-old Virginia militia officer named George Washington to warn the French of the Virginia intentions.

He and six others journeyed from Williamsburg, Virginia to Wills Creek, then by the Monongahela River to present-day Braddock, Pennsylvania. When they arrived in December at Fort Le Bœuf, the French received them courteously, but politely refused to leave the area as Dinwiddie's letter had ordered. The response was humiliating to Washington, but upon his return, Dinwiddie was so impressed with the journal kept by Washington that he ordered it printed.

In response to the French rebuff, Dinwiddie quickly ordered the construction of a fort at the junction of the Monongahela and Allegheny rivers, the site of present-day Pittsburgh, Pennsylvania, a site noted in Washington's journal as a likely spot for an outpost. Dinwiddie then dispatched three companies of provincial militiamen initially commanded by Col. Joshua Fry. When Fry died at Patterson's Creek, the militia companies fell under the command of George Washington. The group was to reinforce the 120 militiamen who were present during construction of the fort.

Isabella McKitrick was standing in the front yard of her father Robert's home at Jenning's Gap in Virginia, when a group of young men approached along the road. She recognized Andrew Fowler, and called to him as he neared. Andrew spoke as he walked, and told Isabella that they intended to join the army to fight the French at Fort Duquesne. There was land to be had for each volunteer. Dinwiddie promised a land bounty to each volunteer who served in the effort. Years later, after Isabella was married and went by the name Isabella McGlamery, she spoke of their encounter that day, before a court hearing intended to sort out the various land bounty claims. Young Andrew and his friends completed their walk and joined the army, serving under Captain Andrew Lewis. John Huston was also among the Augusta County contingent—comprised mainly of the Scots-Irish—that volunteered for the expedition along with Andrew Fowler and his traveling companions in the excursion that became known as Braddock's War.

There were problems before Washington and his men ever reached the head-waters of the Ohio. The French overran the outpost, chasing off the militia Washington was to reinforce. There were no roads across the endless ridges, and the process of hacking out a path quickly exhausted Washington's men. Food and supplies never arrived, and support of friendly Indian tribes in the effort was never negotiated as it had been anticipated.

———

Braddock's War—August County Militia
Bounty Claimant Suit (Coleman vs. Richardson, 1808)

Henry Bailey	Sergeant
John Baynes	Military service, no claim filed
Alexander Bonney	Served at Braddock's defeat at Big Meadows
William Bronaugh	First Virginia Regiment under Geo. Washington
Mordecai Buckner	Quartermaster 1755 under Col. Adam Stephens
Benjamin Bullett	Ensign, First Va. Regiment under Geo. Washington
Thomas Buford	Sgt. under Braddock, Lt. under Washington
John Cole	Served at Braddock's defeat at Big Meadows
Timothy Conway	Military service
Valentine Cooper	Served at Fort Dusquesne 1758
William Cromwell	Military service
Charles Croucher	Soldier, Col. Stephens Regiment
Goodrich Crump	Military service
Mathew Doran	Military service
William Dangerfield	Captain, 1st VA Regiment under Geo. Washington
James Dunlap	Lt. under Cap. Peter Hogg, Rangers, killed 1758
William Fleming	Assistant Surgeon, First Va. Regiment
Andrew Fowler	Capt Andrew Lewis' Company at Big Meadows
John Fox	Military service, no claim filed
Henry Gains	Military service
Joseph Gatewood	First Virginia Regiment under Geo. Washington
Nathaniel Gist	Served under Washington and Cap. Chris. Gist
Peter Hogg	Captain under George Washington
John Horn	Served under Col. Mercer.
William Hughes	Subaltern, Geo. Washingon's Reg. of Regulars
John Huston	Military service
Thomas Kinkead	Cap. Lewis' Co. on Boquet's expedition in 1764
Alexander Kinney	Military service, no claim filed
Francis Kirtley	Military service
Charles Lewis	Captain under George Washington
Thomas Lovett	First Virginia Regiment under Geo. Washington
William Magee	Cadet, Braddock's defeat at Big Meadows

William McAnulty	Served at Braddock's defeat at Big Meadows
George Mercer	Cap. Old Va. Reg. under George Washington
John Fenton Mercer	Ensign, served with bro George in Old Va. Reg.
Thomas Morse	Hip wound at Big Meadows under Cap. Savage
Thomas Moss	Drummer, claimed carried Braddock from battle
Robert Murphy	Served at Braddock's defeat at Big Meadows
George Muse	Lieutenant Colonel, army
Thomas Nappe	Military service, no claim filed
John Neal	With Dunmore 1774, 13th Va. Reg. 1777
John Poo	Military service
John Posey	Military service
Marshall Pratt	Military service
Thomas Rutherford	Military service
James Samuel	First Virginia Regiment under Geo. Washington
John Savage	Military service
Charles Scott	Corp. in First Va. Reg. of Geo. Washington
Jesse Scott	Military service
Robert Scott	Military service
Francis Self	Served at Braddock's defeat at Big Meadows
John Smith	Military service, no claim filed
Hugh Stephenson	Military service
Robert Stuart	Military service, no claim filed
John Thompson	Served at Braddock's defeat at Big Meadows
George Turner	First Virginia Regiment under Geo. Washington
Jacob VanBraam	Military service, no claim filed
James Walker	Military service
Arthur Watts	Military service, no claim filed
John David Wollper	Subaltern, Col. Lewis Reg. of Regulars

On May 24th, when the troops reached a spot that was called Great Meadows, Washington was told by the Mingo Indian chief Half-King that the French were nearby. In a surprise attack, Washington's troops and a half-dozen Mingo warriors moved from the Meadows until the French were overtaken, then killed ten of the French party and accepted the surrender of the remaining twenty-three. It was the first battle for the young officer, and in a later account of the encounter, Washington described the sound of whistling bullets as "charming." He later attributed the statement to his youthful inexperience.

His troops were hungry and exhausted, and Washington returned to Great Meadows, where a stockade he called Fort Necessity was quickly constructed. The French were enraged by Washington's attack, and called the death of one of the slain men "an assassination." Anticipating a reprisal, members of the colonial militia were summoned from across Virginia to aid Washington. Reinforcements sped to Fort Necessity, but the four hundred militiamen who gathered under Washington's command were not nearly enough to hold off the nine hundred French who retaliated.

In the pouring rain on July 3rd, the French attacked. Within hours, nearly half of Washington's troops were wounded, dead, or too sick to fight. He was forced to surrender to the French, although they allowed him to march from the fort with full honors of war. Many of the men were unable to make the journey back with Washington, and others stayed behind to tend the wounded. John Huston, of Captain George Mercer's Company was left "lame on the road," along with John May, John Gollahorn, William McIntyre, and John Clements of the same Company.

The place called Great Meadows, where the first shots of the French and Indian War rang out, was later owned by George Washington, and was referred to in his will. Ironically, a Scots-Irishman named Joseph Huston later came to own the land where one of his namesakes had been left behind.

The battle at Fort Necessity was the first in what would become nearly ten years of colonial fighting between the French and the British.

———

The British had every intention retaking the Ohio Valley, and determined two regiments of British regulars could easily accomplish what the provincial militia had failed to do. General Edward Braddock, a sixty-year-old career soldier, was sent to conduct the campaign. Braddock was well schooled in the gentlemanly art of European warfare, but discounted advice on the tactics of battle used by the native tribes on behalf of the French.

Along with the British 44th and 48th Regiments, members of the colonial militia from Virginia and North Carolina began gathering for the impending battle. George Washington had resigned his command, but offered to serve without pay as an advisor to Braddock. Daniel Boone was among those from the Carolinas who followed Braddock, serving as a wagoner. From Augusta County, Virginia came Mathew Pigg, Major Scot, Audley Paul, William Scot, and others in the county militia. Pigg, who in March had been promoted to Lieutenant of Foot militia, served as a wagoner for John Davis, while Major Scot was a carrier for David Stuart. Archibald Huston had recently been promoted to Lieutenant of Foot, while Israel Christian, William Engles, and James Mitchell were sworn as militia captains. Adam Thompson and Henry Murray had also been given rank, as ensign and lieutenant respectively, just months previous to the start of Ohio Expedition.

There were twenty-five hundred men behind Braddock when he left Fort Cumberland, Maryland in June. Travel through the dense forest took so long, that he opted to detach fewer than fifteen hundred of his best men to advance more quickly on Fort Duquesne, while the remainder continued the march as reinforcements. In leading the column, Braddock envisioned a quick victory over the 800 French at the fort.

Just as the styles of warfare conducted by the Europeans and the native tribes differed greatly, the personal level at which battles were fought during colonial times were vastly different from modern warfare. While propaganda continues to be a device embraced in campaigns of war, Braddock and his men faced enemy taunts as they made their way to Fort Duquesne. In the journal he kept of the expedition, Robert Orme, an aide to Braddock, described a gruesome discovery made during their march in late June.

> *At our halting place we found another Indian camp, which they had aban-doned at our approach, their fires being yet burning. They had marked in tri-umph upon trees the scalps they had taken two days before, and many of the French had written on them their names and sundry insolent expressions.*

When Braddock made camp ten miles from Fort Duquesne, scouts had already warned the French of his location. On July 8, Captain Hyacinth de Beaujeu took two hundred French soldiers to meet Braddock, and managed to persuade an equal number of reluctant Indians to join him.

The next morning, with fifers blowing the "Grenadiers March," the British began splashing across the Monongahela. As they marched into the woods on the other side of the river, they heard shouts ahead and quickly formed a skirmish line, in traditional British battle form. A volley was sent into the direction of de Beaujeu's troops, forcing Braddock and his men to fall back. Suddenly, shots began ringing out from both sides of his column. The main body of French and Indian force had been posted behind trees and in adjacent ravines. As Braddock's men tried to fall back, they ran into the remainder of their own advancing troops as the French ambush continued. Hundreds fell on the spot, unable to escape the gunfire.

For three hours, Braddock wildly rallied his men. On five separate occasions, horses were shot out from under him as he rode among his men, vainly urged them to continue the struggle. Finally, Braddock was hit. As the drums sounded a retreat, George Washington dragged Braddock into a wagon and turned to follow the fleeing British troops.

"Who would have thought it?" Braddock kept muttering, as the wagon rolled through the carnage of the battle.

The French suffered less than sixty casualties. For the British, the losses were massive. Only 459 of the 1,373 privates escaped uninjured, and over 60 of the 86 officers were killed or wounded.

General Edward Braddock died two days later, and Washington ordered his burial in an unmarked grave in the middle of the trail, to disguise its location.

England was shocked at the fall of Braddock to what was considered a lesser force, and Virginia fell into a panic. The frontiers of Virginia, Pennsylvania, and Maryland, primarily settled by the Scots-Irish and the Rhinish Germans, were under the immediate threat of attack. Many in the Shenandoah Valley chose to abandon their homes rather than face the continuing threat of Indian attack, and others were simply driven from their land. Governor Morris of Pennsylvania wrote in November of 1755, "What a vast tract of country has been depopulated by these merciless savages." In western Pennsylvania, some estimates had reduced the number of fighting men in the area from 3000 to a mere 100. Many more opted to remain, facing those who would drive them from their lands with a characteristic determination.

——

During the period that marked the French and Indian War, colonists in the East for the most part learned to distinguish the differences among those inhabiting the frontier. While the Scots-Irish and the Rhinish Germans together settled the Pennsylvania and Virginia backcountries, their reactions to the increasing confrontations with the native tribes were markedly different. In acquiring land for settlement, the German pioneers usually followed the example of the Quakers in Pennsylvania, and worked out agreements with those tribal nations holding ancestral claims to the land. They also withdrew rather than confront members of the various tribes, and were similar to the Quakers in their pacifistic tendencies. The Scots-Irish, on the other hand, were hot-tempered and inclined to jump to defend what they viewed as rightfully obtained land.

Descriptions of the Scots-Irish tenacity contain common threads in regard to their apparent fearlessness. They were called "fighters—wherever courage, activity, and force were wanted—they had no equals." Many of the traits later used to describe Americans in general are the same as those used in describing the colonial era Scots-Irish frontiersman. The bold fighter, quick-tempered, God-fearing, righteous, defender of the faith, was the Scots-Irish frontiersman. It was their ferocity as fighters during the times of continual raids that established them a place when they were newcomers in the colony, and the more pacifistic of their neighbors viewed them as a positive line of defense against attack. The Scots-Irish demeanor—although liable at times to provoke confrontations—was respected when the protection of the settlements was concerned, and it served to lessen the time the Scots-Irish were cast as interlopers in the British colony.

It is an unfortunate aspect of human conflict that compassion and decency as regards the other side are quickly lost. The tribal members who battled to preserve their ancestral lands and the Scots-Irish, who fought to protect the homes they had built in the wilderness, were both guilty of the most vicious types of warfare. The Scots-Irish, as a rule, lived closest to the frontier, and were the primary targets when raids occurred. Given their temperament, they were more than willing to return a fight. Winthrop Sargent, a historian who wrote of Braddock's expedition, described the Scots-Irish: "*Impatient of restraint, rebellious against anything that in their eyes resembled injustice, we find these men readiest among the ready on the battlefields of the Revolution. If they had their faults, a lack of patriotism or of courage was not among the number. Amongst them were found to be men of education, intelligence, and virtue.*" There are accounts of ministers preaching sermons with a gun next to the Presbyterian prayer book in the pulpit, mindful of the possibility of attack even as services continued. It was largely the contributions of the Scots-Irish on the colonial frontier that brought about the eventual ending of the French holdings in the Ohio Valley.

Andrew Fowler and his companions found their way to the enlisting officers the day they passed Isabella McKitrick standing in her father's front yard, and the government made good on its promise to those who volunteered. Among those who volunteered from Augusta County to serve in the French and Indian Wars were many who later chose to take their land bounties in the wilds of Kentucky country. William Dangerfield was allotted 2000 acres in Jefferson County, while other Kentucky lands were deeded to William Bronaugh, Mordecai Buckner, Thomas Buford, Timothy Conway, William Fleming, John Fox, Nathaniel Gist, Peter Hogg, William Hughes, Stephenson Huston, Charles Lewis, George Mercer, George Muse, James Samuel, John Savage, Charles Scott, Robert Scott, John Smith, and John Thompson, all of whom served from Augusta County, Virginia.

———

The Scots-Irish feistiness that was so admired in some arenas served as a strain in others. John Houston, typical of his Ulster brethren—stubborn, quick-tempered, and impetuous—eventually fell into a major disagreement with the other elders of the Providence Church in Augusta County. Rather than settle the dispute and continue his membership, Houston and several other prominent members founded a second congregation, which they called The New Providence Church. He remained active in that church and in the operation of his farm, clearing land even to the age of sixty-four, when he died after being struck by a falling tree limb while working the plantation in 1754. He was buried in the New Providence Church Cemetery.

Custom dictated that the eldest son was the primary beneficiary of a last will, but John Houston bucked tradition by naming his youngest son Matthew to inherit the estate. James, the oldest son, had died in Ulster, leaving Robert as the oldest surviving son. Robert was not even mentioned in his father's will, although he may have already received his inheritance without it appearing in the legal notation.

Robert Houston had a considerable amount of land, likely acquired with the assistance of his father, and like his late father, he shared an avid interest in the affairs of the Presbyterian Church, although he was somewhat less benevolent than his father had been. John Houston donated land and aided in the construction of a church building, but his son Robert may have been more of the kind described by the adage that said "the Scotch-Irishman keeps well the Commandments, along with anything else he can lay hands on." Whatever his motivation, Robert sold "one acre and 9 perches" in November of 1759 to Samuel McDowell, John McClung, John Lyle (Lisle), William Alexander, and John Thomson, who were trustees of the Presbyterian Congregation of Timber Ridge. The price was five shillings. Robert had himself paid only twenty-five shillings a month previously for 95 acres on a branch of "Bufflow Creek."

———

WHILE BRADDOCK was making his ill-fated march to Fort Duquesne, Governor Dobbs of North Carolina was making an expedition of his own. In written remarks to the Board of Trade, Dobbs described his trip to the western edge of the province, and mentioned the Yadkin river as "*a large, beautiful river where is a ferry. It is near 300 yards over, it as at this time fordable scarce coming to the horses bellies. At six miles distance I arrived at Salisbury, the county town of Rowan. The town is but just laid out, the courthouse built and seven or eight log houses erected.*"

Among those seven or eight houses were four that served as public inns. Even as the guns were firing on Braddock at Fort Duquesne, settlement of the Carolina backcountry was in high gear. Those who came to settle in what was now Rowan County, having been divided from Anson County in 1753, could find food and lodging while they constructed homes on their land. Public inns were busy places and already the proprietors faced some stiff regulation by county officials. "Spiritous Liquors" were to be sold at the rate of six shillings per gallon, and small beer for a penny per quart. Even the fare at the inn came under the scrutiny of the county court.

> *Each Dinner of Roast Boiled flesh 8 pence Brakefast and Supper four Pence each Pasturing for Each for the first 24 hours 14 pence and for Each 24 hours afterwards 2 pence, Stableage each 24 hours with good hay or fodder 6 pence…*

The bed, which may have been enjoyed by the weary traveler regardless of condition, was "a good Bed and Clean Sheets Two Pence."

Colonists in North Carolina were also facing somewhat frequent attacks by tribes, included the Catawbas, who had previously been on good terms with the settlers. William Morrison advised the county that several had come to his mill and tried to throw a pail of water into his meal trough. He reported that when he tried to stop them "they made many attempts to strike him with their guns over his head."

Rowan County settlers had agreed to appropriate 500 Pounds "proclamation money" to buy guns and ammunition for the defense of the county. James Carter and John Brandon were entrusted with the money, but the cash proved too great a temptation for Carter. He was accused in 1757 of misappropriating the money and was fired from the position he held as one of the Justices of the Peace. In addition, he was expelled from his seat he held in the Assembly and was later forced to resign his commission as Major in the county militia. Brandon might have faced sanctions as well, but died in the interim period between the raising of the money and the discovery of its misuse.

While they prepared for the worst, diplomatic efforts brought a temporary peace with the Cherokee Nation, and as a result, many of the settlers serving at Fort Dobbs began returning to their homes. By November of 1758, only Jacob Frank and one assistant remained at the fort. Frank was a German settler who owned one of the early inns at Salisbury. The fort was no sooner abandoned than attacks on settlements resumed by the Cherokees in North Carolina. A number of families in the Catawba Valley were forced to withdraw from their homes as a result of the continued attacks. Andrew Morrison, John Oliphant, William Ireland and John Ireland were among the many who fled to other areas for fear of attack.

It was also in 1758 that the British fortunes on the American frontier began to change. British General John Forbes was sent to take Fort Duquesne. He left the site of present-day Bedford, Pennsylvania with five thousand provincial troops and fourteen hundred Scottish Highlanders. They moved with caution across the Ohio Valley ridges and left a string of fortified posts behind them as they progressed. In September, eight hundred of the Highlanders were sent ahead to scout the fort and wound up in a fierce battle with tribal warriors. Both sides lost nearly a third of their parties.

By late November, Forbes had moved to a point within a few miles of Fort Duquesne, and as they advanced nearer, a huge explosion rumbled from the fort. At their arrival the following day, Forbes and his company of men found the fort gutted and abandoned, except for a grisly reminder of the ferocity of the war. The French had left a row of stakes inside the fort, to which were attached the heads of the Highlanders taken prisoner in the earlier battle. Underneath each was a Scottish kilt.

Hugh Waddell, who had left his command at Fort Dobbs to join in the Ohio Valley fighting against the French and Indians, returned in early 1759 and headed a small contingent of Scots-Irish militiamen. Before attacking Fort Dobbs, tribal warriors killed Robert Gillespie of Rowan County, and the fourteen-year-old son of Richard Lewis. A short time later, Waddell, back at Fort Dobbs, noticed activity around the fort, and headed a party of ten men to investigate the matter. In a letter to Governor Dobbs, Waddell indicated his force was greatly outnumbered.

> *We had not marched 300 yards from the fort when we were attacked by at least 60 or 70 Indians. I had given my party orders not to fire until I gave the word, which they punctually observed: we received the Indians fire: when I perceived they had almost all fired, I ordered my party to fire which we did not further than 12 steps each loaded with a bullet and seven buck shot, they had nothing to cover them as they were advancing either to tomahawk or make us prisoners:*

The remainder of the tribe attacked the fort and met with similar fire. Waddell reported 10 or 12 of his enemy killed or wounded, and "on my side I had 2 men wounded one of whom I am afraid will die as he is scalped, the other is in a way of recovery and one boy killed near the fort whom they durst not advance to scalp."

Colonial militias retaliated for the attack on the fort, and Colonel Alexander Osborne, Captain Martin Pfeiffer, Captain John Kerr, and Captain Conrad Michael were among those leading men against the warring Nation. David Houston served in Osborne's primarily Scots-Irish company, with Lieutenant John McWhorter and Ensign Zebulon Brevard. Some fifteen Native American villages were destroyed during the two-year campaign that pushed the tribes westward to the foothills of the Appalachian Mountains. Terms of a treaty reached between the colonists and the Cherokees intended to establish a boundary line between the two groups, but it was a treaty forced upon the Cherokees, who had few other choices. With the French vanished from the Ohio Valley, the English and their colonists had no further use for the tribes earlier been courted as allies.

Scots-Irish Settlement Militiamen from Augusta County Virginia

Jacob Aberman
John Aberman
Gardner Adkins
Archibald Alexander
Francis Alexander
James Alexander
Moses Algier
Hugh Allen
James Allen
Robert Allen
Charles Allison
Chris Amontrout
George Anderson
James Anderson
Robert Anderson
William Anderson
James Anon
Sampson Archer
John Armstrong
Robert Armstrong
George Barclay
Thomas Barrow
John Baskine
Thomas Baskine
Robert Belche
David Bell
James Bell
John Bell
Samuel Bell
William Bell
Henry Beniger
Henry Benningar
Dominick Beret
James Berlane
Christopher Bingaman
John Bingaman
Anthony Black
John Black
Matthew Black
Robert Black

William Black
William Blackwood
James Blair
John Blair
William Blair
Jacob Botters
Henry Bowen
John Bowen
Moses Bowen
Reice Bowen
Thomas Bowens
John Bowin
William Bowin
Thomas Bowne
Robert Boyd
Thomas Boyne
Robert Brackenridge
James Bradshaw
William Bratton
James Bridgetts
Samuel Briggs
John Brown
David Bryans
James Bryans
Alexander Buchanan
Andrew Buchanan
Archibald Buchanan
James Buchanan
John Buchanan
William Buchanan
James Bunton
James Burk
James Burnside
John Burton
William Buyers
James Caghey
John Cain
Andrew Campbell
Hugh Campbell
James Campbell

John Campbell
Matthew Campbell
John Cantley
George Capliner
Patrick Cargon
John Carlile
Robert Carlile
William Carothers
Henry Carr
John Carr
Richard Carr
Samuel Carr
James Cartmill
William Carvin
Thomas Cashaday
Valentine Castle
Thomas Cavon
Edward Cenney
William Christopher
John Clark
William Clark
Mathias Cleeke
Christopher Clement
Arsbel Clendinin
John Clendinin
John Clerk
Joseph Clerk
Daniel Cloud
Phelty Cogh
Hyram Coler
John Colley
James Colter
Woolrey Conrad
Darby Conway
Jeremiah Copper
Martin Cornet
John Cosby
Tetrarch Couch
James Couden
James Cowdown

Alexander Craig
Robert Craig
John Cravens
William Cravens
John Crockett
George Croford
John Crosby
James Cull
James Culton
Andrew Cunningham
Jacob Cunningham
John Cunningham
Robert Cunningham
Walter Cunningham
William Cunningham
John Cunrod
Walter Cunrod
William Currey
George Davidson
James Davidson
Benjamin Davies
James Davis
John Davis
Samuel Davis
John Davison
Robert Dew
Mathias Dice
John Dickenson
Michael Dickey
Hugh Diver
Joseph Dixton
Nathaniel Donlap
Henry Downs
Abraham Duncklebery
George Dunkle
John Dunkle
James Dunlap
James Dunlap
Adam Dunlop
James Dunlop
John Dunlop
William Dyer
Abram Earhart

Michael Earhart
John Early
Michael Eberman
William Edemston
David Edmiston
Moses Edmiston
Samuel Edmiston
Jeremiah Edwards
Frederick Eister
William Elliot
Michael Erhart
Edward Ervin
William Ervin
Daniel Evans
Nathaniel Evans
John Farrell
John Finley
Robert Finley
Christopher Finney
Andrew Fitzpatrick
William Fleming
Samuel Ford
Thomas Ford
James Fowler
Nicholas Frank
John Frazier
Michael Frees
Jonas Friend
Jacob Fudge
John Fulse
John Fulton
Thomas Galbreath
David Gallaw
David Gallaway
James Gamble
James Gatlive
James Gay
John Gay
Dennis Getty
Robert Gibson
Archibald Gilkison
Archibald Gilkson
James Gillaspey

Alexander Gillespie
James Gilmore
John Gilmore
Thomas Gilmore
George Gipson
George Goodman
Jacob Goodman
Daniel Goodwin
John Gordon
Robert Gragg
William Gragg
David Graham
Jacob Graham
John Graham
Robert Graham
David Gray
James Gray
Arthur Greer
James Grimes
Robert Grimes
Jacob Grub
David Guin
John Gum
George Gunn
Robert Gwinn
Benjamin Hagler
Jacob Hagler
John Hagler
Postine Hagler
Andrew Hall
Moses Hall
Robert Hall
Moses Hambleton
Robert Hambleton
William Hambleton
George Hamer
Alexander Hamilton
Andrew Hamilton
James Hamilton
John Hamilton
Thomas Hamilton
William Hamilton
Stephen Hanburger

Benjamin Hansley
Adam Harper
Jacob Harper
Philip Harper
Leonard Harring
Gideon Harrison
John Harrison
Nathaniel Harrison
Nicholas Havener
Andrew Hays
John Hays
Hyram Hecks
Adam Hedrick
George Hedrick
Samuel Hemphill
Daniel Henderson
James Henderson
John Henderson
Michael Henderson
Samuel Henderson
William Henderson
Robert Henry
Caleb Hermon
Leonard Herren
Thomas Hicklin
Nicholas Hoffman
William Hog
Peter Hogg
Michael Hogshead
Robert Homes
William Hook
James Hooks
William Hooks
Archibald Hopkins
John Hopkins
Jacob Hornbery
James Houston
Edward Howard
John Howell
John Hudson
Thomas Hudson
Nicholas Hufman
Philip Hufman

James Hugart
Thomas Hugart
John Hughs
Robert Hunter
Holerick Hushman
Archibald Huston
James Huston
Samuel Huston
John Hutcheson
William Jackson
Andrew Jameson
John Jameson
Joseph Jenkins
John Johnson
John Johnston
Jonathan Jones
George Jordon
Abraham Keeny
Michael Kelly
James Kenaday
William Kenaday
William Kerr
Samuel Kerre
John Kilpatrick
Jacob Kindler
George King
John King
John Kinkead
Thomas Kinkead
William Kinkead
Benjamin Kinley
Conrad Kinsel
William Kinsey
Francis Kirtley
George Kite
Valentine Kite
William Kite
Ralph Laferty
David Laird
William Lapesley
John Lawn
James Lawrence
Thomas Lawrence

Gaun Leeper
Going Leeper
Alexander Legat
John Leonard
Charles Lewis
George Lewis
William Lewis
Matthew Lindsey
Adam Little
Andrew Little
James Lockart
Andrew Lockridge
James Logan
Henry Long
Hyram Long
John Long
William Long
Peter Looney
Ephraim Love
John Low
John Lowry
Patrick Lowry
Robert Lusk
Daniel Lyle
John Lyle
Samuel Lyle
Hugh Mackclure
James Magavock
Robert Magery
John Malcolm
John Malcom
George Malcomb
John Malcomb
Michael Mallow
Michael Malow
Charles Man
George Man
Jacob Man
William Mar
George Marchel
John Massey
George Matthews
John Matthews

Joshua Matthews
Richard Matthews
Sampson Matthews
William Matthews
William Matthis
John Maxwell
John Mayers
John McAlheney
Charles McAnally
Daniel McBridge
Robert McCarney
John McCay
Alexander McClanahan
James McClong
John McClong
Patrick McCloskey
James McClung
Arthur McClure
James McClure
John McClure
Halbart McClurr
Hyram McCollom
Thomas McComb
Thomas McCome
Robert McComey
Adam McCormick
Thomas McCorne
John McCoy
John McCoy
Robert McCoy
David McCroskey
James McCutchison
Samuel McCutchison
William McCutchison
James McDowell
Samuel McDowell
William McFarland
James McFerrin
John McFerrin
Samuel McFerrin
Hugh McGarey
Robert McGarey
William McGill

Thomas McGregor
James McHenry
William McHenry
John McKay
William McKinney
Thomas Mcklemare
Daniel McKnight
James McMahon
Alexander McMullan
Samuel McMurray
Thomas McNamar
John McNeal
Dennis McNely
John Medley
James Meeter
Edward Megary
Robert Megary
John Melcum
Joseph Melcum
Nicholas Mildebarler
Adam Miller
Jacob Miller
John Miller
Patrick Miller
Peter Miller
Robert Minice
William Minter
William Mintor
John Mitchel
Robert Mitchell
George Moffett
George Moffett
John Montgomery
James Moor
David Moore
John Moore
William Moore
George Moses
Peter Moses
George Mouse
Lawrence Murphy
Henry Murray
John Murray

Thomas Nicholas
Samuel Norwood
Poston Nosler
Nicholas Null
John Osborne
Matthew Paten
Thomas Paterson
Charles Patrick
John Patrick
James Patterson
Robert Patterson
Samuel Patterson
Audley Paul
Thomas Paxton
Larkin Pearpoint
John Peary
Jacob Pence
Henry Peninger
Gunrod Peterfish
Edwin Peterson
Jacob Peterson
John Peterson
Martin Peterson
Thomas Peterson
John Phares
Martin Phillips
Gabriel Pickins
John Plunkett
Thomas Pointer
William Polog
John Porter
Patrick Porter
Thomas Powell
William Preston
Daniel Price
Thomas Pritchard
Adam Props
Michael Props
Richard Pryar
Lofftus Pullen
William Purzins
John Putt
John Putt

William Ralston
James Ramsay
Francis Randalls
Archibald Reah
Robert Reah
William Reah
Adam Reburn
John Reburn
Eldad Reed
William Reed
John Reiger
Francis Reity
Daniel Reme
Daniel Remi
Robert Rennick
Jacob Richard
John Richard
James Risk
James Robertson
David Robinson
George Robinson
John Robinson
William Robinson
George Rogers
Matthew Rolestone
William Rolestone
Jacob Rolman
Robert Ross
William Ross
George Rowland
Jacob Runkle
Charles Rush
James Rusk
John Salley
Moses Samble
Patrick Savage
David Sayer
Alexander Sayers
Sampson Sayers
David Scott
Thomas Scott
Thomas Seirl
John Seller

Samuel Semple
Matthew Shaddin
Ludwick Shadow
Edward Shanklin
John Shanklin
Richard Shanklin
William Shannon
William Shanon
Paul Shaver
William Shaw
Paul Shever
John Shields
William Shields
John Shill
George Shillinger
Isiah Shipman
Josiah Shipman
James Simpson
Nicholas Sivers
James Skidmore
Joseph Skidmore
Abraham Smith
Charles Smith
Daniel Smith
David Smith
Francis Smith
Gasper Smith
Henry Smith
John Smith
Thomas Smith
John Snodgrass
Thomas Spence
Thomas Spencer
John Sproul
John Sprout
James Steel
Robert Steel
James Steele
James Steenson
Adam Stephenson
James Stephenson
John Stephenson
Thomas Stephenson

Alexander Steuart
David Steuart
James Steuart
Adam Stevenson
James Stevenson
John Stevenson
Robert Stevenson
James Stewart
William Stewart
John Still
John Stilt
Timothy Stoten
Cornelius Sullivan
Cornelius Sullivant
Alexander Sutherland
William Taylor
William Tencher
Alexander Thompson
John Thompson
Moses Thompson
Robert Thompson
Robert Thomson
Mathias Tice
John Tinley
James Tobit
Samuel Todd
David Tolford
Robert Tolford
Arthur Trader
Robert Tremble
John Trimble
Robert Trimble
Walter Trimble
Peter Trusler
James Turk
Gunrod Umble
Martin Umble
Ury Umble
John Vance
Thomas Vance
Peter Vanimon
Joseph Vauhob
Peter Veneman

Ludowick Wagoner
Alexander Walker
John Walker
James Ward
Joseph Ward
William Ward
James Wardlaw
John Wardlaw
Edward Watts
George Watts
Cornelius White

Moses Whiteside
Jonathan Whitley
Jacob Wiece
Joseph Wiece
John Willey
Robert Willey
John Williams
Charles Wilson
George Wilson
Hugh Wilson
James Wilson

John Wilson
Josiah Wilson
Richard Wilson
William Wilson
John Withlaw
John Wizer
John Woods
William Woods
Richard Yedley
James Young
John Young

CHAPTER SIX

Where There's A Will

TO CALL IT A PEACEFUL LIFE would have been extravagantly optimistic and a good deal misleading regarding the frontier settlements and plantations of the Scots-Irish. The fanfare and ceremony that marked the acquisition of French holdings by the British may have been too far removed from the colonists in Virginia and the Carolinas to make any impression. After abandoning Fort Duquesne, the French fled their western forts as well. For the most part, by 1760, the British were in possession of virtually all of Canada. On the frontiers of Pennsylvania and Virginia, the signing of the Treaty of Paris in 1763 may have raised hopes that the violence of the previous decade had ended. In the agreement, France ceded all of its holdings east of the Mississippi, including Canada, to Britain.

It may have been the religious tenets of the Presbyterian Scots-Irish, and an adherence to the practices that brought them from ignorance and poverty in Scotland to having attained some degree of respectability in the American colonies—over the short term of two or three generations. Whatever the reasons, the Scots-Irish settlers were ready users of the colonial courthouse, and their lives are amply documented in the archived papers of the time. Even those men who had little to declare set aside the time to put on paper a last will and testament, and the religious foundation of the Scots-Irish was almost always noted in their final depositions. The Rowan County, North Carolina will of David Houston is typical of those of the time.

> *In the name of God Amen, the thirteen Day of August one thousand Seven Hundred Sixty one, I David Houston of the County of Rowan being in perfect mind and memory thanks be given to God, therefore Calling to mind the mortality of my Body knowing that it is appointed for all men to Die and afterward the Judgment, Do make and ordain this my Last Will and Testament, first and principally of all I give my Soul into the Hands of God Who gave it, and for my Body I Recomend it to the Earth to be buried in a Christian Manner at the Descretion of my Executors—Nothing Doubting but at the General Resurrection I Shall Receive it. Same again, by the Mighty power of God and as touching such Worldly Estate where with it has pleased God to Bless me with in this Life I Give, Devise and Dispose of In the following manner & form Viz.—*

After naming his wife Mary and son Aaron as executors of the estate, and ordering the payment of all debts and funeral charges, the Scots-Irish farmer considered the disposal of his property.

> *I Give and Bequeath unto Mary my Dearly Beloved Wife forty pounds Ready money, a pacing Mare Called Sorrel, her Choice of my beds and furniture and the use of the plantation whereon I now Dwell During her life, also her Saddle and Bridle, Six pewter plates, a pewter Dish, and a pot which She pleases to Choose—to her, her Heirs and assigns for Ever...*
> *I Give and Bequeath to my Beloved Son Archibald five pounds to be Raised out of my personal Estate...*
> *I Give and Bequeath unto my Beloved Son William that Tract of Land Whereon he Now Dwelleth...and what movables he has already Received in part of his portion and also four pounds in money...*
> *I Give and Bequeath unto my Beloved Son Aaron that piece of land lying between or adjoining to Hugh McQuowns and Thomas McQuowns Land and Ten pounds to take out a Deed for it...also a Tract of Land in the County of Anson Near Twelve mile Creek...and what Stock he has already Received...*
> *I Give and Bequeath unto my Beloved Son John one Half of the Tract of Land Whereon I now Dwell, to be Laid off on the West Side of the Branch to him...*
> *I Give and Bequeath unto my Beloved Son David the other half of the tract of Land whereon I now Dwell, to be Laid off to him on the East Side of the Branch after his Mothers Decease or When at age...*

I Give and Bequeath unto my Beloved Daughter Ann two pounds to be Raised out of my personal estate...

I Give and Bequeath to my Beloved Daughter Mary two pounds together with what she has already Received...

I Give and Bequeath to my Beloved Daughter Jane a Horse Value Eight pounds, a Saddle and Bridle, a Bed and furniture, and four Cows...

Identical bequests to those afforded his daughter Jane were made to daughters Agness, Hannah, Margaret, and Elizabeth, before Houston turned to the subject of education.

I Order my Son John Half a year Schooling, also I order my Son David two years Schooling, and more if my Executors sees need for it—also, I Order my Daughter Elizabeth three years Schooling, and the Cost of Schooling to be Calculated, and taken off the Estate before any publick sale is made of what is not here Willed and Bequeathed.

It is my Will and pleasure, that what of my Estate is not here Willed and Bequeathed, be Sold by Publick Vendue, and the Value thereof to be Equally divided among these of my Children, Viz. Aaron, John, David, Jane, Agness, Hannah, Margaret, Elizabeth to them their Heirs and Assigns for Ever.

It is my Will and pleasure if any of my Children Should Die before they Come to age, that then what I have herein Willed and Bequeathed be Sold By my Executors and Equally Divided, among the Then Surviving Children, Males and females, Except my Son Archibald, & Daughter Ann.

Signed Sealed published pronounced and Declared by the Said David Houston as his Last Will and Testament in presence of us the Subscribers.

Beyond the length of the document, there are several items of note concerning the will. The distinctive handwriting is likely not that of Houston, who signed in his own hand. The paper was folded into quarters, typical of storage methods at early-day courthouses. On the outside edge is the notation:

David Huston's
Last Will &
Testament
Oct Court 1762
Registered Book A Page 63

The standardized spelling of surnames was not formalized until the 19th century, and ironically, the spelling listed reflects the spelling that came to be associated with the family line of David's son Archibald, who was already married and living in Augusta County, Virginia. Archibald and his sister Ann are singled out in the final Item of the will, to be excluded in the division of unclaimed bequests. Since the remaining children are presumed by the wording to be minors, the exclusion of Archibald and Ann may have been a reflection of their ages or marital status. Many married children received anticipated inheritances at the time of their weddings or removal from the family plantation. It was somewhat uncommon that David Houston chose to list the names of all his many children; numerous wills from the same period do not, and many others list only the sons living at home.

Wills of the period, particularly those involving men of some means, generally mentioned the disposition of slaves. The Scotch-Irish were among those who held slaves during the period, but apparently, David Houston did not. It was also a common practice that furniture and like items, generally termed the "movables," that were not specifically mentioned in the will, were sold at a public vendue, or sale. Often, the widow was placed in the position of having to buy back from the estate any items she wished to keep that were not specifically mentioned in the will. Bequeathing items to the widow that presumably were her own, such as kitchen utensils or clothing, was also a common practice. It is a rare will of the period that acknowledges possession of articles by the wife, especially items owned before the marriage.

David Houston died within a year of the filing of the will. When his son Archibald in Virginia received word, he requested that a relative look out for his interests in the probate of the estate. In addition, he made a formal filing at the Augusta Courthouse naming Hugh Houston of "New Providence" as his counsel in the estate of David Houston.

———

A WAR BELT was a string of wampum—small beads made from shells—that could be sent from one Indian tribe to another when assistance was sought for an anticipated war. The war belts were being passed in 1763 among the Delawares, Hurons, Miamis, Ottawas, Potawatomis, Senecas, and Shawnees. It became apparent to the tribes that their status with the English had changed, and that their livelihood on the continent was threatened. War with the English appeared to be the only way to preserve the Indian's position.

Britain and France had just signed a formal peace agreement when a Seneca war belt was sent to the Miami Nation. The Ottawa chief Pontiac called a council in April and urged the tribes to attack the colonists. His plan included a surprise attack on Fort Detroit on the western Great Lakes.

On May 7, Pontiac and 300 warriors, each concealing a weapon appeared at the fort, then under the command of Major Henry Gladwin. The garrison had somehow been warned of the attack plans and, although the gates were left open as usual, the guards there were doubled and armed with bayonets. Pontiac withdrew his force without attacking the fort. Instead, he attacked a nearby farm and killed three colonists, then proceeded to attack other settlements in the area. He ordered Gladwin to surrender the fort, which Gladwin refused, sending Pontiac on a rampage. He attacked in series a line of English forts throughout the Great Lakes, then turned his force toward western Pennsylvania. Fort Duquesne (which had been renamed Fort Pitt by the English), Fort Venango, Fort Ligonier, and Fort Bedford were all attacked. Fort Venango fell in mid-June. Half of the men at Fort Le Boeuf escaped when that outpost was attacked, but the thirty men who surrendered at Fort Presque Isle were taken prisoner and divided among the Ottawas, Hurons, Senecas, and Chippewas. In late June, Delaware Nation demanded the surrender of Fort Pitt, but the captain of the garrison refused, but sent a present to the attacking force. The gift, consisting of several blankets from the fort's smallpox hospital, carrying the illness that later decimated the Delaware Tribe.

The Scots-Irish—who constituted the majority of the settlers at the extreme frontier—suffered greatly during the next months as attacks continued. Some estimates put the number of colonists killed by Indians during the spring and summer at two thousand.

In August, Colonel Henry Bouquet marched with 460 reinforcements from Carlisle, Pennsylvania to Fort Pitt, and came under attack by a war party of Delawares, Hurons, Mingos, and Shawnees. Bouquet and his force fought throughout the afternoon of August 5, but by sundown they were surrounded. When the sun rose the next morning, the tribal leaders saw a thin line of defenders and ordered an immediate attack. Ironically, the tribal tactics used in the earlier defeat of Braddock's force, were used against the advancing warriors. As they rushed from the forest toward the colonial line, they were attacked from both sides by forces that Bouquet had concealed. The Pennsylvania Quakers refused to consider measures against the Native Americans, which only further exasperated the quick-tempered Scots-Irish, who were hearing rumors that the Conestogas were assisting the warring tribes in the attacks on the frontier settlements. The rumors eventually pushed the impetuous Scots-Irish to the boiling point, and on December 14, fifty-seven men from the township of Paxtang (or Peckstang, as Benjamin Franklin called it when he wrote about the incident) surrounded the Conestoga village. The vigilantes did not realize that the entire tribe, with the exception of a few members, was away peddling crafts to colonists. Three men, two women, and one boy had remained behind. The so-called Paxton Boys brutally killed four of the Conestogas and shot the other two. Governor John Penn condemned the attack, and the remaining members of the Conestoga trible were housed in the county workhouse for their own protection. Despite the measures, the Paxton Boys launched an attack on the workhouse two weeks later, killing the remaining fourteen as they knelt in prayer.

It wasn't until two months later that the Quakers at last took up arms, but not against the Native Americans. When the Paxton Boys determined to march on Philadelphia and attack any tribal members living there, the Quakers mobilized to fight the oncoming mob. While the Scots-Irish camped outside Philadelphia, Benjamin Franklin led a delegation to the camp and persuaded the Paxton Boys to return home.

Meanwhile, the tribes involved in the frontier attacks were matched in strength when English reinforcements finally began arriving. Rather than continue the hostilities, many of the tribes began striking deals with the British and pulled out of the war. Finally, with most of his allies gone, Pontiac agreed to stop his attacks, ending what came to be called Pontiac's Rebellion. In 1769, Pontiac was shot in the back and killed, ending perhaps the last real possibility that Native American tribe could halt the encroachment of the frontier settlements.

———

As early as 1762, there were at least 62 families living south of the Yadkin river along the outreaches of Third and Fourth Creek in western North Carolina's back country. Most were Scots-Irish, and many had been in the colonies for a number of years before relocating to the Carolinas. Andrew Morrison was an early settler, dating to 1762, and his property was located in the west part of present-day Rowan County. Nearby property owners were John Kerr, Benjamin Wiley, Robert Morrison, Michael Bird, James Knox, John McElwaith, and David Morrison. Hugh Waddell, who later served the area well in the county militia, bought land just north of the Fourth Creek Meetinghouse in 1756 from John McCulloch, who owned, but never lived on the land. John Jack moved from Chester County, Pennsylvania to settle as one of the pioneers in the fertile savannah between the Yadkin and the Catawba rivers. John Potts and James Potts moved into the area from Maryland at about the same time. Between the forks of the Yadkin and South Yadkin

Thyatira Church - Rowan Co. NC

rivers and Lord Granville's Line to the south was one of the larger settlements in western North Carolina. It was so populated with Scots-Irish that it became known as the Irish Settlement. They were primarily farm families and were largely content in bypassing elected or appointed public office. The town of Salisbury was laid out just north of the center of the Irish Settlement.

It was in Salisbury in 1763 that a change was in store for Elizabeth Gillespie. Her husband Robert had been involved in a business venture with Thomas Bashford, and their enterprise had become quite successful. Robert Gillespie was scalped and killed during a Cherokee attack in 1759, and the following year, his widow bought a lot in Salisbury from William Williams to operate a public inn. She apparently possessed a business savvy that equaled that of her late husband, and over the next two years, Elizabeth became one of the continent's early female business success stories. She later bought a second lot in Salisbury, and a 275 acre tract of land adjacent to the town proper. She ran the public house and managed the land purchases alone for three years, until she married William Steele, a recent emigrant from Pennsylvania who bought sixteen lots that adjoined Elizabeth Gillespie's property at the north edge of Salisbury. Together the couple prospered, and raised a son—John Steele—who became a public figure in his own right, then serving the young state of North Carolina in the legislature and as a member of the first Congress of the United States. President George Washington appointed Steele as the first Comptroller of the Treasury, and he served in that capacity until 1802. Elizabeth's daughter by her first husband also faired well, marrying Samuel Eusebius McCorkle, who co-founded the University of North Carolina.

The same year Elizabeth Gillespie remarried, more than 150 people were living in Salisbury and more than 74 of the original 256 lots laid out had already been sold. There were houses, shops, inns, a doctor, lawyers, a candlemaker, three hatters, a butcher, a tailor, a wagonmaker, and two general stores. The news still came from the courthouse steps though, and it was well after the Revolution that a newspaper began printing locally. John Baker of Salisbury was missing part of his lower ear, having had it bitten off during an argument some years earlier. Most of his Rowan County neighbors were aware of the cause, but Baker had petitioned the court for a certificate to prove that the loss was not an "ear-cropping"—a common punishment for larceny during colonial times.

The Presbyterian congregations of the Scots-Irish met at Thyatira Church, which was one of the focal points on the western fringe of the Irish Settlement. John Thomson was a Presbyterian preacher, and among the first to minister in the northwest part of the province. Before the meetinghouse at Thyatira was constructed, he conducted frontier services at the homes of William Morrison, Osborne's meetinghouse, Cathey's place, and Samuel Young's settlement—later, the site of the Fourth Creek Church.

Changes in the frontier community were also reflected in the variety of community offerings among the Scots-Irish. A small library was kept at Thyatira Church, where volumes such as Butler's *Analogy of Natural and Revealed Religion*, and Mosheim's *Ecclesiastical History* could be referenced. A classical school called Crowfield Academy was established near the home of Alexander Osborne. Pupils at that school included Adlai Osborne, Aaron Houston, Samuel Eusebius McCorkle, and Ephraim Brevard, the son of John Brevard. Ephraim Brevard became involved politically and served as secretary in a group that composed a treatise that for years was called the "Mecklenburg Declaration of Independence."

———

In Virginia during the same period, life in Augusta County was returning to a calmer form of frontier life, but again, other changes were in store. Thomas Gilmore lost his mother and father—both were killed during an Indian raid, and although less dramatically, the county lost one of its early pioneers when William Stephenson died in 1759. He did not live to see it, but his sons would serve the county as he had, and several won respect in the Continental Army during the Revolution. His widow Sarah, and son Adam served as executors of his estate, including a tract of land on Gum Run Meadow, which he divided among his children; Adam, John, James, William, David, Elizabeth, Mathew, and Sarah.

Another stalwart of the community was in poor health at the time of Stephenson's death. Robert Houston was married to Mary Davidson, the daughter of another Scots-Irish colonist, Samuel Davidson and lived in an inspired two-story house on Timber Ridge complete with white columns and a gallery. In September of 1760, just six years after the death of his father, Robert was "sick and weak of body" at the age of forty-one. He died the next spring, leaving his plantation to his youngest son Samuel, whose own son would later become the President of the Republic of Texas. Sons James and John were given land, while the eldest daughter, having already received her share in the form of a dowry, received five shillings. Daughters Anne, Esther, Margaret, and Mary divided two-thirds of the household goods and the twelve pounds in cash that were included in the estate. Robert's widow received the remaining third.

John Paxton headed another Scots-Irish family that settled in the Shenandoah Valley by way of Pennsylvania. He farmed the land until 1761, when he opened a tavern in Rockbridge County. Paxton is said to have been the richest man in the county, and his daughter Elizabeth would later become one of the most sought-after of the young women in Rockbridge. After the Revolution, she married Samuel Houston, who was by then a Major, and thoroughly entrenched in the life of the colonial military.

Farming was generally a prosperous enterprise in the areas of Rockbridge, Rockingham, and Augusta counties, and landowners were expected to contribute a part of their harvest toward the needs of the county, a tax the colonists called a tithe. Considerable land was added in 1763 to the county tithables, including 320 acres of Thomas Stevenson, 241 acres of William Erwin, the son of Jane Erwin, 550 acres belonging to John Kilpatrick and 500 acres of James Green. James Huston and Archibald Hamilton qualified that same year for the position of "Inspectors of Flour."

While residents of tidewater Virginia continued to view those in the west as backward farmers, life in the Shenando had advanced significantly from its crude beginnings. Unlike the "Irish Settlement" in North Carolina, where many of the Scotch-Irish had just arrived and had small farms and little money, many in the Virginia valley managed much larger farms. While the term plantation was often used interchangeably with the word farm, some of the Shenandoah farms were large enough to justify the term. The Harrison brothers managed huge operations in Rockingham County, and opted to use slaves to assist in the field work. John Stephenson, without the typical large Scots-Irish family, took on both slaves and indentured servants to assist in the operations. Families such as the Paxtons, Harrisons, Houstons, Stephensons, and others enjoyed a position of respect that held them up as part of a local "gentry" of sorts—gentlemen, or squires, as they were sometimes called—whose success and resulting relative wealth formed a basis for some esteem.

———

Not all violence in the Valley could be attributed to raids or ambushes. During the January court session, there were two cases dealing with county murders. Paul Armstrong was tried and acquitted in the death of Thomas Hicks, and despite the injustices perpetrated against slaves; there are cases of prevailing justice. Fanner, the Negro slave of John Harrison, who had been charged with aiding and abetting in the death of his master, was judged innocent of the crime.

The raids on the settlers during the French and Indian war caused a hardship for many of the colonial children. A child was considered orphaned at the death of their father, even if the mother was still living, and officers of the court would name guardians to oversee the upbringing of the orphans in the county. In March of 1770, Alexander McClenachan was appointed guardian of John, Andrew, James, Elizabeth, and David Black, the orphaned children of David Black. John Stephenson was appointed guardian that month to James Rusk, the orphaned son of James Rusk Senior. Archibald Huston was chosen as guardian for Esther Boyd, the orphan daughter of Robert Boyd, and in 1773, Huston was appointed guardian of Henry Stalp, whose father William died in January.

Archibald Huston had also answered the county's call for appraisers, and had already worked with colonists Gasper Kinder, Peter Funk, Mathew Thompson, and John Stewart in evaluating the estates of John Faught (Bellfaught), John Sheldon, and Robert Cravens, among others. When the estate of William Adair was listed, one of the larger private libraries of the county was made available, and its titles give an indication of the reading material of the time: Watt's *Philosophical Essays*, a medical dictionary, *Baley's Dictionary, The Art of Surgery, Confession of Faith, Death and Heaven, The Interest of England, Psalm Book, Durbam on Death, The Wars of England, The Free Nonconformist*, and an arithmetic book. In the matter of the estate of Alexander Anderson, the legal activities included the authorizing of payment for six gallons of peach brandy consumed during his illness and at his funeral.

When John Taylor made his will, he called on his neighboring relatives to witness the document, and their signatures represent three generations living in the area. Taylor was married to Esther Waite, the daughter of John and Catherine Waite, who lived nearby on Mill Creek. John Waite signed as a witness, as did his son-in-law John Stephenson, and Stephenson's son-in-law Archibald Huston. Stephenson was married to Waite's other daughter Sarah. In March of 1774, Archibald Huston made out his own last will, with instructions on the division of his considerable estate, including nearly one thousand acres in Augusta County, Virginia. John Stephenson served as a witness, and James and George Huston were listed as executors, along with militia Captain David Laird. Following his father's death, Stephenson Huston began working the farm of his grandfather John Stephenson. It was a working relationship that was to benefit both parties. John Stephenson in August of 1774 gave Stephen Huston charge of his Augusta County concerns and filed the agreement in County Court on March 6, 1775, retroactive to the previous summer. In consideration of Huston's faithful oversight of John's affairs, including four grown slaves, John granted Stephen 250 acres, which included the plantation house.

Stephenson Huston—along with brothers John, James, Archibald, George, Nathan, and his six sisters—inherited substantial holdings in Augusta County, but most of the family gave up that land to join the growing number of their Scot-Irish neighbors who were heading through the Cumberland gap for life on a new frontier—in the wilderness of Kentucky.

CHAPTER SEVEN

Dunmore's War

WHEN JOHN MURRAY, the fourth Earl of Dunmore, became Governor of Virginia in 1772, one of his first official travels took him along Braddock's Road to Fort Pitt on the western frontier. Dunmore was a brash, outspoken man and had bold designs for the Province of Virginia. At Fort Pitt, Dunmore persuaded Dr. John Connally to act as his agent in a scheme to establish a more northern boundary for the Virginia colony. The Governor had already made an impact on the area, by issuing land grants in the Ohio Valley to veterans of the French and Indian campaigns, although the grants were in clear violation of treaties negotiated with the Shawnees and other tribes.

Connally posted an announcement at Pittsburgh in January of 1774, informing of his appointment to the position of "Captain, Commandant of the Militia of Pittsburgh and its Dependencies," although shortly after the posting, Connally was arrested by Pennsylvania justices and was held at Hanna's Town, near present-day Greensburg. Connally persuaded the justices to release him, on a promise that he would return in April, when the next court would be convened.

In early spring, the Shawnees, who were most affected by the encroachment of Dunmore's veterans, began attacking the settlements. Volunteers were sent by Dunmore to reinforce those living in the troubled area. Meanwhile, another group of militia was sent with Connally in April when he returned to Fort Pitt, and the 175 militiamen arrived "with their colors flying," and the captains with "their swords drawn." He took possession of the fort and renamed the outpost Fort Dunmore. The following day, April 8, three Pennsylvania justices who lived near Fort Pitt, but were in session at Hanna's Town, returned home, where Connally had them arrested.

The border dispute was only part of the conflict; Dunmore called on the Scots-Irish militiamen to counter the Shawnees who were raiding colonial settlements, and authorized the movement of several companies under the command of General Andrew Lewis. It became known as Dunmore's War—a brief but vicious campaign that involved some fifteen hundred militiamen against the Shawnees. That Nation was alone in facing the colonial militia, after unsuccessfully attempting to bring in the Iroquois as allies.

The Scots-Irish had pushed the frontier well into Shawnee territory in present-day Virginia and Tennessee's Holston River valley. As early as 1772, the Scots-Irish crossed the New River west of the Iron Mountains in southwest Virginia, and cleared land at Wolf Hills for a settlement. Another twelve miles to the west, Captain Evan Shelby staked a site, and to the south, in what is now Tennessee, other Scots-Irish banded together for the purpose of self-defense and self-government, naming the collective the Watauga Association. It was at the onset of Dunmore's War that the Pennsylvania rifles and their owners were forced to defend themselves against the Shawnee's retaliation for the loss of their ancestral lands.

Daniel Boone and Micheal Stoner were sent by Virginia authorities in 1774 to warn settlers in the Watauga and surrounding regions that Dunmore intended to attack the Shawnees. On September 24, 1774, the Shawnees attacked the cabin of John Roberts on Reedy Creek. Roberts, his wife, and three of their four children were killed, and a young boy who was the lone survivor was taken prisoner. The raid ooccurred in the jurisdiction of the redheaded Scots-Irishman, Arthur Campbell, a major in the Augusta militia. When the boy was found scalped—but alive—the troops carried the lad to Campbell's home at Royal Oak, just east of the Scots-Irish settlement, where he was able to describe the massacre, but died of his injuries shortly afterward. The southern raids were originally attributed to the Shawnee, but Campbell soon learned otherwise. He struggled to protect settlers along the Tennessee—Virginia line while Dunmore ordered other Virginia companies to a point some eighty miles to the north.

Dunmore made his way through the wilderness into present-day West Virginia and made camp on the south banks at the juncture of the Ohio and the Kanawha

Rivers on October 5, 1774. John Stephenson led a company of militiamen from Augusta County, Virginia. Officers serving under him included Robert Bell, Benjamin Harrison, George Shilling, John Morgan, Robert Vance, and Jesse Wheeler.

Captain John Stephenson's Company

John Beck
Joseph Beckett
William Bennett
James Blackstone
Richard Blackstone
James Boswick
Daniel Bradley
Samuel Bradley
Henry Broyles
William Burns
Jesse Buzan
Thomas Clifton
Betts Collier
Patrick Collins
Leven Cooper
John Cox
Samuel Cornwell
John Crawford
William Darville
Joseph Davis
Kinsey Davis
William Davis
Henry Dawson
John Dawson
Frank Duke
Osborne Flynn
Thomas Foster
William Foster
Nathaniel Fox
Thomas Gwynn
Joseph Hall
Lawrence Harrison
Nicholas Harrison
William Holliday

William Hollis
Philip Jackson
William Jeffries
William Juks
Absolom Kent
Henry Kersey
William Kersey
John Knight
Hancock Lee
Daniel Leet
Kiah Lindsay
John Lion
James Little
William Lock
George Main
John Marks
Thomas Marks
James Mason
Forence McCarty
William McIntire
Jacob Meek
William Miller
John Minter
James Moody
Charles Morgan Jr.
Samuel Murphey
John Moore
Thomas Moore
Joseph Mount
Hugh Newell
Hugh Newell Jr.
William Newell
Gariot Nugent
James Parks

William Phillips
Charles Poague
Jonas Potts
George Pretty
Tom Ravenscroft
Thomas Reagan
John Reardon
Thomas Reardon
John Redman
Isaac Scissal
Linsfield Sharp
John Smith
Peter Stacy
William Stephens
Hugh Stinson
Edward Stuart
William Taylor
Philip Thompson
James Trimble
James Vaenscraft
William Vineyard
Thomas Waller
Peter Warren
Samuel Wells
James Whaley
Moses White
John White
David Williams
James Wilson
William Wilson
James Winkfield
James Wood
Robert Worthington

The place where the men made camp came to be called Point Pleasant, a dramatically ironic name, given the wild emotions of the following morning. The Shawnee warriors were led by their chief, Cornstalk, and silently crossed the Ohio at daybreak, catching the militiamen by surprise. The men sprang to arms and flew into a lengthy battle in which both colonists and Shawnees fell at an alarming rate. The skirmish lasted throughout the day, and by late afternoon the colonists held an advantage. When the sun finally set at Point Pleasant, the Shawnees were defeated, at a cost of some fifty men among the militia and a similar number among the Shawnees. Records indicate another 150 colonists were wounded.

Dunmore arranged terms with the Shawnees that allied them with the British and Dunmore himself remained loyal to the crown. Ironically, the militiamen who had served under him against the Shawnees would—almost to a man—fight against the British as colonial militiamen.

The attacks on the southern Scots-Irish settlements were the result of a vengeance-minded Mingo chief called Logan, who turned south instead of joining with Chief Cornstalk in the finale of Dunmore's War. The Mingos believed militia Captain Michael Cresap was behind a murderous attack and when the Shawnees were defeated, the Mingos refused to sign the treaty. Their chief sent a message through Dunmore's emissary:

> *I appeal to any white man to say if ever he entered Logan's cabin hungry and he gave him not meat; if ever he came cold and naked and he clothed him not? During the course of the last long and bloody war, Logan remained idle in his camp, an advocate for peace. Such was my love for the whites that my countrymen pointed as I passed and said: "Logan is the friend of the white man!"…Colonel Cresap, the last spring, in cold blood and unprovoked, murdered all the relations of Logan, not even sparing my women and children. There runs not a drop of my blood in the veins of any living creature. This called on me for revenge. I have sought it. I have killed many. I have fully glutted my vengeance.*
>
> *For my country, I rejoice at the beams of peace; but do not harbor a thought that mine is the joy of fear. Logan never felt fear. He will not turn on his heel to save a live. Who is there to mourn for Logan? Not one!*

His defiance of Dunmore is often quoted as one of the finest examples of Native American oratory of the time. The revenge he achieved gave a brief respite for those Scots-Irish in the Holston Valley, including Arthur Campbell, who remained in the area and watched as a steady stream of new frontiersmen passed before his door on the trail to Kentucky.

In the final month of 1774, Dunmore ordered county records at Staunton, in Augusta County, be removed to Fort Dunmore. The new jurisdiction was called the District of West Augusta and encompassed much of present-day western Pennsylvania. A new commission of the peace was formed and its first court term was held February 21, 1775.

Daniel Boone always seemed to be on the move, and in March had taken on the task of cutting a path through the Cumberland Gap into Kentucky. He was to soon discover that Dunmore's treaty was no guarantee of peace.

Southwest of the Scots-Irish settlement, Boone and his brother Squire, along with thirty recruits, hacked through the mountainous forests for nearly two weeks. Several acquaintances from the Yadkin River area of North Carolina joined Boone's party, including Colonel Richard Callaway, and Captain William Twetty's Rutherford County militia company: Samuel Coburn, James Bridges, Thomas Johnson, John Hart, William Hicks, James Peeke, and Felix Walker. After fourteen days of chopping underbrush, trees, and cane, the party emerged from the mountains and camped among the trees south of present-day Richmond, Kentucky—just fifteen miles from their intended destination. Exhausted and relieved, the men slept through the night, without sentry, only to be surprised before daybreak by a band of Shawnees. Boone and his men were surrounded and gunshots rang out in the pre-dawn darkness as the Shawnee warriors fell on the campsite. Twetty was hit in both knees and could not run with the others, who scattered wildly into the woods. Squire Boone grabbed his rifle, but missed his powderhorn, and could only drag the useless gun at his side as he crawled through the underbrush.

After several wild minutes, Daniel Boone rallied the men out of hiding and managed to drive off the Shawnees. Unable to continue with two wounded men—Felix Walker was shot in the hip, in addition to the injury to Twetty— Boone had the men hastily build a small enclosure of stacked logs. Twetty died several days after the raid, and was buried at the site. Walker survived, and was carried for twelve days to a place that was later called the "Colony of Transylvania."

It was weeks later that the frontier skirmishes took on a different light, with news of the British attacks on April 19, 1775, at Lexington and Concord. Shortly thereafter, Dunmore, ever the Loyalist and therefore concerned for his safety, retreated with his family to a British man-of-war on the Chesapeake.

Four days before the attacks on Lexington and Concord, Benjamin Logan was striking out on a thin trail leading away from Daniel Boone's crude road. Logan was the son of David Logan, another Augusta County Scots-Irishman, and he was searching for a suitable location to build a "plantation house" for Anne

Montgomery, his wife. The two were among the Scots-Irish settlers at Wolf Hills in the Holston Valley.

The point where he left the path is near present-day London, Kentucky, and the trail Logan followed from there to the Falls of the Ohio made up the final leg of what was called the Wilderness Road. Logan was joined by William Gillespie, and the two were following as carefully as possible a nearly hidden trail—or *trace,* as they were called—that had been made by three Scots-Irishmen who had already spent a good amount of time in Kentucky. The trail was Skaggs' Trace, named for Charles, Henry, and Richard Skaggs. It was the aim of Logan and Gillespie to follow the path of the three brothers as long as they could before eventually branching off to explore the Dick's River area. After working their way through hilly forests, the pair finally emerged to find a rolling valley filled with wild crab apple trees. It was a spot that had been used by hunters, and when settlers later followed Logan's path and began settling throughout the grove, it was called Crab Orchard.

After a restful stay of several days, Logan and Gillespie again pushed on, moving through the grassy valleys bounded on one side by rugged hills. The ground was fertile and suitable for planting, and a stream wound its way through the valley, providing needed water. It was the spot Logan intended to build his plantation; the settlement came to be known as Stanford, the seat of present-day Lincoln County, Kentucky, although it wasn't the first name for the community. A Welshman, who was one of Logan's first visitors, mentioned that May first was the day a Welsh monk was canonized as a saint, and since Logan founded his settlement on that day, the settlement should be called St. Asaphs. Logan is said to have agreed with the idea, but the name did not stick, and the settlement was commonly referred to as Logan's Station.

Frontiersmen sent word for a meeting among the various settlements, and Alexander Spotswood Dandridge, John Floyd, John Todd, and Samuel Wood represented Logan's Station as delegates to what was called the Transylvania convention.

Logan brought his family out the following spring, and by that time there was already a community of Scots-Irish settlers.

CHAPTER EIGHT

Beginnings of a Revolution

CHARLOTTE HAD BEEN FOUNDED as a town in 1767, located in North Carolina's newly-formed Mecklenburg County. It had become a major traffic area for travel south of Salisbury to South Carolina and also had become a center of population and commerce. As the county seat, Charlotte became a natural gathering point for settlers in the area, and when the news of the day was to be heard, someone standing on the courthouse steps called out the latest in a loud voice.

The political climate was already tense by 1775, and a series of events involving taxation—including the Boston Tea Party—led to a political climate that had both colonists and the Crown considering the possibility of rebellion.

Nine years earlier a Scots-Irishman himself caught in a disagreement over his position as Stamp Master for the Province. While the British were long accustomed to the practice affixing stamps on official documents, the colonists met the passage of the Stamp Act of 1765 with outrage. It required a tax stamp on any document that was intended as an official record. Opposition was immediate and unruly; many of those who had been newly appointed to oversee the stamp distribution faced angry neighbors who began calling themselves "Sons of Liberty." When the British sloop Diligence anchored on the Cape Fear River with tax stamps intended for the Virginia Province, the Virginia "Sons" advised the ship's captain that they intended to resist the unloading of the stamps. One of the ship's boats was seized and served as a rallying point through much of the night. The next day, militia Colonel John Ashe led a procession to the Governor's house and challenged any effort to enforce the Stamp Act. The crowd demanded that the appointed Stamp Master, James Houston, be brought before the crowd, which the Governor refused. He changed his mind when the mob began preparing to set his house ablaze. When Houston was finally brought before they crowd, he was swept ahead of the gathering to the Brunswick market, where he was ordered to take an oath swearing he would never execute his duties as Stamp Master.

Similar occasions had warranted the gathering of Mecklenburg County residents to discuss effects on that county, and Colonel Thomas Polk had already been given authority to call conventions that consisted of representatives from each of the county's militia companies. There was such a convention underway in mid-May, when a rider burst in among them carrying news of the attacks by the British at Lexington and Concord. The excited crowd settled at last, and in discussions among the convention principals, including Thomas Polk, Abraham Alexander, Hezekiah Alexander, John McKnitt Alexander, Dr. Ephraim Brevard, John Phifer, Waightstill Avery, and Rev. Hezekiah James Balch, a decision was reached to form a committee to write a response.

The outcome of the committee's effort—The Mecklenburg Resolves—is a document that has been debated since that day in 1775, with such illustrious citizens as John Adams and Thomas Jefferson weighing in on the discussion. The debate centered on the purported existence of a paper called the Mecklenburg "Declaration of Independence," said to have been written more than a year before the official American document of 1776, and to contain similarly worded phrases throughout. There is a consensus that the convention at the courthouse in Charlotte—before a crowd estimated by some as being almost half the men of the county—named Dr. Ephraim Brevard to head a sub-committee along with Colonel William Kennon, who was an attorney from Salisbury, and Rev. Hezekiah Balch. The three were to compose a response reflecting the attitude of the citizenry. The group labored long in preparing the set of resolves, finally returning to the convention with the document. The crowd at the courthouse had steadily increased, and the group buzzed in anticipation, until at last, Ephraim Brevard began speaking. At once, the room fell silent, as the resolutions were read aloud by Brevard. When he finished the oration and looked up, the room erupted in cheers and applause, and the measures were unanimously adopted. The following day at noon, Colonel Polk read the Resolves from the steps of the courthouse before a gathering of the county residents, and his delivery again met with cheers from the colonists.

The Mecklenburg convention was largely that of the Scots-Irish. They voted to have the Resolves carried by messenger to the Continental Congress. Captain James Jack, of Charlotte, was prevailed upon to ride to Philadelphia with a copy of the document. Captain Jack mounted his horse, waved goodbye to the crowd of well-wishers, and set out on the Wagon Road with orders to deliver the Resolves to the North Carolina delegation. When he arrived at Salisbury a short time later, court was in session and he was compelled to read the document for those assembled. The response was again supportive, but two attorneys—John Dunn and a Mr. Booth—claimed the Resolves amounted to treason and moved to have Captain Jack detained. Before anyone could move, Jack drew his pistols and threatened to kill anyone who tried to keep him from his duty, then raced from the courthouse to his horse. He packed the papers in his saddlebag and spurred his way onward to Philadelphia.

When word reached Charlotte that two men had attempted to stop Captain Jack, a party of nearly a dozen armed horsemen rode to Salisbury for retribution. Dunn and Booth were brought before the Mecklenburg committee; Dunn convinced the group to let him return to Salisbury, and George Graham and Col. John Carruth escorted Booth to Camden, South Carolina. That action has been described, in some seriousness, as the first military expedition from Mecklenburg County in the Revolutionary War.

John Dunn served as the first clerk of the court for Rowan County and was a registrar of deeds for Anson County. He maintained his law practice in Salisbury until the Revolution.

The *South Carolina Gazette and Country Journal* printed the resolutions:

Charlotte-town, Mecklenburg County, May 31, 1775

This day the Committee of this county met, and passed the following Resolves:
WHEREAS, By an Address presented to His Majesty by both Houses of Parliament, in February last, the American colonies are declared to be in a state of actual rebellion, we conceive; that all laws and commissions confirmed by, or derived from the authority of the King or Parliament, are annulled and vacated, and the former civil constitution of these colonies, for the present, wholly suspended. To provide, in some degree, for the exigencies of this county, in the present alarming period, we deem it proper and necessary to pass the following Resolves, viz.:

I. That all commissions, civil and military, heretofore granted by the Crown, to be exercised in these colonies, are null and void, and the constitution of each particular colony wholly suspended.

II. That the Provincial Congress of each province, under the direction of the great Continental Congress, is invested with all legislative and executive powers within their respective provinces, and that no other legislative or executive power, does, or can exist, at this time, in any of these colonies.

III. As all former laws are now suspended in this province, and the Congress have not yet provided others, we judge it necessary, for the better preservation of good order, to form certain rules and regulations for the internal government of this county, until laws shall be provided for us by the Congress.

IV. That the inhabitants of this county do meet on a certain day appointed by this committee, and having formed themselves into nine companies (to-wit), eight in the county, and one in the town of Charlotte, do chuse a Colonel and other military officers, who shall hold and exercise their powers by virtue of this choice, and independent of the Crown of Great Britain, and former constitution of this province.

V. That for the better preservation of the peace and administration of justice, each of those companies do chuse from their own body, two discreet freeholders, who shall be empowered, each by himself and singly, to decide and determine all matters of controversy, arising within said company, under the sum of twenty shillings; and jointly and together, all controversies under the sum of forty shillings; yet so as that their decisions may admit of appeal to the Convention of the Select-Men of the county; and also that any one of these men shall have the power to examine and commit to confinement persons accused of petit larceny.

VI. That those two Select-Men, thus chosen, do jointly and together chuse from the body of their particular company, two persons property qualified to act as Constables, who may assist them in the execution of their office.

VII. That upon the complaint of any persons to either of these Select-Men, he do issue his warrant, directed to the Constable, commanding him to bring the aggressor before him or them, to answer said complaint.

VIII. That these eighteen Select-Men, thus appointed, do meet every third Thursday in January, April, July, and October, at the Court-House, in Charlotte, to hear and determine all matters of controversy, for sums exceeding forty shillings, also appeals; and in cases of felony, to commit the person or persons convicted thereof to close confinement, until the Provincial Congress shall provide and establish laws and modes of proceedings in all such cases.

IX. That these eighteen Select-Men, thus convened, do chuse a Clerk to record the transactions of said Convention, and that said Clerk, upon the application of any person or persons aggrieved, do issue his warrant to one of the Constables of the company to which the offender belongs, directing said Constable to summons and warn said offender to appear before the Convention, at their next meeting, to answer the aforesaid complaint.

X. That any person making complaint upon oath, to the Clerk, or any member of the Convention, that he has reason to suspect, that any person or persons indebted to him, in a sum above forty shillings, intend clandestinely to withdraw from the county, without paying such debt, the Clerk or such member shall issue his warrant to the Constable, commanding him to take said person or persons into safe custody, until the next sitting of the Convention.

XI. That when a debtor for a sum below forty shillings shall abscond and leave the county, the warrant granted as aforesaid, shall extend to any goods or chattels of said debtor, as may be found, and such goods or chattels be seized and held in custody by the Constable, for the space of thirty days; in which time, if the debtor fail to return and discharge the debt, the Constable shall return the warrant to one of the Select-Men of the company, where the goods are found, who shall issue orders to the Constable to sell such a part of said goods as shall amount to the sum due; That when the debt exceeds forty shillings, the return shall be made to the Convention, who shall issue orders for sale.

XII. That all receivers and collectors of quit-rents, public and county taxes, do pay the same into the hands of the chairman of this Committee, to be by them disbursed as the public exigencies may require; and that such receivers and collectors proceed no further in their office, until they be approved of by, and have given to, this Committee, good and sufficient security, for a faithful return of such monies when collected.

XIII. That the Committee be accountable to the county for the application of all monies received from such public officers.

XIV. That all these officers hold their commissions during the pleasure of their several constituents.

XV. That this committee will sustain all damages that ever hereafter may accrue to all or any of these officers thus appointed, and thus acting, on account of their obedience and conformity to these Resolves.

XVI. That whatever person shall hereafter receive a commission from the Crown, or attempt to exercise any such commission heretofore received, shall be deemed an enemy to his country, and upon information being made to the Captain of the company in which he resides, the said company shall cause him to be apprehended, and conveyed before the two Select-Men of the said company, who, upon proof of the fact, shall commit him, the said offender, to safe custody, until the next sitting of the Committee, who shall deal with him as prudence may direct.

XVII. That any person refusing to yield obedience to the above Resolves, shall be considered equally criminal, and liable to the same punishment, as the offenders above last mentioned.

XVIII. That these Resolves be in full force and virtue, until instructions from the Provincial Congress, regulating the jurisprudence of the province, shall provide otherwise, or the legislative body of Great Britain, resigns its unjust and arbitrary pretensions with respect to America.

XIX. That the eight militia companies in the county, provide themselves with proper arms and accouterments, and hold themselves in readiness to execute the commands and directions of the General Congress of this province and this Committee.

XX. That the Committee appoint Colonel Thomas Polk, and Doctor Joseph Kenedy, to purchase 300 lb. of powder, 600 lb. of lead, 1,000 flints, for the use of the militia of this county, and deposit the same in such place as the Committee may hereafter direct.

Signed by order of the Committee.

Eph. Brevard,
Clerk of the Committee.

Some argued at the time that the document was drawn up May 20, 1775, before the official Declaration, but that the proof was lost when the document was burned in a fire at the home of John McKnitt Alexander in 1800. The North Carolina Historical Commission has no official policy concerning the Resolves, which collectively were touted as the first step toward independence and referred to as the "Mecklenburg Declaration of Independence." The Resolves were republished in the Raleigh Register on April 30, 1819 and again in the June 5, 1819 edition of the Essex Register. Although claims regarding the validity have been vehemently argued through the decades, complete with sworn statements from several men said to be in attendance, the "Mecklenburg Declaration" remains as folklore reflecting the genuine historical patriotism of citizens of North Carolina.

There are a number of documented Scots-Irish among those listed as signers of the Mecklenburg "Declaration." Ezekial and Thomas Polk, were sons of Robert Polk of Northern Ireland, who settled in Somerset County, Maryland in 1735. John McKnitt Alexander bore the middle name of an Ulster ancestor. Rev. Hezekiah Balch was a licensed preacher of the Everlasting Gospel by the Presbytery of Donegal in 1766. William Graham was Scots-Irish, as was John Flenniken, who arrived in Pennsylvania and later settled near Beattie's Ford on the Catawba River in North Carolina. Robert Irwin was an elder in the Presbyterian Church and served as a member of the Provincial Congress from

Mecklenburg County in 1776. Mathew McClure was born in Ulster and settled near the site where Davidson's College was established. Neill Morrison was the son of James Morrison, who was among the many Morrisons who had emigrated from Northern Ireland and settled early near the Iredell—Rowan county line. Benjamin Patton was descended from Scottish Covenanters who moved to Ulster, then to America, where he settled in what is now Cabarrus County. John Queary was Scottish and may have emigrated from Northern Ireland to the colonies. David Reese owned extensive land on Coddle Creek in North Carolina and was born in Pennsylvania of Scots-Irish ancestry. John Davidson and William Davidson were among the earliest to settle in the North Carolina backcountry, and the Davidson's Creek settlement became the location of the Centre Presbyterian Congregation, established before 1755.

Signers of the Mecklenburg Resolves

Abraham Alexander	William Davidson	Duncan Ochletree
J. M. Alexander	Henry Downs	John Phifer
Adam Alexander	John Flenniken	Thomas Polk
Hezekiah Alexander	John Ford	Ezekiel Polk
Ezra Alexander	William Graham	Benjamin Patton
Charles Alexander	James Harris	John Queary
Waightstill Avery	Robert Irwin	David Reese
Ephraim Brevard	William Kennon	Zacheus Wilson, Sr.
Hezekiah J. Balch	Matthew McClure	William Wilson
Richard Barry	Neill Morrison	
John Davidson	Samuel Martin	

Five days after the date ascribed to the fabled "Mecklenburg Declaration," the winds carried the British Ship *Cerberus* into the Boston Harbor. On board were three generals sent by the Crown to bring the colony back into order. General William Howe was the senior officer and in his company were Major-General Henry Clinton and General John Burgoyne.

The people of Boston watched from the rooftops and gathered along the hills near the shore as British troops rowed longboats from the ships to make their landing. The thunder of the fleet's cannons rolled across the water as a cover fire was directed on an area known as Copp's Hill. Nearby was Breed's Hill, where the colonists dug their hasty fortification. Behind that was Bunker Hill, the site of the British landing and where a thousand militiamen were dug in as reinforcements.

The men on Breed's Hill were armed with muskets, determination, and fifteen musket balls apiece. John Stark, who was commanding, gave orders to hold fire, given the shortage of ammunition. Dirt and grass were punched into the air as the British fire thudded into the fortification around the militiamen, and as the three lines of Redcoats clambered up the hillside toward them, they finally passed a stake that had been driven into the ground by Stark. Behind the rebels, the sky was thick with flames and smoke from the burning buildings, having been set afire by the British shot. Cannons continued their roar, and as the British crossed the line of Stark's wooden marker, the rebel muskets barked at once, immediately dropping dozens of those advancing. Others attempted to retreat, but were prodded forward by the officers.

The rebels were without firepower by the time General Clinton reached the battle with his troops to reinforce Howe. Seeing the advancing British troops, the militia was forced to give up the hill. The men fell hurriedly back toward Bunker Hill, where their fellow colonists still stood. They had hesitated to joint in the front line battle, and at the sight of the scattering troops, they joined in the mad retreat.

The British declared victory in the Battle of Bunker Hill, but it came at a tremendous expense. Casualties amounted to nearly forty percent of the total force—226 killed and 828 wounded. The colonial losses were high as well, with more than four hundred militiamen either killed or injured.

George Washington was not the unanimous choice to head the Continental Army, nor was it a position he had campaigned to achieve. The army he inherited was more an assemblage of men than a disciplined fighting unit. There was little or no training among any of those initially under Washington's command at their encampment at Cambridge, near Boston.

Descriptions of the soldiers pointed out their "wretched" state of dress, and—owing to their lack of laundry facilities—the general filthiness of both the men and the camps. Most of the men had come from farms and were used to a diet consisting primarily of vegetables, and some were taken ill by the change to a meat-laden diet. The traveler riding into camp would pass through a wide range of sights, few of which resembled anything military. Soldiers, to fend off the weather, had thrown up primitive huts constructed of scrap boards, or made tentlike shelters of cloth and stakes. Still others had tossed together a dirt home not unlike those that would have been found in the Scottish Lowlands, made of sod and turf. There were others better equipped. A group from Rhode Island that brought proper English tents was as well organized as the British in the arrangement of their campsite.

When the troops showed little improvement even after weeks of training, Washington determined to affect a gradual replacement of the unruly troops, with other recruits that could be brought in with a better understanding of what was expected of them. Discipline was renewed and a strict line was drawn between the officers and the enlisted men, with both sides expected to act according to their position, or take "forty or fifty lashes according to his crime."

Recruitment began in earnest in the summer of 1775, and by July, some three thousand men arrived from Pennsylvania, Maryland, and Virginia. Washington's affection for the Scots-Irish as fighters was already well established, they formed the bulk of his troops in militia companies during the French and Indian campaigns. From the Scots-Irish stronghold in Augusta County, Virginia came a number of men who would later fight in Daniel Morgan's Virginia Rifle Brigade. Samuel Houston, the son and principal heir of Robert Houston enlisted with the Continental Army, and went on to serve as an officer and paymaster in Morgan's Brigade. John Stephenson and brother Adam elected to stay in Virginia and served the Revolutionary cause from that area of the colony, while their brother David Stephenson joined Houston in volunteering to serve as part of Washington's Continental Army. By February, there were more than seventeen thousand men under Washington's command.

The British, meanwhile, had twelve thousand troops under General William Howe. His men had little to do, not enough to eat, and continued illnesses during the winter months in Boston, and as a result, morale was exceedingly low, and hopes for improvement were slim.

From the safety of his ship off the coast of Virginia, John Murray, the Earl of Dunmore, attempted to conduct business as usual with the House of Assembly meeting at Williamsburg. The burgesses responded by declaring that Dunmore, by his actions, had abdicated, leaving power with the Committee of Public Safety. Dunmore retaliated against the colonists by gathering a collection of ships that could move up and down the coast, attacking settlements and plantations. Prisoners, including two women, were taken, tobacco crops were confiscated, and offers were made to Virginia slaves for their services. Dunmore promised freedom to any slave who would join his "Loyal Ethiopian" regiment. Enough of them were lured to service that, in December of 1775, an armed party of slaves and Loyalists attacked a militia force of more than nine hundred men under the command of Colonel William Woodford. Many of Woodford's men came from the Virginia backcountry and were experienced fighters and experts with the long rifle.

Woodford and his Scots-Irish sharpshooters were entrenched behind a seven-foot-high barricade while Dunmore's troops were forced to march single file to reach the fort. It was an attack Dunmore had been warned against, and an easy victory for the colonists. As the Loyalists moved nearer the fort, those at the front were simply picked off by the rebels. The commander, leading his men, was hit numerous times and died on the spot. A British soldier wrote of the surprising compassion displayed by the militia following the rout. "The Rebels behaved with the greatest Humanity, ceasing to fire when we were retreating with the wounded." In addition, the colonists buried the body of British Captain Charles Fordyce—who led the attack and was among the first to fall—with full "Honours of War." The rebels suffered a single casualty; one of the militia fighters was shot in the hand.

The renewal of an old feud was in the making in North Carolina. Allen and Flora MacDonald emigrated from the Scottish Highlands and settled with a number of fellow Highlanders in the upper reaches of the Cape Fear River. Despite the death of her husband, Flora maintained a high profile and was appointed by North Carolina Governor Josiah Martin as a brigadier general. Ironically, the Highlanders were staunchly loyal to the Crown, and Flora McDonald took her position to heart, traveling through the Cross Creek settlement urging the Scots to take up the Crown's battle.

The North Carolina governor had assured the British that Loyalists were to be found in great numbers in the province, and that the defense of the Crown's interests would be easily managed. There were many Highlanders among those recruited, but number of Loyalist recruits fell far short of the North Carolina Continentals who were already marching with regularity. At Widow Moore's Creek, in one of the early battles of the Revolution in North Carolina, the colonial militia handily defeated their Loyalist neighbors, and the British determined that the use of local troops would be an insignificant addition to their own forces.

The beginning of the revolution put emigration to the colonies on hold for all practical purposes. Although there was an understanding at the time of the origins of the various groups, the term Scots-Irish was not used in contemporary descriptions. They were called Irish, although they were of Scottish ancestry. They no longer shared ideals or the culture of their lowland ancestors. They were a distinct and separate race of people who left for America before the revolution. Those who remained in Ulster were assimilated into the Irish culture, and when boatloads of new arrivals landed on American shores during the potato famines of the mid-1800's, those arrivals were simply—*Irish*.

CHAPTER NINE

Year of the Sevens

IN THE AMERICAN REBELLION, there were significant differences between troops originating in the established eastern towns and villages, and those who kept homes on the frontier and the backcountries of the provinces.

Patriotism was not an issue and bravery was found throughout the reaches of the colony. Despite the confusion that reigned at Bunker Hill, even Burgoyne conceded the retreat "was no flight; was covered with bravery and even military skill."

Washington was authorized to raise a force of twenty thousand men, but he was successful in recruiting only about half that number. The Continental Congress had provided that for their three years of service, each recruit would be given a bounty of twenty dollars, one new set of clothes per year, and a one-hundred-acre land grant. Since the provinces were offering as much as thirty dollars for a shorter period of service, many colonists opted to stay closer to home and serve in the local militia companies. Serving in the Continental Line posed an additional hardship; service pay was delayed for months and much of the promised clothing was never delivered.

Experience on the front lines may have favored those on the frontier as well. Many had fought to protect their homes and families from raids, and had endured the rigors of organized campaigns during the French and Indian Wars. The backcountries of both Virginia and North Carolina were populated with experienced fighting men, and they were particularly numerous in the settlements of the Scots-Irish. Among George Washington's papers containing the accounts and pay rolls of the French and Indian campaigns are listings of recruits, their enlistment dates and places, and descriptions, many of whom were drawn from eastern locales, but even among those were men of Ulster. Some listed their place of origin as Scotland, and may have been Ulstermen as well, as the number of emigrations from Scotland directly to the American colonies before the Revolution is known to have been small.

From Captain William Cock's Rangers, 21 Oct. 1755
Thomas Watts, Corp., 1 Sept., 33, 5'6", fair, saddlemaker, Ireland
Dennis McNamara, 1 Sept., 25, 5'5", fair, planter, Ireland
John Gill, 4 Sept., 24, 5'9", black, tanner and currier, Ireland
Daniel Lasley, 1 Sept., 27, 5'4", fair, planter, Scotland
George Hill, 17 Sept., 30, 5'7", brown, planter, Ireland
Matthew Linch, 26 Sept., 21, 5'7", fair, planter, Ireland
Thomas Carr, 9 Oct., 40, 5'4", brown, piper, Scotland
Laurence Higgins, 16 Oct., 40, 5'5", brown, planter, Ireland

From Captain David Bell's Company 13 July 1756
Thomas Ferguston, (recruited at) Williamsburg, 31, 5'9", Scottish
Francis Ryan (recruited at) Amelia, 21, 5'9", butcher, Irish
John Dennochy (recruited at) Richmond Town, 22, 5'1", Irish
Daniel McFain (recruited at) Winchester, 26, 5'7", planter, Scotch
Whitnell Warner (recruited at) Albemarle, 20, schoolmaster, Irish
Peter Mullen (recruited at) Yorktown, 23, 5'6", sailor, Irish
William Colbert, (recruited at) Westmoreland, 22, planter, Scotch
Lawrence Johnston, 35, 5'6", joiner, Irish, fair and light hair
Charles Travis (recruited at) Richmond, 23, 5'5", planter, Scottish
James Young (recruited at) Albemarle, 38, merchant, Scottish
David Collins (recruited at) Yorktown, 21, 5'7", sailor, Irish
Charles Bruce (recruited at) Albemarle, planter, Scottish
John Hooper (recruited at) Yorktown, 26, 5'4", shoemaker, Irish
John Cotter, (recruited at) Chesterfield, 36, planter, Irish

Fourteen of the forty-four listed in Bell's Company are designated as Scottish, Scotch, or Irish. While that number is a considerable percentage, even that may not reflect the total Scots-Irish in the company. Fourteen others are listed as English and two carry a Dutch designation. The remaining fourteen other may have originated in Ulster as well.

The Size Roll of Captain Mercer's Company 2 Aug. 1756 includes similar percentages of Scotch-Irish from Tidewater counties such as Prince William and Prince George; and eastern areas such as Chester County, Pennsylvania. Although their features varied widely, the listing for Archibald Lockard is fairly typical of the Scotch/Irish/Scotch-Irish on Mercer's roll:

Archibald Lockard, 19 Oct. 1755, Prince William, 23, 5'6", planter, Scotland, dark complexion, smooth face, short curled hair, speaks upon the brogue...

Perhaps the most significant of the differences of the colonial fighting men was their temperament. The same mannerisms and habits that led the established colonists to point the newly arrived Scots-Irish to the frontiers became sought after traits for the rebel army. Any earlier disaffection for their quick-tempered bravado was lost when the cause of freedom swept through the Provinces. Accounts of the Scots-Irish participation in the Revolution range from those that imply the Ulster descendants single-handedly turned the tide, to those indicating their involvement was just part of the total picture. Regardless of the account, however, there is a singular vein of description regarding the Scots-Irish as fighters. From the Watauga and Yadkin River settlements in North Carolina to the Shenandoah Valley and backcountry of Virginia, there were no hardier men than the Scots-Irish. Many recorded their signatures on official records at the courthouses with an X and had little desire to interact beyond their own circles, but they were quickly and vehemently incensed by any injustice—real or imagined—and possessed a brash temperament that prompted action regardless of the odds. They possessed a bravery discovered in the kingdoms of Ulster and forged in the regular battles at the front doors of their settlements on the frontiers of America. They were stubborn, fiercely independent, toughened by decades of hardships, and skilled in the use of their deadly long rifles. The Scots-Irish were frontiersmen, and were comfortable in the woods with nothing more than a pouch of dried corn for their meal. They were excellent hunters and when the corn was gone, wild game was plentiful and easily had by them. They were at ease on the back of a "horse creature," as many of the Scots-Irish called their animals. On the rebel's side, the Revolution was fought from behind the rocks and trees of the forests, and the majority of the Scots-Irish in America were children of the forests and farms.

Finally, the trade tools of the Eastern colonists were the hammers and implements required to serve the needs of an urban community, while the primary tool on the frontier was almost certainly always the long rifle. It provided food, sport, and protection.

Weapons were scarce for the rebels, and except for the rifles of the frontier, the rebels primarily owned the muskets that were slangly called "Brown Bess." The flintlock gun weighed fourteen pounds, and had a three-quarter-inch-wide barrel that was forty-four inches long. To fire Brown Bess, gunpowder was poured onto a shallow metal pan with a trailing fuse leading into the barrel. There, more powder was packed along with a wadding of paper, and a lead ball. The flintlock sparked the powder in the pan, which ignited the trail of powder into the barrel, and the resulting explosion fired the ball from the barrel. There was little requirement for aiming the musket; troops stood in a line and waited until the enemy was close enough that the volley of musket balls was bound to hit something or someone. Since reloading took so long, the muskets were often fitted with bayonets and after the initial firing the troops charged the enemy with blades extended. Often, bayonets were nothing more than thin blades jammed into the musket barrel, and such a fitting had to be removed before the gun could again be fired.

Colonists continued to use the British method of loading and firing the muskets for nearly two years after the Declaration of Independence. Loading the musket was dangerous in itself. If a powder horn was not closed, the "flash in the pan" could ignite the entire horn, burning the man with the gun as well as anyone nearby. Brown Bess had such recoil that some rested the stock against a tree, and there are accounts of injury and even death, when the kick of the gun hit a man's chest instead of his shoulder. Before colonists began manufacturing their own replicas of the British Brown Bess, small arms were in such short supply that Benjamin Franklin suggested troops be outfitted with bows and arrows, or spears. At one point, militiamen were called out and ordered to bring with them shovels, axes, or scythes to serve as weapons. On the frontier, however, Brown Bess had been made a stranger by the introduction of a refined version of the weapon. It was called the Pennsylvania long rifle, or as it became known in later years—the Kentucky rifle.

In the hands of the Scots-Irish, it was simply a "rifle gun." It was the same tool purchased at the trading camps at the beginning of the Great Philadelphia Wagon Road, as families set out for the frontier. It was the weapon that saved homes from attack, and invaded the lands of the Shawnees in the French and Indian War. Often, when wills were recorded, the "rifle gun" was among the first items listed in bequests to the older sons. It was an extremely accurate weapon in the hands of a skilled marksman, and the men of the frontiers of Virginia, Pennsylvania, North Carolina, and Western Maryland were sharpshooters.

Ironically, in the hands of men considered nothing more than backwoods farmers were the finest weapons of the time. The difference was in the barrel design. While the Brown Bess had a smooth bore, the frontier gun had a rifled barrel—thus, the name *rifle*. A groove inside the barrel spun the bullet as it was ejected, which gave it an accuracy far superior to the musket. The design was known in Europe, and it was the Pennsylvania Germans and Dutch who recreated it in America, but it was the "backwoods farmer" who ingeniously wrapped the bullet with a swatch of greased linen that allowed the irregular size of the lead shot to perfectly match the barrel. If the man at the trigger of a flintlock musket was brave enough to aim, it might be accurate at fifty yards; the Pennsylvania rifle, easily and regularly aimed by the frontiersmen, had a deadly accuracy at distances approaching one hundred fifty yards. When a captured long rifle was sent back to England for demonstration, potential soldiers were so dismayed at seeing its accuracy, the recruiting effort suffered tremendously.

Meanwhile, when a call was sent out along the Virginia frontier for five hundred marksmen to serve in the Revolution, so many volunteered that contests were held to determine the most accurate sharpshooters. From a distance of some one hundred yards, the marksmen aimed at an outline of a nose, drawn on the center of a piece of wood. Before fifty shots had been fired, the center of the target was nothing more than a hole in the wood. Once selected, some fifteen hundred of the Virginia marksmen marched nearly six hundred miles to the camp at Cambridge. Ninety-six men under the command of Captain Daniel Morgan made the march in twenty-one days and upon their arrival were described as "remarkably stout and hardy men." Not one had fallen out of the long march. They were soldiers who wore leather shirts on their backs and moccasins on their feet, and the "rifle guns" they carried were such a part of their existence that they gave them names like "Sweet Lips" and "Hot Lead."

Their look was anything but that of an army. They were lacking uniforms and as a result, troops varied in appearance from location to location. Many of those fighting from the militia ranks were seasonal soldiers who had to return to the farms to harvest or plant. The fighting accommodated such practices. Though the Revolution lasted eight years, fighting was intermittent throughout that span and battles were located across a fairly wide geographic region. The British considered the appearance of the militia and completely unmilitary, and were equally critical of their battle tactics.

The Scots-Irish and others who inhabited the frontier and served in the French and Indian campaigns had learned much from the Native American style of combat. The British generally considered the American tactics cowardly or unfair, and at odds with all the "proper" methods of waging a war.

The demeanor of the troops also presented occasional problems for General Washington. Since many of the soldiers under his command had joined from the same areas, many knew each other well. The temperament of the frontiersmen made it difficult to take orders from one of their neighbors. Conversely, the Scots-Irish were quick to watch out for the welfare of their own, even going so far as to surreptitiously free the occasional acquaintance being held under military guard for a breach of discipline or other misdemeanor.

Washington sent most of the Continental Army to New York, correctly anticipating a British landing at Long Island. Success was mixed for the remainder of the year and losses were extensive to both sides in battles from White Plains, New York to Trenton, New Jersey. Daniel Morgan's company was among those sent to fight in the North, where the major battles of the Revolution were centered for the next twenty-four months.

By the winter of 1777–78, Washington's troops were gathered at Valley Forge, twenty-two miles northwest of Philadelphia, and were haggard and nearly frozen from inadequate clothing. Washington reported to the Congress that some twenty-nine hundred men were "unfit for duty because they were bare foot and otherwise naked." As the winter months progressed, so did the number of men who were incapacitated by the cold. Blankets were used as coats, five hundred horses starved to death, and the men were ravaged by smallpox and typhus. For a three-month period during the winter at Valley Forge, Congress left vacant the post of Quartermaster General and supplies to the army became virtually nonexistent. More than two thousand men died during the encampment over the Pennsylvania winter months that closed the year of the Bloody Sevens on the frontier.

For the Scots-Irish in closest proximity to the wilderness, there were daily reminders of the allure of Kentucky. There were groups of travelers passing regularly along the Wagon Road, heading for that point where a branch led to the Cumberland Gap, the closest break in the mountains for passage out of Virginia. Financial considerations were always a factor, and many who could not afford to purchase land in the quickly filling areas of Virginia looked to the wilderness of Kentucky.

The dissention among family members was even recorded in the wills of those early settlers who had expected to leave their farms in the hands of the sons and grandsons. The will of John Stephenson of Augusta County, present-day Rockingham County, Virginia attests to the divisive nature of the allure of the frontier. Stephen Huston is documented as having been among the earliest in Lincoln County, Kentucky, and the majority of his siblings, along with his widowed mother, joined him on that frontier.

His previous agreement with his grandson Stephen notwithstanding, John Stephenson left the majority of his estate to his second wife, and two of his stepchildren.

> *...I give and bequeath to my dearly beloved wife one third of all my estate both real and personal, the real estate during her Natural life, and the personal forever and do request my executors, hereafter mentioned, that when her third is laid off of the Plantation whereon I now live which contains upwards of 700 acres by Patent, the dwelling houses and out houses Together with the clear land and other improvements may be included in that part assigned to her, I give and bequeath to Jonathen Taylor and Easter Taylor, two of my wife's children, the sum of fifty pounds each, I give to my Daughter Mary Huston, widow of Archibald Huston Deceased, the sum of one Hundred Pounds.*

The slap Stephenson intended in his small bequests to his grandsons is made clear by his description of their behavior.

> *I give to my grandsons John Huston, Stephen Huston, George Huston and Nathan Huston one Shilling each if they demand the same, they and each of them having proved very undutiful to me.*

There were better provisions for the other grandchildren, including Archibald Huston Jr., who was considerably younger than his brothers.

> *I give and bequeath to my other six grandchildren to wit, Ann, Abigail, Sarah, Jane, Elizabeth, and Archibald Huston the sum of Sixty Pounds each. I desire that my Executors as soon as conveniently may be after my death sell both my real and personal estate including the Division of the thirds of my real estate delivered to my wife and to make proper & Sufficient conveyances to the purchaser or purchasers and to place out the money arising from such sale or sales on Interest on good security till such time my said six grandchildren and two Step children shall arise to their Respective ages as Managers.*

One of the executors named was Felix Gilbert, who operated an ordinary or store at an area called Peale's Crossroads, near the Cross Keys cemetery where John Stephenson was buried. Gilbert was a character in his own right, and was mentioned in one of George Washington's journals after encountering him on a foray through the area.

In Kentucky, the year of the Bloody Sevens saw Benjamin Logan moving his wife and two sons from his Station to Harrodsburg, a larger settlement that offered greater protection. Boonesborough had already been under a three-day siege, although the attacking braves finally withdrew into the forest when they could not break through Boone's fort. When Harrodsburg was attacked, Logan knew the safety of his settlement was in jeopardy. He had only fifteen men with rifles to protect the women and children who had been brought back from Harrodsburg. No one was allowed to leave without guard, and lookouts kept a constant vigil for possible raiding parties. While in the company of a sentry on May 20, a number of the settlers were outside the walls when the attack finally came; the clap of flintlocks broke the morning stillness and shot pounded against the wooden fort. John Kennedy tumbled back inside the walls with four wounds, William Hudson was killed immediately, and Burr Harrison dropped to the ground wounded and unable to move. The women scrambled to the safety of the fort, along with James Craig, who escaped injury.

Later that afternoon, Logan dashed outside the gate and dragged back the bodies of Harrison and Hudson. Surprisingly, Harrison was still alive when Logan carried him behind the wooden walls. Hudson was buried inside the stockade, as Harrison was later—he lived only a few days after the attack.

For days, a siege was maintained around Logan's Station, with occasional gunshots sounding against the timber walls. When the settlers returned the fire, time after time, and day after day, it became apparent that the supply of powder and shot would soon be exhausted. Logan took on the task of going for help. In the dark of night, he slipped from the stockade, and made his way south through the forests, leaving Skaggs' Trace for the security of the deep woods on his way to the Holston Valley. He was gone for ten days, but returned with a pack full of supplies and word that men from the southern settlements had volunteered to give assistance. Two companies of militiamen eventually arrived, and the threat of attack was lessened.

Residents of Logan's Fort were not told of the note passed to Logan from Sir Guy Carleton, the head of the British forces in Canada. It was addressed to Logan specifically, but intended for all Kentucky settlers, and offered a land bounty for each man who surrendered his rifle and pledged allegiance to the King. The note specifically offered Logan a commission in the British army; he chose to keep its contents secret for fear some of his fellow settlers might desert.

In June, Sir Carleton sent word to Henry Hamilton, the lieutenant governor of Detroit, to enlist the aid of the native tribes in staging raiding parties and "employ them in making a Diversion and exciting an alarm upon the frontiers of Virginia and Pennsylvania." The frontier lands of Kentucky were considered a single county of Virginia at the time, and would be included in Carleton's order.

The first big raid was delayed several months, but it was of major consequence when it occurred. Daniel Boone and several companions were gathering salt at

Blue Licks when he was captured by the Shawnee and was taken to one of their villages in Ohio. He was adopted by Chief Blackfish, and was taken to Detroit where the British questioned him about the strength of the forces in Kentucky. When the chieftains and Boone returned to Ohio, he learned of a planned attack expedition through Kentucky. He managed to escape and return to Boonesborough. The ensuing attack lasted three weeks, and although the settlers successfully repelled each assault, food was running short and the water they had hoarded was nearly gone. Chief Blackfish, with plenty of powder and shot but unable to break through the walls and its defenses, decided to tunnel underneath. The settlers could hear the activity, and opted to dig their own tunnel at a right angle, hoping the Indians would break through and be caught defenseless. Those who weren't digging could hear the shouts of the warriors outside the walls, "Digging Hole! Blow you to hell tonight!"

When night fell, the roaring commenced, but instead of a powder explosion from a tunnel under the fort, it was the rumbling of a thunder from a storm that brought torrential rains. The next morning, the settlers looked outside at the tunnel; it had collapsed under the torrent of water. The enemy had vanished. One by one, the men crept out of the fort and wandered around the stockade, surveying the area and digging the lead shot from the outside walls of the log fort. In all, they gathered 125 pounds of lead, which they were able to melt down to make ammunition for their own use.

As the tribal warriors departed the Boonesborough stockade, they divided and went separate ways; one band was to strike Logan's station. Benjamin Logan was warned in advance of the attack and made extensive preparations for defense, and for storing supplies to carry them through in the event of an extended siege. The settlers had a herd of cattle grazing about two miles from the Station, and Logan decided to bring as many inside the stockade as he could, and chose to run the risk alone. When he neared the herd, the Indian party spotted him and fired; Logan was hit in the chest and his arm was broken. Severely wounded, he gave rein to his horse and galloped back to the fort, outpacing the pursuing warriors. While his wounds were dressed, Logan sent a messenger to the Holston Valley asking for reinforcements, and conferred with the men of the settlement on the need to hold out until help arrived. Logan and his small community waited for three weeks for the attack that never came. When the men from Holston finally arrived, they were ready for a fight, and not finding one at Logan's Station, they traveled first to Boonesborough, then to Harrodsburg hoping to find support for a counterattack. After discussion, the men from the South agreed it was too late in the season to start anything, and they returned to their Valley.

The events that preceded the attack on Boonesborough and the attack that never materialized at Benjamin Logan's Station caused a major controversy on the frontier. There are differing opinions as to Benjamin Logan's position; some say he was upset with Daniel Boone and accused him of surrendering at Blue Licks and then consorting with the British at Detroit. Others say Logan was merely asked to sit in as part of a general court martial proceeding. Regardless, Colonel Richard Callaway, a one-time friend of Boone's, believed the frontiersman had acted improperly, and convinced Logan that a court martial should be held at Logan's Station. Boone was shocked at the charges leveled against him. Not only were Logan and Callaway men he considered friends, Boone had recently rescued Callaway's daughter who had been captured by tribal raiders; furthermore, Boone's daughter Jemima had married Callaway's son Flanders.

It was a low period for Boone. Even though he successfully argued the reasons for his actions, and was acquitted of wrongdoing, he hated being accused by his companions. In addition, Rebecca and his children, believing he had been killed, had left for North Carolina months before his return. When Boone left the tribunal at Logan's Station to retrieve his family, he also severed his ties with Boonesborough in disgust. He later founded another settlement, Boone's Station, north of the Kentucky River, but—as though those events weren't enough to deal with—there were a number of discrepancies among land warrants drawn by Boone, and settlers could not be sure of holding clear title to their land. As a result, he sold major portions of land he owned in Kentucky, raising $20,000. He collected $30,000 from friends and set out in 1780 for Richmond to settle the claims. On his way, he stopped at an inn at James City, Virginia, where a thief crept in and stole his saddlebags. There were friends who commiserated with Boone's unenviable position and forgave him any debt of repayment. Others, however, believed he pocketed the money. His reputation was severely damaged by the scandal.

CHAPTER TEN

Through the Gap

BLOSSOMS PAINTED THE VALLEY, in the springtime along Mill Creek, and for many Scots-Irish it was the spring of a new adventure. Among those documented to have left present-day Rockingham County, Virginia for the area of present-day Lincoln County, Kentucky were the sons of Archibald Huston. Of the several brothers, only George Huston remained in Virginia, although John Huston later returned.

Archibald Huston Jr was legally under the guardianship of his brother John, the eldest of the siblings. As 'orphans' left by the death of their father, Archibald and his sisters might live with their mother, but they were the legal responsibility of their respective guardians until they came of age. On March 22, 1779 Thomas Hewitt was appointed guardian of Anne Huston, while her sister Abigail chose James Brewster. John Huston returned to the courthouse April 27 to again declare as the guardian of Archibald and brother George posted the required three-thousand-pounds bond. That same day, Abigail had her guardian bond renewed with James Brewster, and her sister Sarah was placed in the care of Captain David Laird, who posted six-thousand-pounds in bond money on behalf of the two sisters. May 24, 1779, and again in Rockingham County Court, Elizabeth Huston was placed in the legal care of her mother, while Jane chose John Magill as her legal guardian.

Although the distance between the Shenandoah Valley and the Kentucky frontier was substantial, and the geography rugged, trips between the two locations were being made with regularity. John, Joseph, and Abraham Bowman, whose family was among the pioneers of the Bluegrass State, made several trips beginning in 1775 when they were located near Harrodsburg. Joseph Bowman also maintained his home on Cedar Creek, some miles north of the Huston's plantation on the Wagon Road and made several trips between the Valley and Kentucky in the years 1775, 1776, and 1777. When a number of families from Rockingham County began moving with their wagons and animals toward the Indian Road, a new urgency swept the Scots-Irish community. The Bowmans and others were surveying land along the frontier and the on the frontier the best land would quickly be taken up by the first settlers; the countryside of Rockingham was a testament to that fact. The spring planting was completed. The time to travel had come at last—and, there was a deadline of sorts. John Stephenson had served in the French and Indian Wars under Captain McClanahan in Colonel Bouquet's campaign. Eight months after the treaty was signed, King George III issued a proclamation that rewarded all men who had served from 1754 until their unit was disbanded. The acreages were determined by rank, and as private, John Stephenson was entitled to 50 acres in the western section of Virginia, or present-day Kentucky. Shortly after his death, the Virginia Legislature placed a one-year time limit on receiving the land. The claimant, or his representatives, could present the certificate from Lord Dunmore or from the County Court where the military service had been performed. Between 1779 and 1783, the Commonwealth of Virginia issued more than 1,400 land bounty grants. In March of 1780, a grant was issued in the name of John Stephenson of Rockingham County.

It would require a new wagon and plenty of supplies. There were several wheelwrights in the Valley that could complete construction of a pair of suitable wagons, large enough to carry goods to sustain the party until a crop could be put in the ground. The wagons would have to be of sturdy design, since the Wilderness Road—as it came to be known years later—was still Boone's Trail, and once the brothers reached the frontier's edge there would only be the faintest semblance of a trail near their home site.

Groups of families were leaving regularly for Kentucky and passed nearby on the road near Harrisonburg. Safety was an issue, and reports of new attacks on the frontier had begun to filter back. Despite the risks, families continue to migrate. Wagons would be loaded with bags of flour, sacks of corn and salt. Bags of seed would be required to start their planting in Kentucky. Stores of gunpowder and lead would be stacked where they were readily accessible. There would be little room for trinkets, given the amount of required goods and the distance to be traveled.

———

Moving was becoming nearly commonplace among the Scots-Irish settlers of Augusta County. Colonel James Knox was one, having courted Miss Anne Montgomery before she married Benjamin Logan. Knox, in 1775, followed the Logans and made the move himself, traveling to the far reaches of the region before settling near the falls of the Ohio River. He was still traveling between the two locations, as many did, for supplies or business—or both. Often Knox served as 'officer in command' when making the trip with a large party of families. Like the Bowman brothers, Knox knew the territory along Boone's Trail and could advise travelers of the best course. As the summer months began to slip away to fall, thirty families joined to make the long haul to Kentucky with Colonel Abraham Bowman, who had decided to end his frequent trips to the frontier by making Kentucky his home.

Along the trail, horses would look like pack-mules. Light pieces of furniture would be strapped across the backs of some animals, while others bore leather saddlebags outfitted with straps that carried an assortment of farming tools. There were crude baskets made of thin hickory that could be balanced on the sides of some horses and in which could be stored any bed linens or clothing, and occasionally a small child or two. Tied behind the wagons were milk cows and the spare horses, and in the hand of each adult was a rifle or a pistol.

As they moved along the road from Harrisonburg to Staunton to Lexington, more and more families joined in, some hurriedly gathering their belongings to take advantage of the opportunity. There were men who joined by themselves—single men, or those scouting a homestead for their families—who took a position at the front or the rear of the caravan as guards. After passing the Natural Bridge in Rockbridge County, and heading through Roanoke, they would have covered over a hundred miles but remain hundreds of miles short of their destination. The scouts and guards at the head of the party would be spread thin as the caravan forded streams and rivers, leaving men at the water's edge to make sure that each wagon and pack animal successfully managed the crossing.

As they families moved deeper into the wilderness, the sounds of the forests would make sleep difficult for many. Wolves were said to howl relentlessly, the underbrush rustled with the movements of night creatures, and owls hooted throughout the dark hours. Since native tribes were known to travel the trail, many believed the sounds were human-made and an indication of imminent ambush; regardless, it was uneasy time spent in the dark forests between the warm glow of the hearths in the Valley, and the relative safety of the Kentucky stations. During the night, guards were posted at the outer edges of the caravan, and spies or scouts slipped through the darkness looking for signs of trouble. In the morning, the men would return with their reports, and the day's travel was charted accordingly.

Caravans moved parallel to the Holston River from Marion to Abingdon, to the edge of Bristol, and then generally camped at the Block House. The house of Colonel John Anderson marked the end of the Great Road and the true start of

Boone's Trail. Anderson was also from Augusta County, and had built the unusual house two years earlier. It was made of logs laid on top of one another, each successive trunk set slightly off-center so the house was wider at the roof than it was at the floor. The Block House not only attracted attention because of its looks, but also because of its location at the edge of the wilderness. It was becoming an almost mandatory stop for groups of travelers on the frontier, and was a point of reference that found its way into conversations, recollections, and diaries. Beyond the Block House was Boone's Trail, a thin trace that would lead travelers across the Clinch River to the Cumberland Gap, and onward into Kentucky.

After resting for the night, the families gathered their belongings and their courage, and set out for the frontier. From the Block House, the wagons could roll several abreast, allowing company and conversation between the drivers, but as the trail became narrower, the wagons were forced to move single file. Eventually, the caravan of animals and wagons grew to more than a mile in length as they drew nearer the Clinch River. Scouts moved ahead to locate a suitable crossing, and upon their return, the wagons followed them, the driver of each hoping that the crossing would be as uneventful as possible. The men began urging the horses and wagon drivers onward, quickening the pace, in an effort to ford the river before dusk, giving the families time to erect tents and make camp before nightfall. Each night, men were posted as guards in a wide circle that surrounded the sleeping camp, watching over the women and children, and keeping a vigilant watch against anything that might move furtively through the underbrush.

All along Boone's Trail, the men would spot signs that offered proof they were not alone on the path. Sometimes it was heavy-footed tracks left by buffalo or animal carcasses left by wolves. Other times, there were indications natives might be near, if only in small numbers. Generally, when the men suspected an ambush was possible, wagons were halted and gathered into a defensive position—as best as could be managed in the wild terrain—since no one wanted to place the women or children at additional risk.

As they drew nearer the Cumberland Gap, as many as two-dozen men might be sent ahead to scout the rocky overhangs and high terrain surrounding the narrow passage. It was hoped the scouting party would be large enough to deter any thoughts of ambush, but small enough that they could quickly move along the ridge over the Gap.

The caravan would be extremely vulnerable as it passed through the Cumberland Gap; although they moved as quickly as possible, it would take time to navigate the entire group through the narrow mountain pass. Orders would be barked and reins snapped in reply; alongside the wagons, men on horseback would whistle and yell to urge the animals more quickly onward.

Once through the Cumberland, the remainder of the trip seemed of little consequence. The Cumberland River was forded, as was Stinking Creek and Rockcastle River. Big Laurel and Little Laurel were successfully crossed. With each river crossing, the caravan could stop on the far banks to camp for the night. Once the majority of the wagons had passed through the running water, men began chopping trees and dragging them along the edges of the camp. The branches were stripped for firewood and the trunks were stacked into a crude wall to serve as additional security; with the river at their backs and a wall of timbers in front of them, each of the travelers could feel somewhat more secure in lying down for the night.

There was one more stop for the caravan as a group. At a place called Hazel Patch, a narrow path led away from Boone's Trail that created a fork in the road. The path leading to the northwest was Skaggs Trace, and men looking at each path for the first time could only imagine what might lay at the other end. Along Boone's Trail to the north, travelers would eventually reach Boonesborough. If they followed the more narrow of the two forks, the travelers would pass through Crab Orchard and Logan's Station on their way to Harrodsburg. Some intended to continue past Harrodsburg for the Falls of the Ohio. The Huston brothers followed the trace leading to the settlements along Dick's River, and Benjamin Logan's fort.

——

New settlers searched for land that would serve well for their purposes. They needed a nearby water source, and enough ready accessible timber for building houses and outbuildings, but not so many that farming would be difficult. Elbowroom between the neighbors was also a prerequisite. Logan's settlement filled rapidly with the new families that were pouring into the Kentucky territory.

A single man that was good with an axe could fell enough trees to build a house for himself in two week's time. Cabins were becoming numerous along Dick's River, back toward Boone's Trail east of Logan's. Just beyond a fork in Carpenter's Creek, named for another pioneering family, was another thin trail that crossed from near the Kentucky River southward to the Green River Valley. The Hustons settled at a location called Hanging Fork, the site where exhausted and exasperated Virginia lawmen decided to enact frontier justice rather than continue to escort two unruly prisoners back home.

It was an appropriate time to be sizing up a homestead in Kentucky; in an effort to straighten out some of the problems with land surveys, the Virginia Land Commission planned hearings at Logan's Station, Louisville at the Falls of the Ohio, Boonesborough, Harrodsburg, and at Bryan's Station.

Raids on the settlers happened with regularity, and it was important to construct a structure sturdy enough to provide some security, and have construction completed as quickly as possible. In the meantime, the wagons and the supplies were hidden in the nearby woods, and the horses tied nearby. If they felt threatened, frontiersmen in Lincoln County could take the horses and ride for the safety of nearby Carpenter's Station, or the added security of Logan's Station.

Since the logs were uneven and large gaps remained, river mud would be mixed with dried grasses to form a paste that would fill the gaps. Rocks would be collected and used to build a fireplace and chimney. Until a crude cabin was completed, families were forced to sleep outdoors or in what space could be arranged in a wagon. Once completed, the work would begin again. Cabin rights were still being claimed, although the survey teams would not support many of them. In Kentucky's frontier, officials hoped to avoid some of the earlier disputes among frontier landowners. By 1780, Kentucky settlers had pushed some fifty miles southwest of the first Kentucky settlement at Harrodsburg, into a then-forested region, with prairie grass valleys along the Green River.

Stephenson Huston's land claim in 1780 was among the early deeds recorded in the Green River—Dick's River watershed. There were earlier settlers in the territory to be sure—Boone, Logan, Harrod, Bowman, the Hite's, and others who made the early trails and the several forts, but as a frontier family establishing itself in 'Kaintuck,' the Hustons and their party would initially have few close neighbors. In 1779, 200 acre bounties to many settlers in the area "bounded by the Green River, the Cumberland Mountains, the Carolina line, the Tennessee River, and the Ohio River." In addition to the military bounties, there were tracts deeded to settlers who had "really and bona fide settled themselves" in the area by building cabins "upon any waste or unappropriated lands." The second tracts were up to 400 acres in size. After statehood, land in the valley sold for thirty dollars per one-hundred acres, and anyone living on unclaimed land could buy up to two hundred acres. In 1794, the Kentucky legislature passed an act "encouraging and granting relief to settlers" by selling up to two-hundred acres to anyone who had cleared and fenced two acres, and had grown a crop of corn before 1798, with the land sold at a price of forty dollars per one-hundred acres.

Benjamin Logan, whose St. Asaph's settlement was the center of activity for many incoming families, was deeded 200 acres on a branch of the Kentucky River in 1775, but many of his early holdings were in the Hanging Fork/Dick's River area. In 1781 alone, Logan was deeded more than 5,600 acres along the Hanging Fork branch, St. Asaph's Spring Branch, and the Dick's River. Hugh Logan had 1,000 acres at Hanging Fork in 1781, while James Logan had 800. John Logan, another major Lincoln County landowner, was deeded his first 1,400 acres on Dick's River on April 12, 1781, just days before a similar grant to Nathaniel Logan. William Montgomery—the father-in-law of Benjamin Logan—was one of the first settlers in the upper Green River Valley, claiming a 1,400 acre tract "over the Knobs" from Logan's Station. At the time of his settlement, he had seen no signs of Native Americans, and built his settlement without a stockade fortification, said to be a contributing factor in his death during an attack in 1781. John Montgomery was granted deeds that same year for land on Carpenter Creek and Dick's River, as was William before his death, along with his son William Junior. Thomas, John (Senior), and Joseph Montgomery were all listed on deeds by 1784.

Two highly visible pioneers owned land at or near Hanging Fork; Isaac Shelby, the man who would be sworn in as Kentucky's first governor in 1792, and Colonel William Whitley, a fearless leader of men on the frontier. Shelby had five separate deeds originally issued to him that amounted to more than 1,900 acres on "Nob Lick Br. Hanging Fk. Dicks R." Despite the impressive holdings, he later built a home northwest of Stanford that he called "Traveler's Rest." Whitley's home, built east of Logan's Settlement, remains as an outstanding example of architecture and construction on the frontier. Whitley was deeded 400 acres along the creek that bore his name in 1780, and nearly 2,000 additional acres on Dick's River before 1787.

Henry Boughman was granted 400 acres on February 15, 1781, and another 1,000 acres on Dick's River was dated February 17. The Boughman family was among those that found a home in the lush valley, becoming prominent as mill owners and businessmen over the next two centuries, with descendants living for generations near their ancestral lands at Hanging Fork. A watercourse named for them, Boughman Creek, became the home of James Renffro in 1784 when he was deeded nearly 2000 acres there.

The Carpenters were a frontier family that arrived early enough that the creek came to be called for their settlement. Conrod Carpenter had two separate deeds issued for land at Hanging Fork on Dick's River, one for 400 acres and another for 1,000 acres. Between 1781 and 1787, more than four thousand acres were added in separate deeds to Adam Carpenter, Coonrod (likely Conrad, in a second variation) Carpenter, George Carpenter, and John Carpenter, all in Lincoln County, and all primarily in the Hanging Fork area.

By 1781, Nathan Huston had also established a separate deed for 150 acres on Dick's River, and in 1783 was deeded 250 acres in Lincoln County. Brothers John, Nathan, George, and Stephenson were all listed on deeds by 1784, from Rolling Fork on Salt River in Jefferson County, to Nelson County to the Green River in Lincoln. Brother George, who remained in Virginia, was named on the deed to a 923 1/2 acre tract on Scagg's Creek in 1784. By 1785, Stephenson Huston was listed on deeds totalling 1,600 acres.

Nathaniel Evans was a major landowner that began his holdings with deeds at Hanging Fork. His first four properties in early 1781 totaled more than 2,000 acres but his lands eventually extended from the Crossroads at Hanging Fork through Nelson and Fayette counties. Seventeen additional deeds granted Evans more than 10,000 acres.

Abraham Miller began with 1,000 acres at Hanging Fork in 1781, while Andrew Miller was deeded 100 acres nearby the same year. Alexander and John Miller also owned land in the Green River—Dick's River area by 1787.

Thomas Ammons was granted 200 acres at Hanging Fork in 1783. A year later, David Anderson had a 1,000 acre grant on the Green River, and in 1785 he was granted another 1,000 acres, while nearby, Richard C. Anderson received a grant for 9,000 acres. William Monger settled on Green River in 1784, the same year Alexander Montgomery built on land nearby.

The Allen family was granted land when it was a part of Virginia called Fincastle County, although the grant named the location as Kentucky County. Hugh and James Allen had three thousand acres along Beargrass Creek and Salt River as early as 1774, and Thomas Allen found a spot along Hanging Fork in 1785.

John Bowles, sometimes spelled Bowls, settled on 400 acres along Dick's River in 1783, although a few years later, he became a major landowner in the Rockcastle

Creek area with a grant of 6,751 acres in 1786. Squire Boone, Daniel's brother, settled on land north of the Huston's location at Hanging Fork. Deeds were issued to George Boone, Hugh, Isaac, Jacob, Jonathan, Levi, Ovid, Samuel, Samuel Jr., Sarah, and Thomas Boone in Fayette and Jefferson counties, but Squire Boone had 400 acres issued to him in Lincoln County in 1786, near Silver Creek.

The Bowmans were among Kentucky's pioneer families; Joseph was deeded 837 acres on Cane Run in Lincoln County in 1781, while brother James owned land in the Green River area by 1786. John Bowman, along with Isaac Hite and Company, were speculating in land and were deeded 2,000 acres along Clark Run and Knob Lick Fork in Lincoln County on March 9, 1784, and another 1,000 on March 15 at Hanging Fork.

The Lee family, including Hancock and Willis, were among the first in the area of present-day Frankfort, founding a settlement in that area called Leestown. Hancock was deeded land on Elkhorn Creek in 1780 as was John Lee. Some of their many relations and namesakes migrated southward to settle the Dick's River (or Dix, as it is spelled in the early Kentucky deed book) valley at the same time. Thomas Lee had 500 acres on the Dix in March of 1781, while Jacob Lee had 375 acres Paint Lick Creek in Lincoln County that same year. William Fleming Lee was deeded 1,400 acres at the same time on Huston Fork in Bourbon County. Brothers William and Henry are jointly listed on two deeds on the North Fork of Licking Creek in 1980, totalling 1,500 acres, where a third brother, Richard Lee, also settled. Before 1785, Richard acquired land on Rowling (Rolling) Fork, as did Samuel, Joseph, William, and Henry Lee. William's son Richard H. Lee bought land in 1797; his daughter Jane married into the Huston family years later at Stanford. Henry Lee was deeded 4,000 acres on the Cumberland in 1788, while Charles Lee settled on a 4,000-acre tract on Woods Fork years earlier, in 1783. George Lee built a home at Hanging Fork by 1791. Ambrose Lee bought land by 1800, and later added to his holding when he acquired several tracts from the Montgomery brothers on Green River.

Thomas Gay originally settled in Fayette County around 1784, but was in the Hanging Fork area by 1790, and was among those of that name that had settled the Pastures in the early Virginia grants. Richard Clark had 666 and 2/3 acres on the Green River in 1784, while Jesse Clark settled on the Dick's River and 500 acres in 1785. Other early landowners in the Hanging Fork area were William Moor (1783), Daniel and John McCormack (1781), John McGuire (1783), James McKenny (1781), John Patterson (1781), John Reins (1783), George Reynold (1781), Joseph Russell (1781), John Rutherford (1781), Zachariah Smith (1781), George Spears (1784), James Speed (1782), and John and Spencer Stone (1781, 1783).

———

Rough times awaited those who made it to the end of the Wilderness Road by that fall. It was bitterly cold during the winter of 1779–80—it was not just a typical winter cold snap or an unusual amount of snow that settled over the cabins. It was an extended spell that saw temperatures drop below zero and stay there, day after day, week after week, and month after month. Those who suffered through it and survived would comment for years that that it was the coldest weather ever faced on the American continent. As it turns out, it was not the coldest ever, but at the time, in the threat of armed attack, on the leading edge of the sometimes-lonely frontier, it may have made the frigid temperatures feel all the colder. In the wilderness of Kentucky, those who had already arrived were struggling to survive, and many who were on the Wilderness Road would not make it past the Cumberland Gap. From the middle of November 1779 to the end of February 1780, Kentucky was suspended in a brittle landscape of ice and snow. Sap froze in the trees and burst the trunks; creeks and streams were nothing more than thin ribbons of ice, and even the Kentucky River was frozen to a depth of more than two feet. Settlers melted snow for drinking water and cooking, but animals in the forest were not so fortunate; even many of the settler's horses and cattle froze to death.

From Logan's Station to Harrodsburg to Boonesborough, people were waiting for the break in the weather, trying to survive just one more day in the unforgiving new country. Until the bitter weather settled in, each day seemed to bring more families through the Cumberland, but one Scots-Irishman wanted only to be back in Virginia.

Colonel William Fleming was the Chairman of the Virginia Land Commission, and his job was to sort out the various land claims and warrants in Kentucky. Not all the deeds transferred by Daniel Boone and the Transylvania Company met Virginia requirements. Fleming was advanced in years and had been quite content on his estate near Christiansburg, serving as a Senator in the Virginia Assembly from Augusta County. He had seen the wagons and pack-horses as they rolled along past his home, heading for Kentucky; then, at the Assembly's urging, he had reluctantly joined them just before the winter set in and travel became hazardous.

Working with Fleming were Colonel Stephen Trigg, Edmund Lyne and James Barbour. The four commissioners met at Logan's Station, where they listened to a steady stream of claims and accusations regarding deeds to land on the frontier. In six months of work, Fleming and Company adjudicated 1,328 claims that involved over a million acres of land. Along with the records of his group's work,

Fleming was meticulous about keeping a journal. He detailed aspects of life at Logan's Station, on the frontier in general, and noted the hardships facing new settlers during the particularly rough weather.

> *The effects of the severe winter was now sensibly felt, the earth for so long a time being covered with snow and the water entirely froze, the Cane almost all kiled, the Hogs that were in the Country suffered greatly, being frozen to death, in their beds, the deer likewise not being able to get either water or food, were found dead in great numbers, tirkies dropt dead off their roosts and even the Buffalos died starved to death, the vast increase of people, near three thousand that came into this Country with the prodigious losses they had in their cattle and horses, on their Journey, and the severity of the winter after they got here killing such numbers, all contributed to raise the necessaries of life to a most extravagant price.*

Many considered themselves fortunate just to be alive to struggle through the winter. The Davis family, trying to find land and build a structure to before the weather worsened, may have let haste overcome their caution. They stopped near Rockcastle River, and barely had time to stretch after the day's ride, when they discovered the water was rising around them. Before they could gather themselves and their belongings back into the wagon, they found themselves completely surrounded by swirling water, marooned on a thin strip of land. David hoped that with the help of several men he would be able to rescue his family and tried to swim for help, but the cold and savage river proved to be too much; he was swept downstream to his death. His wife and children, huddled together without a campfire, froze to death during the night.

Despite Fleming's note that frozen deer were found "in great numbers," meat was such a rarity during those winter months that it could scarcely be had at any price. Instead, settlers were forced to eat the horses that had died from the cold. Others brought the horses and cows inside the cabins to keep them alive. Sanitation was deplorable.

> *The Spring at this place is below the Fort and fed by ponds above the Fort so that the whole dirt and filth…putrified flesh, dead dogs, horse, cow, hog excrements and human odour all wash into the spring which with the Ashes and sweepings of filthy Cabbins, the dirtiness of the people, steeping skins to dress and washing every sort of dirty rags and cloths in the spring perfectly poisons the water and makes the most filthy nauseous potation of the water imaginable.*

As would be expected, many settlers were suffering from frostbite and exposure, with the frigid temperatures affecting both the first arrived and the recent arrivals to Kentucky. Just to survive was a testament to the hardiness of the frontier families.

CHAPTER ELEVEN

Revolution on the Frontiers

WHEN THE HARD WINTER FINALLY thawed, settlers again began making the trip along Boone's Trail to Kentucky, something made possible by the efforts of a man named George Rogers Clark. He was a Virginian from Albemarle County who had taken up farming near the site of present-day Wheeling, West Virginia. He was tall and thin, red-haired, and in love with the westward country. He joined the county militia, and in 1774, found himself one of those marching in Lord Dunmore's column in the French and Indian campaign. He also discovered he had an ability to lead men.

The next year, as a surveyor with the Ohio Company, accompanied John Gabriel Jones rode from Kentucky to serve as delegates to the Virginia General Assembly— at least that was the intention. By the time Clark and Jones reached the Assembly, the group had already adjourned. Clark did managed to convince Governor Patrick Henry to provide 500 pounds of gunpowder for the defense of Kentucky.

When Kentucky County was formed in December of 1776, Clark was granted a commission as a major in the militia, and since there was no one on the frontier with a higher rank, the commission effectively put him in charge of Kentucky's militia. In early spring he called out the men, and counted some 140 serving in the new county, including Daniel Boone, James Harrod, and Benjamin Logan, who were among those named as militia captains. All men between the ages of eighteen and fifty were then considered to be part of the county militia, unless exempted. The men provided their own rifles and were required to have a pound of lead and a half-pound of powder.

Clark and his men were the primary defense against tribal raids that were being prompted by the British with the intention of exciting "alarm upon the frontiers of Virginia and Pennsylvania." Rather than wait for the settlements to be attacked, Clark undertook the offense in a campaign that took his men northward into Illinois country. He intended to march all the way to Detroit, but the winter weather forced him back to Fort Nelson at the Falls of the Ohio. There, he waited with his men during the extended winter of 1779–1780.

Springtime found the Scots-Irish in the Dix River Valley trying to turn the land into suitable farms getting, and working to complete the structures of their cabins after the long winter. When the freeze finally ended at the end of February, those who had been encamped at the various stations through the winter moved back to their settlements and began preparing their home sites. Vegetation was brought to life early by the mild weather, as though bursting forth from the long and oppressive freeze. Normally, farmers would have chosen to wait until the threat of frost had passed to put a few crops in the ground, but many used the early mild spell to plant seed and were rewarded. Corn planted after the thaw was "half a leg high" by the middle of April. Peach trees that had been planted by earlier settlers were already bearing fruit, and apple trees that had been placed in the ground before the winter and intended for transplanting, had grown so quickly that some were too large to move.

Along with the mild weather came a renewed British offensive against the Kentucky settlements, and George Rogers Clark was hurrying to head them off. Clark and his men moved to meet the enemy, but they were too late to prevent the British capture of Martin's Station and Ruddle's Station. British Colonel Henry Bird led an alliance of British troops and tribal warriors in taking those two stations. The movement of Clark's troops alone stopped Bird's advance, however, and the British force began to retreat toward Detroit.

Clark intended to follow Bird's warriors toward Detroit, and ordered the land office at Harrodsburg closed, in addition to sending men ahead to prevent the eastward "fleeing" of any men of military age. The Scots-Irish formed a large percentage of the one thousand men who assembled at the fork of the Licking and Ohio rivers and began moving toward the Shawnee villages in Ohio. Benjamin Logan was led a group closing up the flanks, but their delay allowed most of the warriors to escape. Clark was unable to provoke any direct confrontation and returned having covered 480 miles in thirty-one days.

Capt. William Oldham's Company, Col. William Linns Battalion
July 20–August 20, 1780

Lt. Jos. Brown	Joseph Johnston	Daniel McKenzies
Ens. George Wilson	John Massie	Josias Phelps
Serjt. Amara Fizelle	James Happy	Richard Rue
Serjt. Dennis Purcel	Thomas McMullin	George Dickins
Thomas Whitlidge	Thomas Helm, Junr.	John Tewell
James Purcell	Abraham James	Edward Murdock
Thomas Purcell	Jacob Fronch	Robert Hamilton
Henry Frinch	John Foakes	John Severns
John Johnston	John Crawford	John Huston
James Brown	William Stevens	Thomas Fennel
David Standeford	George Hendricks	Charles Lecount

While the hard winter had settlers in Kentucky cabin-bound, the activity in Rockingham County, VA continued much as usual. It was November 23, 1779 that the court for Rockingham County met in session, and recommended the "building of a court house be let." In addition, the body recommended Josiah Harrison, Richard Reagan, and George Huston as the captains of that county's militia. Andrew Shanklin was named as First Lieutenant, John Huston as Second Lieutenant, and Daniel Nelson as Ensign in George's company.

Things were not going well for the rebels against the British. The victories of Cornwallis at Charleston and Camden had families nervous all along the North Carolina frontier; people gathered at the courthouse steps to wait for any word from beyond the line. South Carolina had fallen back to the British. They knew Major-General Charles Cornwallis would not be content at Charleston, and an invasion of North Carolina could come at any time. Already, rebel troops under Abraham Buford were headed toward the border; he had arrived too late at Charleston to keep it from falling to the enemy, and with too few men to take on the British, he was retreating to North Carolina. The Continental Army was in a state of disarray. Benjamin Lincoln and Horatio Gates were removed from command and Nathaniel Green was being sent to take charge of the Southern Campaign. Green was not only having trouble getting enough troops, the guns he requested for them were in short supply, uniforms were absent, and he was being asked to take on Cornwallis with only six cannons.

Meanwhile, Cornwallis had heard that Buford's Virginia infantry was not that far away, and could be caught if he immediately dispatched a force. Serving under Cornwallis was just the man for the job: Banastre Tarleton. It was exactly the sort of mission Tarleton loved—a furious, adrenaline-charged, fox-and-hound action with little time for regrets or second-guesses. Tarleton quickly gathered his mounted British Legion and a detachment from the 17th Light Dragoons. The 270 horsemen thundered off, men shouting and the hooves of their horses pounding the north-bound road, racing against time to overtake Buford before he could reach safety beyond the border. The horses tired, but still Tarleton pushed his men to continue, until a number of the mounts simply dropped to the ground from sheer exhaustion. Before the cloud of dust around the fallen animals could settle, Tarleton obtained a replacement for each by "procuring" replacements from settlers living along the road.

Colonel Abraham Buford had just four hundred men; his Virginia Continental regiment had nearly reached Charleston before the rebels had been forced to surrender it to the British. Buford's long ride with the men had been for nothing. Now, they faced the added danger of the British combined forces, without any hope for assistance should they be engaged in battle. They had been marching for days, and presumably, were beyond the reach of the British back at Charleston. On May 29, Buford learned otherwise; Tarleton had covered a distance of 105 miles in 54 hours, most of it ridden without a break. With no other choice available to him, Buford turned his Continentals around and dug in to face the expected attack. He set a line at a place called the Waxhaws, along the border between North and South Carolina. Tarleton, after having spent so much time in chase, opted to charge the rebels immediately.

Since muskets were the common weapon of the continentals and they had such little accuracy—except at close range—it was a common order to "hold fire" until the enemy was well within range. Buford's men crouched as Tarleton's cavalry galloped toward them, occasionally hearing the order repeated in a hiss— "Hold fire!"—until the horses were nearly on top of them. Buford finally screamed his order to fire, but it was seconds too late. The momentum of the racing horses carried them well into the rebel's line, even as the muskets blasted toward the charge. Several of the horses fell, and Tarleton lost his mount, but his men were quick with their sabers and Buford could see his chances for victory were slim. Although reluctantly, he quickly gave an order and an ensign began to raise the white flag of surrender, but it was barely unfurled when Tarleton's men shot down its bearer. Realizing at once there would be no surrender, the rebels scrambled for their lives; the British regiment began mercilessly swinging their sabers as they rode on horseback through the scrambling rebel troops. A surgeon named Robert Brownfield was present at Waxhaw when the white flag was shot down:

> *Viewing this as an earnest of what they were to expect, [the Virginians took up their arms again] to sell their lives as dearly as possible; but before this was*

fully affected, Tarleton with his cruel myrmidons was in the midst of them, when commenced a scene of indiscriminate carnage, never surpassed by the ruthless atrocities of the most barbarous savages.

The demand for quarters, seldom refused to a vanquished foe was at once found to be in vain. Not a man was spared...[Tarleton's dragoons] went over the ground plunging their bayonets into everyone that exhibited any signs of life, and in some instances, where several had fallen over the others, these monsters were seen to throw off on the point of the bayonet the uppermost, to come at those underneath.

Tarleton's massacre of Buford's Scots-Irish regiment at Waxhaw had a profound effect on the colonists, both the rebels and those who were Loyal to the Crown. The loyalists were called Tories, and were in the minority in most areas and many had been in hiding for months. They rallied after witnessing the strength of the British army. Filled with new courage, they emerged from hiding to settle scores with those neighbors who had joined the rebellion. On the other hand, the rebellious Whigs were hardened in bitterness over Tarleton's treatment of Buford and his men; "Bloody Tarleton" was ominously hissed through clenched teeth, and "Tarleton's Quarter" became synonymous with the merciless treatment of men seeking terms of surrender. Between the Whig's anger and the newly inspired boldness of the Tories, riots broke out that included armed fighting among neighbors and some attacks that were nothing more than outright murders.

Two weeks after Buford's defeat at Waxhaws the militia was called out in the southwestern part of North Carolina. Tarleton's massacre of the Continentals had occurred just forty miles south of Charlotte, and the Scotch-Irish settlers in Mecklenburg County began gathering. By June 3, there were nearly nine hundred men milling around the courthouse. Brigadier-General Rutherford ordered the men to be ready, since it was expected that Cornwallis would eventually enter North Carolina.

One of the men marching northwest ahead of Cornwallis was a Tory by the name of John Moore who had grown up near the south fork of the Catawba River in North Carolina. He had joined the British army the year before, and on June 7, he arrived back at his father's home, wearing a suit of regimentals and carrying a sword. He told them he was now Lieutenant Colonel of the North Carolina Loyalists Regiment, and called a meeting of Tories in preparation for the arrival of Cornwallis.

Some days later, rebel General Rutherford was advised of Moore's gathering of Tories at Ramsour's Mill, near the present-day site of Lincolnton, North Carolina. Rutherford ordered Colonel Francis Locke of Rowan and Major David

Wilson of Mecklenburg County to raise as many men as possible to put down the Tory gathering, which by June 20 numbered nearly thirteen hundred men.

Locke and Wilson, along with Major Joseph McDowell, and Captains Falls and Brandon, marched their force of four hundred men along the east side of Mountain Creek to a point sixteen miles from the Mill. Their first intention was to camp at the site, but after the officers conferred, it was considered too danger-ous to wait so close to the Tories. Instead, they hoped the element of surprise would work to their benefit, and planned an immediate attack. It was the most basic of strategies: they would march through the night to within a mile of the Tories, and then the companies commanded by McDowell, Falls, and Brandon would take the point in front of what men remained.

Locke suspected the Tories had found out about their presence in the area, but as the rebels moved toward Ramsour's Mill, sentries fired into the air—a warning of a surprise attack. The picket of twelve men who had served as guards began running back to the Tory camp, and the mounted rebels directed their horses after them. The troops on foot hurried to keep pace with the point companies, but when the fighting actually began, the rebel forces were widely scattered between the lead man on horseback and the last infantryman huffing and puffing to catch his company.

The Tories had no time to form a proper line, but the first shots they unleashed against the oncoming horsemen were extremely deadly—resulting in heavy casualties for the rebels. Captain Falls was shot and killed in the first charge, and as the rebels dropped back, the Tories gathered themselves and moved down the hill after them. The fighting continued for several hours with no clear advantage taken by either side. Finally, the Tories retreated up the hill, only to discover the rebels had begun closing from another side. The two groups fought at close quarters, but having no bayonets and no time to reload, the men were forced to swing the stocks of their guns at each other, like clubs. By the time the Whigs finally realized they were in possession of the hill, the remaining Tories had fled beyond a nearby pond.

Both the Whigs and the Tories who fought at Ramsour's Mill were sons of North Carolina. There was no physical distinction between them, and neither side had uniforms. The only badge of identification was found on the soldier's caps: the Tories stuck a sprig of pine top in their caps, while the Whigs placed a piece of white paper on theirs. As the battle began to turn and the momentum began to shift, many of the Tories simply removed their identifying mark, and slipped in among the Whigs until they could safely flee the area. Since many of the fallen troops lost their caps, and since there was no return muster to account for troops after the battle, the exact number lost by both sides is unknown.

It is known that some seventy men from the Scots-Irish settlement in North Carolina lost their lives in the Battle at Ramsour's Mill, and another two hundred or so were wounded. In Locke's attack plan, the officers did not watch the battle from a distance issuing orders, but instead, fought like common soldiers—many officers died as soldiers in the battle. In addition to Captain Falls, who was shot at the outset of the battle, Captains Dobson, Smith, Bowan, and Armstrong were also killed. Captains Houston and McKissick were wounded—both shot in the thigh—but both later recovered.

Captain James Houston's Muster Roll
Lieutenant William Davidson

John Beard	David Evans	John Singleton
Benjamin Brevard	Nat. Ewing	Thomas Templeton
Robert Brevard	James Gray	John Thompson
Daniel Bryson	James Gulick	Adam Torrence, Jr.
David Byers	John Hovis	Adam Torrence, Sr.
Robert Byers	Philip Logan	William Vint
John Caldwell	Angus McCauley	Moses White
John M. Connell	Joseph McCawn	Alexander Work
William Creswell	John Poston	James Young
Paul Cunningham	Robert Poston	
William Erwin	Charles Quigley	

Most of Houston's company came from Iredell County, North Carolina, and many remained there after the Revolution. Robert Brevard—one of the men in Houston's company—was serving under his son-in-law. Houston was married to Brevard's daughter Arsenath.

The Scots-Irish faced hostilities regularly at their homes on the frontier and as a result, were qualified to draw their rifles in the service of their new homeland. There were scattered Loyalists among the Scots-Irish, but their number was small compared to those who fervently backed the rebel cause. The Houston families were typical of the Scots-Irish participation, more than two hundred men bearing the name are listed as having fought in the Revolution.

Abraham Houston re-enlisted in Captain Williams' Company, NC Regiment.
Archibald Houston, private, North Carolina Unit, married Rosannah Cunningham.
Christopher Houston, private, Capt. Richard Pearson's Company of North Carolina Minutemen, battle of Ramsour's Mill, died Houstonville, NC 1839.
Daniel Houston, Salisbury District, North Carolina.

David Houston, corporal, infantry, Virginia.

David Houston, Salisbury District, North Carolina.

Edward Houston, Wilmington District, North Carolina.

Elijah Huston, Kentucky militia.

Captain George Houston, Rockingham Co. Virginia, married Susanna Snapp.

George Houston, supplier, NC, married Margaret Ware.

George Houston, Capt. Samuel Martin's Company, Lieutenant William Polk's Regiment, light dragoons, in Gen. Thomas Sumter's Brigade.

Henry Houston (Huston), lieutenant, North Carolina, married Sarah Elizabeth Miller.

James Houston, captain, North Carolina Rangers, wounded at Ramsour's Mill, married Arsenath Brevard.

James Houston, private and ensign, Rockbridge County, VA, married [first] Esther Houston, [second] Polly Gillespie.

James Huston, Captain Tate's Company, Augusta County, VA.

James Huston, supplier to Virginia militia, married Nancy McCreary.

James Huston (Houston), private, Virginia, married Anna Braddock.

John Huston, ensign, 9th Virginia Regiment, 1776–1777.

John Huston, Captain McCutchin's Company, Augusta County, VA.

John Huston, 2nd lieutenant, Rockingham County, VA militia, private Cap. William Oldham's Co. Kentucky County, married Mary Ann Miller.

John Huston (Houston), private, Virginia and North Carolina, married Rachel Balch.

Joseph Huston (Houston), deputy commissary for Militia, Rockingham County, VA.

Mathew Houston, Captain McCutchen's Company, Augusta County, VA.

Nathan Huston, Captain Hewett's Company, August County, VA, captain, Lincoln Militia, Northwest expedition 1782.

Neil Huston, private, North Carolina, seven years service, heir Daniel Huston received a 640 acre land bounty.

Peter Huston, Battle of King's Mountain with father, Samuel Huston.

Samuel Houston, commissary department, NC and VA, married Sarah Henderson.

Samuel Houston, captain, Morgan's Rifle Brigade, Virginia militia, married Elizabeth Paxton. (Father of Gen. Sam Houston).

Samuel Huston, private, Reuben Taylor's Company, Col. Moses Hazen's North Carolina Regiment, married Mary Hamilton.

Samuel Huston, Battle of King's Mountain with son, Peter.

Samuel Houston, private, Rockbridge County, VA, Battle of Guilford Courthouse, married [second] Margaret Walker.

Stephenson Huston, Captain Hewett's Company, Augusta County, VA; ensign, Cap.Robert Barrow's Company, VA; scout for Captains John Martin and Captain Samuel Kirkham, Lincoln County, Kentucky under Colonel Benjamin Logan.

William Houston, private, Salisbury District, NC, seven years in the Continental Army, heirs received a land bounty of 640 acres.
William Houston, captain, North Carolina Regiment, married Margaret Williams.
William Houston (Huston), private, North Carolina, married Susana Allen.
William Houston (Huston), private, Virginia, married Hannah Sherrill.
William Huston, Captain Shield's Company, Augusta County, VA.

———

Cornwallis entered Charlotte on September 20, 1780, and designated the town as his headquarters during the campaign to bring North Carolina back under the Crown. He set up camp in the middle of Mecklenburg County, where Colonel Davie and a force of one hundred fifty cavalry and fourteen volunteers planned a welcome for him.

Davie knew he could do little against the superior numbers of the British, but opted to confront Cornwallis regardless. He positioned a company at the courthouse behind a stone wall and sent two other companies about eight yards ahead, where they hid among the houses and gardens.

Cornwallis sent Tarleton's Legion to disperse the militia, and the troops formed a line in the road just three hundred yards from Davie's front men. The charge was sounded, and the cavalry stormed toward the courthouse. From their spots in hiding, Davie's Scots-Irishmen fired at the advancing brigade. The cavalry met the fire and turned, but the British infantry continued its advance. The cavalry regrouped and attacked several times, each meeting with rebel fire and keeping Davie's men occupied as the infantry marched up the road. There was little Davie could do but withdraw. His men moved back along the road to Salisbury.

The skirmish at Charlotte was brief, but carried a stiff toll. Among the Mecklenburg men killed were Lieutenant George Locke and four privates; Major Graham and five privates were wounded. The British lost twelve men and had more than thirty wounded.

Cornwallis was in possession of Charlotte, but it was not a position of security. Rebel snipers regularly picked off the sentries who were stationed at the edge of his camp, and eventually Cornwallis ordered the digging of holes in which the guards could hide. Davie continued his assaults, and continued the fashion of his assaults, which included a quick ambush and then immediate disappearance into the woods.

Tarleton later wrote of the period of time spent among the Scots-Irish in Mecklenburg County:

It was evident, and had been frequently mentioned to the King's officers, that the counties of Mecklenburg and Rohan (sic) were more hostile to England than any others in America. The vigilance and animosity of these surrounding districts checked the exertions of the well-affected, and totally destroyed all communication between the King's troops and loyalists in other parts of the province. No British commander could obtain any information in that position which would facilitate his designs, or guide his future conduct.

When the British sent men out to forage for food, they did so at personal risk. Rather than following the custom of remaining at home to be paid for any supplies that were taken, the Scots-Irish fled to the woods and fired at the British companies as they approached their farms. Express riders who carried information to and from Cornwallis were regularly ambushed at the outskirts of town. There was a substantial skirmish between the rebel militia and the British at Polk's Mill, some two miles from Charlotte. The British troops located in Mecklenburg County were described as being in the middle of a hornet's nest, and the "Hornets" were greatly aroused.

On October 3, a British foraging party under Major Doyle was sent along the road leading to Beattie's Ford. By now, the troops were accompanied by armed troops for protection, and along with sixty cavalry troops and forty wagons, some four hundred fifty British infantrymen marched beside Long Creek to gather supplies from nearby farmhouses.

James Thompson lived in the area and served as Captain of the militia company along the creek. Anticipating the British supply expedition, Thompson had called out the thirteen men in his company early in the morning, and assembled at Mitchell's Mill. Thompson's group came to be called the "Hornets" and all of them were intimately familiar with the terrain. In addition, they were all crack shots with a Pennsylvania rifle. The rebel company hid quietly in the woods for nearly an hour before the British regiment marched by, and as they passed, Thompson had his men keep pace with the British; the rebels scampered stealthily through the woods alongside the road. From tree to tree they moved: George and Hugh Houston, Thomas McClure, Francis Bradley, George Graham, James Henry, Thomas and John Dickson, George and Edward Shipley, John Long, and John Robinson.

McIntyre's farm was located some seven miles from Charlotte, and from there Thompson watched as Major Doyle ordered half his troops to stay behind in gathering supplies from the farmhouses. McIntyre was warned of the impending British arrival and fled his house into the woods. After seeing Thompson and his men moving through the thicket near the house, McIntyre crept out of the trees and joined them. He had grabbed his rifle before fleeing the house and was eager for an opportunity to fire it.

Thompson's men clenched their teeth and watched the British for several minutes. Grain was being carried from the barn; there were men inside the house, and others in the yard chasing chickens. When a beehive was knocked over by one of the men in the yard, the bees swarmed, sending the closest soldiers running—much to the amusement of the remainder of the troops. In the midst of the British laughter and vandalism, the rebels could hold themselves back no longer. Thompson whispered coarsely, "Boys, I can't stand this any longer! I'll take the captain, each of you choose his man, and look out for yourselves." With that, he gave a nod and the rifles erupted flame and smoke. The commander of the troops was hit in the chest as he stood at the door of McIntyre's barn, and he dropped on the spot. The men in the yard scrambled for cover, but another eight men and two horses were shot and killed before the British could react.

Doyle would be bringing the rest of the troops back to help, and Thompson set his men along the road with orders to fire as the force approached. When the gunshots began, many of Doyle's men were so frightened they cut the horses free from the wagons, hopped on their backs and fled. Many others were not as fortunate. By the time Thompson ordered his Hornets back into the woods, Doyle had lost at least twenty men.

————

When the county militias gathered across North Carolina and Virginia, the talk eventually turned from drills to exploits like those of Thompson's "Hornets." Sooner or later, someone would mention Patrick Ferguson. The British Major was in charge of a regiment of Loyalists headquartered at the Ninety-Six settlement in South Carolina. Comparisons were made between the British commander and colonist Daniel Morgan. Morgan was an older man and Ferguson was only thirty-six, but even the most cynical of the talkers had to admit that similarities existed.

Both men were skilled at firing the long rifle. Ferguson had gone so far as to invent a rifle that improved on the Pennsylvania model being carried by Morgan's Brigade. The British officer's version was a breech-loader, which did away with the long rod to tamp the wadding and the powder, and allowed the firing of five or six shots per minute. By comparison, some skirmishes involving troops carrying the so-called Brown Bess musket had soldiers getting fewer than ten shots over the course of an entire battle due to the time required to reload. Compared to the Brown Bess, Ferguson's Breechloader rifle resembled a machine gun. Unfortunately for Ferguson, the company he had put together to use his new weapon was recruited without the consent of the officer above him. To pay back Ferguson for his insolence, the officer had the rifles placed in storage, and ordered the company disbanded.

Both Ferguson and Morgan were headstrong men. Morgan initially declined to serve under a younger man who he felt was less qualified than he—being a veteran of numerous campaigns and a boisterous leader of men. Like Morgan, Ferguson was self-confident to the point of being cocky. He was called "Bulldog," but probably only behind his back. Ferguson was the son of a Scots-Irish lawyer, and although physically small, he was extremely clever and accustomed to having his way.

Cornwallis ordered the Bulldog to join him at Charlotte. Ferguson had a relatively large force under his command at Ninety-Six, but he decided to divide the troops into two groups. He took the smaller of the two with him, leaving a good-sized force to guard Ninety-Six. The British still believed there were plenty of loyal colonists who could be recruited to join with them as they marched through the backcountries of the Carolinas. Ferguson also intended to increase the size of his force by enlisting local support for the Crown's cause. Along the way he rousted Whigs from their homes, and after plundering the valuables he ordered the houses burned. One young Whig was driven from his home and was coerced into traveling over the Blue Ridge Mountains to deliver a message to Colonel Isaac Shelby, the man who would later become the first governor of the State of Kentucky. Shelby and several other officers were located at the point where the present-day states of Virginia, North Carolina, and Tennessee meet. When the young militiaman arrived at Shelby's camp he breathlessly told the colonel about Major's tactics against the Whigs, and delivered Ferguson's message that Shelby should surrender at once or Cornwallis "would come over the mountains and put him to death, and burn his whole country."

When he took the smaller group from Ninety-Six instead of the larger, Ferguson committed a serious military blunder. However, the biggest mistake of his career was making threats against the lives and homes of the backwoods Scots-Irishmen.

The Scots-Irish were used to dealing with threatening situations; their lives on the frontier attested to their success in handling adversity. When the young man delivered the message for Ferguson, the men from "over the hill" were not in the least bit intimidated—they just got mad. The hills were filled with families of Scots-Irish, and there wasn't a Scots-Irishman born that could easily turn away from a threat. As a group they were almost always predictably drawn to an immediate and undiplomatic response to such actions. Knowing the Scots-Irish, Ferguson should not have been surprised that instead of reaching for the white flags, the mountain men reached for their long rifles hanging above the mantle.

They gathered up shot, powder, and cornmeal rations and stuffed them into saddlebags. News of the threat swept through the settlements like a fire, and in response, the mountain men poured from the hills, armed and mounted, and growing in number as they descended the back country to "settle up" with Ferguson.

By September 20, 1780, when the men met at Sycamore Shoals, their force numbered more than one thousand, including 400 militiamen under the command of Colonel William Campbell. Settlers in Augusta County, Virginia were familiar with a Colonel William Campbell who was later referred to as General Campbell. In deference to the size of Campbell's contingent of riflemen, Shelby suggested that Campbell be given overall command of the force. The other commanders agreed, which amounted to a grand gesture among the backwoods leaders, who tended to be jealous of other commanders and protective of their own troops.

Following the Doe River, the party entered a pass between the Roan and Yellow Mountains in present-day Tennessee, and then moved south into present-day North Carolina. After riding three days through an early mountain snow, they managed the tough crossing of the Blue Ridge Mountains at a place called Gillespie's Gap. Once past the mountains, traveling was easier through the Catawba River watershed, and at Quaker Meadows, a Colonel Benjamin Cleveland was waiting with 350 North Carolina volunteers. The force continued to grow in size as it moved toward the South Carolina line, where they finally stopped at Cowpens on October 6th, after having covered well over one hundred miles. At Cowpens were another four hundred armed men who joined Shelby and Campbell, along with John Sevier, Benjamin Cleveland, and Charles McDowell, who were the other primary commanders. There were no recruits for the British Major, no Loyalists, and no fighting Tories to be found anywhere along the route that might fill out the size of his force. Instead, the people he encountered were "the most violent young rebels" he had ever seen—"particularly the young ladies." A scout sent ahead of the troops came galloping back, shouting and waving his arms as he searched for Ferguson. It was bad news: there were two to three thousand men just ahead on horseback, all armed with rifles and waiting for Ferguson to march into their midst.

The size of the force wasn't necessarily what concerned Ferguson. It was more the attitude of the backcountry men he had already had the chance to encounter. They were young and rough, and man-for-man they were extremely deadly when armed with a rifle. Ferguson was smart enough to know that he was in trouble. He sent several couriers back to Ninety-Six, sending them by several different routes. He hoped to have reinforcements hurried to his aid, but not one of the riders made it out of the countryside. The Bulldog hurriedly turned his men around, and headed back south where he could meet his phantom reinforcements. The Scots-Irish rebels stalked him like hungry panthers. By the time they had stopped at Cowpens, they were already close enough that Ferguson ordered his men into a defensive position on a flat hill called King's Mountain. The long, narrow hill was protected on one side by a rocky bluff that even the mountain men would find difficult. He was confident his Loyalists could easily defend such a position against the rebels, even if their force been twice its size.

The mountain army had its scouts as well and when they captured two Tories, the loyalists revealed Ferguson's location and how his troops were situated on the plateau. Not only did the Tories reveal Ferguson's location, but they also told the rebels that the British commander was wearing a multicolored hunting shirt that would make him easily distinguishable. Campbell and Shelby took 900 of their best men and immediately set out through the rain and darkness for King's Mountain. Nearly fifty of the men lacked horses, but promised to keep pace with the mounted army, and trotted alongside throughout the night. With only occasional stops to rest, they continued moving toward Ferguson's location, and reached King's Mountain shortly before noon.

Among the men at the base of the hill, there was seething anger that was ready to strike like a coiled snake. The men were anxious but held in check by Shelby and Campbell. As the commanders dismounted and tied their horses to the trees, the wild-eyed young men followed suit. They quietly and quickly removed their powder and shot, took their rifles in hand and began darting from tree to tree, making their way up the side of the mountain. They clambered over boulders and scrambled behind fallen logs, steadily advancing up the slope, until they were at the edge of the plateau on all sides but the bluff.

Captain Alexander Chesney was a Loyalist from South Carolina, and later recounted the attack:

> ...*Going towards my horse I found he had been killed. King's Mountain, from its height, would have enabled us to oppose a superior force with advantage had it not been covered with wood which sheltered the Americans and enabled them to fight in their favourite manner. In fact, after driving in our pickets, they were enabled to advance to the crest of the hill in perfect safety, until they took post and cover.*

From the safety of the trees, the mountain army were well camouflaged in their buckskins and tan jackets, and at the order, began firing. The orders were to strike, move, then strike again. The tactic stymied Ferguson, who had ordered his men in line for bayonet charges. Even as Ferguson called to his Loyalists, they began dropping around him; he ordered a charge at the trees, and plunged with his men part-way down the side of the hill after Campbell, but by the time they reached the trees, Campbell's men had long since disappeared. At the same time, Shelby's force was racing up behind Ferguson on the other side of the hill. Many of Ferguson's men realized the hopelessness of their cause. Two men tried to raise a white flag of surrender, but Ferguson galloped his horse across the plateau and knocked it down with his sword, yelling "Hurrah, brave boys, the day is ours!" He tried vainly to rally his men, running his horse among them, even as the rifle shots whizzed through the air around him. Ferguson was hit once in the arm, then again—but he still galloped through his men hoping to inspire a battle.

From the side of the hill, a young rebel under John Sevier, clambered with his loaded rifle to the edge of the summit where he recognized the hunting shirt worn by a man on horseback. He watched as the British commander crossed the plateau. Atop the horse—waving his sword and shouting—was the very man who had threatened to burn the homes of the frontiersmen. The barrel was raised and with squinted eye lowered along the barrel of the long rifle, the flintlock was snapped back and released. Ferguson immediately jerked back in the saddle, and then fell from his horse to the ground.

The young rifleman was not alone in recognizing Ferguson. The British Major had been hit a total of seven times, with a number of shots passing completely through his body. His hat and shirt were completely tattered from rifle shots that had narrowly missed their mark. Once Ferguson tumbled from his horse, his men immediately raised the white flags of surrender.

Amidst the fire and the shouts, some of the rebels were unaware of the surrender request. Others were still angry at Ferguson's threat and continued to fire despite the raised white flags. Some fired in revenge for Buford's men at Waxhaws, and began shouting "Tarleton's Quarter! Tarleton's Quarter!" while reloading. The firing continued from the trees onto the plateau at Loyalists who were by now in complete disarray.

The brutality of the continued assault shocked even Shelby and his fellow officers. He began moving among the men shouting at them to hold fire, but it was a good while before order was managed. The cease-fire came with some argument and considerable difficulty. James Collins was sixteen years old when he climbed the side of King's Mountain behind Shelby, and later wrote of what he saw that day:

> *The dead lay in heaps on all sides, while the groans of the wounded were heard in every direction. I could not help turning away from the scene before me, with horror, and though exulting in victory, could not refrain from shedding tears.*

The nine hundred Scots-Irish backwoodsmen herded 716 remaining Loyalists down the mountain as prisoners. 225 had been killed and 163 were badly wounded. Shelby lost 28 men, with 62 wounded. Cornwallis, who had reached Charlotte just before the Battle of King's Mountain, panicked at the news, and immediately withdrew his troops back into South Carolina.

The mountain men, having settled the score with the man who would make threats against them, lowered their rifles and returned to their horses, mounted up, and rode back to their homes in the hills.

CHAPTER TWELVE

Early Day Kentucky

THE MEN WHO WERE MAKING HOMES along Dick's and Carpenter's Creek in the Kentucky back country were expected to do their part when fighting men were required. On February 21, 1781, Colonel John Bowman sent Captain Kinkead's Company of Light Horse to defend settlers to the north in Fayette County. Each man was to bring his own horse and provisions, and although some of the men joined after the company was already on its way, most men served nearly five weeks before they returned on March 28th.

During the summer, George Rogers Clark ordered the construction of a riverboat that could be used in defense of the settlers along the river. In addition, the men were to carve canoes from trees to serve as a part of the crude navy. Another party of Lincoln County men was called out, to guard men "Digging Canoes." The companies under Samuel Kirkham and John Martin would march from Lincoln County to Leestown, at the north edge of present-day Frankfort, with Stephen Huston and James Gilmore riding ahead on horseback. Each was classified as a "Spy" with orders to "Discover the approach of the Indian Enemy." Stephen Huston mounted his horse on April 25 and rode north from Hanging

Fork as the company began its march from Lincoln County. He and James Gilmore spent the remainder of April, all of May and all of June, scouting the areas around the militia and riding back to report their findings. The company completed their mission completed and returned to Lincoln County on July 2. While scouting at Leestown, the ground under surveillance by the spies changed its designation: Virginia had officially organized the frontier as the "District of Kentucky" on May 1.

Captain Kirkham's "Pay Role"

Lieut. William Givens	William Campbell	William Laurence
Sergeant John Popham	William Crawford	Moses Lucas
Sergeant John Smith	Robert Flemming	James Mcphaddan
William Addams	James Gilmore	Henry Miller
James Alley	Henry Grider	Hugh Rosan
Elkaner Allen	John Harbison	David Smith
John Anderson	Samuel Hines	Richard Stearman
Robert Armstrong	Jacob Holefelaws	John Summit
Joseph Ayers	Patrick Hurrigan	George Watts
John Bohannan	Stephen Huston	Edward Willis
James Bradley	John Kelly	Samuel Wilson

The rate of pay differed greatly from the Captain to his privates; Kirkham was to be paid eleven Pounds, Virginia currency per day, while most of the foot soldiers received two Pounds, eight Shillings per day. Possibly, since they had the luxury of riding on horseback, Stephen Huston and James Gilmore were paid at a rate lower than any man who served the entire campaign, at two Pounds, four Shillings per day. If they might have felt slighted at the time, they were compelled to action ten years later to receive payment for their efforts. For their back pay, Huston and Gilmore were obliged to formally petition the General Assembly of Virginia.

TO THE HONE. THE SPEAKER & HOUSE OF DELEGATES—
The petition of James Gilmore and Stephen Huston, Humbly sheweth—

That your petitioners were employed in Lincoln County By Capt. John Martin and Capt. Samuel Kirkham as scouts to Discover the approach of the Indian Enemy That they served as such from the 25th Day of April untill the 2d day of July in the year 1781 and that they never Received any Compensation for their services—and prays that your Honorable body may take their case into Consideration and grant them such Relief as you may think Just and Right And your petitioners in Duty Bound shall ever pray

In October of 1781, the Battle of Yorktown was to have been the conflict that ended the Revolution, the following year in Kentucky, settlers began to call 1782 "The Year of Blood." News to and from the frontier still took time, and the native Nations that had been encouraged by the British continued raids against settlers and travelers along the trail. In addition, the end of the conflict east of the mountains allowed the British to better concentrate on George Rogers Clark in the west.

Raids by Cherokees were occurring from the Block House to the Cumberland Gap and as a result Colonel Arthur Campbell had taken 150 volunteers through Cherokee lands in an attempt to move them out and retrieve those kinsmen who had been taken captive. At the mouth of the Powell River, Captain Joseph Martin led 65 men against a band that had been staging ambushes on Boone's Trail. Benjamin Logan, by now a Colonel, ordered a company of men from Lincoln County under David Cook to defend settlers on the frontier of that county. Four days later, Colonel John Logan took another group of men from Lincoln County along Skagg's Trace to the Falls of the Ohio. The attempts by the Indian tribes to drive the intruders from their lands was having some effect; families hoping to move to Kentucky were being told that it was unsafe to cross the Gap.

Log House on Grounds of Stephenson Huston Plantation House
Described both as a slave house and a smoke house, this small cabin stood just east of the main house at the western edge of Hustonville Kentucky.

Captain Robert Barnett began the campaign on March 15, and had Nathan Huston serving as his Lieutenant, while John South served as Ensign, and Stephen Huston held the rank of Quartermaster Sergeant. The mission was to aid in the protection of General Clark's headquarters at Fort Nelson, at the Falls of the Ohio. British General Sir Frederick Haldimand, who was in command of Detroit and Canada, was planning a major assault on Fort Nelson.

Haldimand was sending Captains William Caldwell, Alexander McKee and Matthew Elliot, along with the Girty brothers against Clark's fort. He intended the assault to begin in August, but on March first, 25 Wyandottes attacked John Strode's Station killing two men. The band then crossed the Kentucky River and attacked Estill's Station near present-day Richmond, Kentucky. After determining that Estill was well armed, they turned north toward the Ohio River. James Estill set out with a band of men in pursuit, and caught them at Hinkston's Creek. Estill and five others were killed.

Pay Roll for Capt. Robert Barnets Company of Militia drawn into actual service to the Falls of the Ohio under the command of Colo. Jno. Logan

Capt. Robert Barnet	John Mitchal	Richard Holly
Lieut. Nathan Huston	John Sertin	Benjamin Molton
John South, Ensign.	Daniel Higgens	Amos Terry
Stephen Huston, QMS	Abner Heyden	Samuel Rice
Sgt. Archibald Belt	James McCord	William Watts
James Heynes	Randol Smith	Andrew Olliver
Daniel McKinny	William Crawford	Green Clay
George Welch	Amaziah Vardiman	Abram Estridge
Joseph East	Kaleb Masterson	William Garner
Wily Espy	William Richards	
Clayburn Duncan	Hickison Grubs	

In August, more than 400 Ohio Indians under the leadership of Simon Girty intended to raid Bryan's Station, north of Boonesborough. Bryan's Station was set inside a formidable stockade, and Girty intended to lie in wait until the men came out into the open. Inside the stockade, the settlers somehow learned that they were about to be attacked, and assumed the warriors were waiting for the men to come out. At dawn, the gates of the stockade were eased open and the wives and daughters of the settlers sauntered out as those nothing was suspected. They filled pails of water from a nearby stream and returned to the stockade; Girty and his warriors allowed them to pass by, presumably to preserve their element of surprise. Once the stockade gates were again closed, the 44 men inside began firing their rifles at intervals, the successfully repelled Girty and his warriors when they attempted to breach the stockade.

The retreat from Bryan's Station by Girty and his men was so obvious that some of the settlers were suspicious. Major Hugh McGary of Lincoln County was among the 200 mounted men under Lt. Col. John Todd who began a pursuit of the force. McGary suggested that Todd wait for Benjamin Logan who was leading some 400 men up from Lincoln County in support. Daniel Boone was among those riding under Todd, and he pointed out that, generally, Indians in retreat simply split up to avoid the enemy; the trail left by the Ohio warriors even included the blazing of trees. Boone suggested that two brushy ravines among the hills just across the Licking River were a likely spot for an ambush and that as many as 500 warriors could be hiding there in wait.

Todd took their comments as an insult and turned to his men, his face flushed in anger, and yelled "By Godly, what have we come here for? All who are not damned cowards follow me!" He held his rifle aloft and plunged his horse into the stream; behind him, his backwoods army began to whoop loudly and fell in behind him to cross the water. Nearly too late, Todd realized the disorder he had provoked and immediately ordered the men off their horses and into three companies. The men met no resistance as they climbed the first hill, but as the first men reached the crest, the Ohio warriors—hiding in the ravine, just as Boone had suggested—jumped to their feet and swarmed forward.

Todd's companies were overwhelmed by the huge force, and began to flee for their lives; those at the front were quickly overrun, while those just reaching the water were cut off by another force that had moved down to the water's edge. Boone's son Israel was badly wounded, and as he fell, Daniel tried to carry his son toward the stream to escape. Daniel was attacked as he ran, and was forced to leave Israel behind as he directed the other men back across the river. The attack lasted five minutes and ended once the frontiersmen crossed the stream—the warriors did not give chase.

Five days later, Logan arrived with his force of men from the Dick's River area of Lincoln County. Advancing with Logan to the place of the battle at Blue Lick's, Boone found the body of his son. For the rest of his life, Daniel Boone carried a sense of guilt at failing to convince Todd to delay his attack at Blue Licks, and he could never discuss Israel's death without breaking down into tears. In all, the frontiersmen buried 43 men that day, all casualties of the ambush at Blue Licks.

After Todd's defeat on August 19, George Rogers Clark ordered a series of attacks on Shawnee villages. By October, Nathan Huston had been promoted to captain of the Lincoln County Militia, and had been given a company to lead on an expedition against the Shawnees. On the 22nd, the company riding out from Hanging Fork included Captain Huston, Phil Morrison, Privates Hayden,

Williams, and Cook, Joseph Hagen, Henry Cook, John Shadrick, Abraham Millar, Joseph Dillon, John Craford, Patrick Welch, James Haydon, John Long, and Frank Miller. A Shawnee village was burned on November 10 and Nathan acquired the services of Michael Stoner to scout the locations of the warriors from the village. Stoner joined the company as a "Spie" on November 12, 1782, as Nathan Huston's company continued as part of the expedition against the Shawnees.

Brigadier General George Rogers Clark was leading the expedition through Ohio, conducting what amounted to a reign of terror against the native tribes in the area in hopes of driving them to submit to a treaty or to move westward. There were "deprivations" on all sides, as is typical when cultures collide. The Shawnees and other Indian Nations were only trying to protect land that they had lived on throughout their ancestry, while the settlers considered their own claims to land as legally secured. Both considered the other as intruders to be driven out at the very minimum.

Among the many companies following Clark's command was that of Captain Robert Barnett, under whom Stephen Huston had served in the spring and early summer. On October 23, 1782, Barnett called his company out and shared his orders to join Clark on the expedition through Ohio. Most of the men were Scots-Irish who were settled near Hanging Fork, with David Evans, Conrad Carpenter, and William Evens among them.

Capt. Robert Barnets Company under the Command of Geo. Rogers Clark B.G. on an expedition against the Shawnees October 23 to November 23, 1782.

Robert Barnet Capt.	Wm. Moor	Coonrad Carpenter
Benj. Pettit Lieut.	Jno. Welch	Wm. Evens
Wm. Casey Ensn.	Benjn. Briggs	Sam. Low
Stephen Huston QMS	Adam Carpenter	Geo. Duncan
Edward Low Serjt.	David Evens	Jno. Jones
Jno McKiny	Ebenezer McKiny	Hugh Leper
Joseph Martin	James Barnet	James Birten
Jno. Littler	Charles Runnels	Josiah Huntsman
Phillip Patton	Wm. Patton	Isom Meadlock
Saml. Bell	Robert Harrall	

As the expedition ended, Nathan Huston and his company began working its way back toward the Dick's River valley, and Hanging Fork, continually alert as they traveled. Nathan brought his men back to their farms on November 24, just six days before a preliminary peace treaty was signed between Britain and the

United States. News of the treaty—like all news on the frontier—was slow in coming; the Kentucky settlers got word of the peace agreement in early spring.

Conducting raids against the Indian Tribes, while an often-reported activity, was hardly the entire focus of life on the frontier. Living as they did at the edge of the wilderness, Scots-Irish families expected hardships and were regularly subjected to them. Homes were attacked at intervals, and livestock was lost to natural predators as well as tribal attacks. Expeditions against local tribes were continued by Clark and Benjamin Logan well into the next decade, although Clark was never regained the high esteem he enjoyed in 1779. Raids along the Wabash River were conducted in September of 1786, less than a year after Clark signed a treaty at Fort McIntosh with various tribes. Logan's force marched along the Miami River at the same time, burning the villages of New Piqua, Mackacheck, Wappatomica, Will's Town, McKee's Town, Blue Jacket's Town, and Moluntha's Town. Following the Battle of Fallen Timbers in 1794, when General Anthony Wayne was victorious over tribes in the Northwest, the Treaty of Greenville was signed by twelve separate tribes that established yet another line between the settlers and the Indians. Like all lines drawn by treaty, they were only held in regard as long as the apportioned land was beyond the current reach of the new frontiersmen.

When Thomas Feland and his many sons and daughters moved into the Hanging Fork area, they settled on a tract of land not far from the cabin of Stephen Huston and his brother Nathan Huston. Stephen began courting Thomas' daughter Jane and early in 1783, the two were married in Lincoln County.

Nathan Huston was no stranger to those at the court sessions at Stanford, including Benjamin Logan, John Logan, Hugh McGary, and Stephen Trigg, who had been named as Justices of the Peace. The first county court was formed in January of 1781, and the following month Benjamin Logan donated ten acres that could serve as a location for a courthouse. Nathan Huston worked with William Montgomery in the appraisal of estates for probate. Montgomery had settled with his father and brothers at the headwaters of Green River, about twelve miles from Benjamin Logan's fort. William the elder was Benjamin Logan's father in law, and four cabins were built in the same area for family members, including the families of William Sr. and William Montgomery Jr.—the grandson of William the elder, John Montgomery, Thomas Montgomery, and Joseph Russell. Nathan Huston married Anne Montgomery, a daughter of Thomas Montgomery who had served with Nathan under Captain Joseph Kinkead. Anne was fortunate to be alive. Just after the Hard Winter had broken, in March of 1780, four cabins of the Montgomery family were surrounded by during the night. The next morning, when William the elder and one of the slave children stepped outside the front door, they were both shot and killed. While one of William's daughters closed the door and called for a rifle, another daughter scampered out of the cabin through the short chimney and ran the two miles to Pettit's Station, where a messenger was sent to Benjamin Logan. By the time Logan and his men arrived, John Montgomery had also been killed, and the remaining family members taken captive, with the exception of Joseph Russell, who escaped. Logan discovered the trail and as his men drew near, the Montgomery family captives were released.

Families moving to Kentucky continued to increase in number and in 1780, settlers petitioned the Virginia Assembly requesting that Kentucky County be divided into three smaller counties, to make it easier for the settlers to conduct business:

"the setled part of the County of Kentuckey is of Late grown so Extensive that in a time of pace it would be extremly inconvanient for your petitioners to attend at the Courthouse mutch more so at present when an invetorate War rages with unremited violance."

Stephenson Huston house, built circa 1790, also known as the
Stoner Stephenson house for a later owner.

Twenty residents, including John Huston and Levi Todd, signed the petition on May 1. The Assembly returned a favorable ruling, dividing Kentucky County into the smaller counties of Lincoln, Fayette, and Jefferson, with county seats at Harrodsburg, Lexington, and Louisville. By 1784, Nelson County was formed, followed shortly by the creation of Bourbon, Mercer, and Madison counties in 1785. Mason and Woodford were also created before end of the decade—in 1788.

Another petition was passed around years later when settlers at Lexington sought their own local government. Archibald Huston was among those who signed the petition asking for the right to form a town to levy taxes, improve the streets, establish peace, and the "power to remove and prevent Nusances."

The petitions of the early day Kentucky residents to the Virginia Assembly are filled with the names of Scots-Irish, including many who followed the same route as the Hustons from the Shenandoah Valley. In addition to the sons of Archibald Huston of Mill Creek Valley in Augusta County (later Rockingham) there several other Huston families living on the frontier; Archibald Huston of Fayette County, and James, John, Samuel, and William Huston, who lived in the area that later became Bourbon County. Joseph Huston headed a party of fourteen men in 1775 that headed into Kentucky from Pennsylvania, and founded Huston's Station in 1776 at the site of present-day Paris, Kentucky. He returned to Pennsylvania and died shortly afterward, leaving his lands in Kentucky to his sons William, John, and Joseph, Jr. Huston Creek, which still runs through the area, was named for the founder of Huston Station. Samuel Huston and his father Peter removed from North Carolina where both served at King's Mountain, and later settled in the area called Cane Ridge, near present-day Paris, Kentucky.

Against Whiskey!
February 1912, Hustonville Kentucky
Saloons and taverns became the focus of Temperance Societies that promoted demonstrations such as this one in front of the Newton Hotel in Hustonville. Building to the left: Corner of the National Bank—Rontenberg Store. *Courtesy: Baughman Family*

Peter was interviewed some years later by Lyman Draper, an historian who was collecting information about the settling of Kentucky who recorded that James was born April 5, 1769 in Iredell County, North Carolina. He married Nancy Alexander, born February 1765, also at Iredell County, North Carolina, on May 18, 1790, and the two moved to Kentucky in September of 1793, settling near Col. James Smith and Stephen Riddle.

The presence of the Scots-Irish as a separate, isolated community of settlers may have diminished with the lessening threat of attack on the frontier. As communities became more populated, more stable, and—most importantly—more civilized, persons who "removed" to areas along the edge of the frontier became much more diverse. Presbyterian Churches were no longer the only meeting places in extremely rural areas. Where the children of Scots-Irishmen had been inclined to marry the children of other Scots-Irishmen because they were the nearest families, the rule no longer applied. As more families moved to the frontier areas of the country, intermarriages of faiths and nationalities became commonplace, though many of the frontier home sites bordered on land settled by previous neighbors or acquaintances. The Scots-Irish brogue became a wilderness colloquialism as children born along the frontier were exposed to other dialects, but some of the Ulster bloodlines remained intact well into the mid nineteenth century. As the country emerged from its infancy and the interactions of the populace were no longer limited to those living in immediate proximity to each other, the cultural separation of the Scots-Irish diminished.

The continued migration of families to the frontier was still a rigorous undertaking. Although traveling the wilderness was becoming easier, the system of trails constituted one of the primary problems facing the settlers—they were still too primitive to even be called roads. As cabins sprang up throughout the area, there were more complaints about the difficulty in getting from one place to another, particularly traveling to some of the larger settlements like Danville. Several men were ordered by the court to survey the lands from Danville to the mouth of Hickman Creek, and report back to the court the best route for a road. At the same time, Stephen Huston, Isaac Shelby, Jacob Spears, Robert Barnett, William Reed and William Warren were asked to look at how a road might best be laid from Danville to Widow Carpenter's land, on Carpenter's Creek. The court had reason to select the men they did, since the road would pass on, or near, the lands of the men doing the surveying. Several weeks later, Huston, Shelby, and Reed returned with their report, and the court ordered the establishment of a road to run from Carpenter's Creek near the plantation of Thomas Feland, passing near William Warren's house before heading in a line to Danville.

On February 16, 1785, John Cowan entered the Lincoln County court bearing a commission from the Governor that appointed him Sheriff of the county. Before moving to Kentucky, John Cowan had wed Mary Craig, the daughter of John and Sarah Craig who lived in the McGaheysville area of Rockingham County, VA. Cowen recommended as deputy Nathan Huston.

It wasn't always the Sheriff or his deputy that received the first notification when trouble was at hand. In Lincoln County, the man who lived at Sportsman Hill was often the first to know when an event had occurred, especially those that victimized families on the Wilderness Road. Colonel William Whitley was a Scots-Irishmen who had come to Kentucky early, but had sacrificed a good part of his early land holdings to pay for the construction of a fine house between Logan's Station and Crab Orchard. There was no house like it in the entire county, and it remains as the legacy of early Kentucky craftsmen. The walls are of red brick carried in from Virginia, and the exterior walls are decorated with a series of lighter bricks forming a diamond pattern. Above the door, white bricks outline the initials of the home's owner—W.W.—and on the wall on the opposite side of the house, Whitley had his wife's initials inset using the same color bricks. The windows on the bottom floor high above the ground, intended to protect the

Whitley's from being fired upon from outside. In addition, Whitley had a secret panel placed in a wall on the third floor where women and children at the house could hide in the event of an attack. It is said to be the first brick house built in Kentucky, and served as the site of some lavish parties and barbecues for people of the county.

Colonel Whitley, as part of the county militia, was regularly called upon when attacks occurred on the Wilderness Road. Invariably, he would quickly gather a group of men and set out for the site of the attack. Whitley believed the militia should be strong enough in number to discourage the ambushes, but said more than once that his troops did little more than "bury the dead."

————

The Kentucky Gazette began publishing in 1787, and each issue warned families moving out by way of the Wilderness Road to come fully armed and in large groups where possible. The paper had also begun printing the names of parties that were heading west. Families on the trail were familiar with the names of those that had left Virginia with similar hopes and dreams, and had met with tragedy on the road. There was Mrs. McClure, who escaped with one of her slave woman during an attack in 1784, but six others in the party were not as fortunate. In 1786, several families and their servants were moving westward from Rockbridge and Botetourt counties and stopped to camp for the night. After dark, a band of Chickamauga warriors descended on the campsite, slipping past their posted guards. Twenty-one persons were killed, five women were taken prisoner, and the horses, mules and household goods were spirited away. One of the women escaped detection by hiding in a hollowed-out tree trunk. She was pregnant, and during the night, while huddled all alone in the dark, went into labor and gave birth. She was found the next day and reunited with her husband, who had escaped.

Maggie Lee Quaite, age 14, circa 1885; her grandfather
David Quaite was from Guilford County NC.

William Whitley had shown that it was possible to build a fine home, even at the edge of the frontier, when he completed construction of Sportsman Hill. Whitley's home was an expensive endeavor, with bricks for the walls carted all the way from Virginia. About the same time as Whitley's construction, Isaac Shelby completed his home, which he called "Traveler's Rest," and was located about eight miles from Stephen Huston's land. From his leadership in the Revolution and on the frontier, Shelby had earned enough respect to be selected as Kentucky's first governor. "Traveler's Rest" was a frontier home outfitted to suit a man of position. On the first floor walls Shelby had waist-high paneling of polished cherry wood, and throughout the house woodwork consisted of fine cherry wood and walnut. Unlike Whitley's house, Shelby used native stone and the mason who pieced the rock together claimed to have had a special formula for his mortar, which he never revealed. The hand-hewn stone was carefully stacked and cemented over the exterior of the two-story house. It was a house that befitted its name, and it, along with Sportsman Hill, was the envy of the county.

The Huston brothers replaced their early cabins with structures built from stone, and turned to the builder of Traveler's Rest for the stonework. The stone was quarried from the riverbanks at Hanging Fork and Carpenter's Creek. The same mixture of hogs-hair mortar used at Traveler's Rest was repeated in the Huston houses, along with a good many other features of Shelby's home. The first floor windows would be high enough above the ground to discourage attack. The chimneys would rise through the house with fireplaces and hearths on both floors. They anticipated the possibility of an attack on the house, and had the builder construct an attic hideaway—similar to the hidden room behind Sportsman Hill's secret panel—that could be reached by climbing a retractable ladder. Once inside, the ladder could be withdrawn and the hatchway closed, enabling the women and children to hide in the uppermost reaches of the house. The features of Shelby's house influenced the Huston's houses, including the design and placement of the windows.

Early on, even before statehood, Stephen Huston operated a public house where any traveler could get rest and a meal. In addition, he began a new enterprise, listed in the census as manufacturing, but better known as a distillery.

The home of Nathan Huston was constructed just over a mile east of his brother's, and when completed, the two homes served as bookends for the small town that grew up between them. The house built at the east end was destroyed by fire, but the plantation house of Stephenson Huston survived the more than two hundred years since its completion and was still standing at the end of the twentieth century.

CHAPTER THIRTEEN

Out of Shenando

THE MAJORITY OF THE SHENANDOAH Valley men served during the
Revolution as part of the county militia, and except for a couple of notable
exceptions, were fighting Whig rebels who sought separation from the Crown.
Felix Gilbert, who owned a general store at Peale's Cross Roads, brought trouble
upon himself when he sought to raise a company of Tories in the area that would
later become Rockingham County, but his attempt was short-lived amongst his
Whig neighbors. Felix Gilbert was also the exception among the county men
concerning choices of occupations. There was little in the way of hard commerce
in Rockingham before the Revolution; Andrew Johnston had a store in the Dry
River area around 1755, and John Grattan had one at Mt. Crawford before 1770.
Felix Gilbert's store at Peale's Cross Roads was one of the early mercantile stores
and as such was often referenced as a landmark of sorts for travelers. Most of
Gilbert's neighbors were farmers, and although they also belonged to the county
militia, they were farmers first and soldiers later.

Nearly every man in the county served in the militia at some point and there
were thirteen times that the governor officially "ordered out" the Augusta County

militia to take up active duty. Militia companies were comprised of some sixty men commanded by a captain, who were expected to show up in full gear—primarily their rifles—for a monthly readiness muster. If a man failed to appear, his name was reported for court martial, and he was later called to explain his whereabouts. If a valid excuse could be produced, the absence was forgiven, and the case acquitted; otherwise, a small fine was levied. Since time was valuable, and the monthly muster often degenerated into what amounted to a men's social gathering, many of the farmers chose to pay the small amount and tend to their farming or other pressing business. Most of the names of the Rockingham area farmers found their way to the court martial list at least once.

To be "ordered out" meant official business was at hand and all farming and local affairs were to be immediately ended. The Governor's call set the militia companies from Rockingham County into motion, gathering gear and preparing for the long march to battle. As part of the final county based efforts during the American Revolution, many of the Rockingham militiamen headed east, where Cornwallis was fortifying Yorktown. Arriving at the Head of Elk, the Rockingham militiamen joined other militia companies, swelling the total to about three thousand men. They were to march with General George Washington and some six thousand of his Continental troops. Before the Army reached Williamsburg, the British fleet had already been driven back to New York, leaving Cornwallis completely cut off and vulnerable to attack.

On October 9, 1781, General George Washington fired the first shot from an American battery of cannons directed against those still held by Cornwallis at the outer edge of Yorktown. The French were already firing at Cornwallis from the opposite side; a total of fifty-two big guns were battering the town, and within days, Cornwallis realized his resistance would be futile. The siege of Yorktown lasted until the morning of October 17, when one by one, the British cannons fell silent. Their ammunition supplies were exhausted, their earlier efforts to escape from Yorktown had been driven back, and their attempts at an assault on the American and French forces had been unsuccessful. October 19, 1781, Brigadier General Charles O'Hara rode out of Yorktown to formally surrender to George Washington on behalf of Cornwallis, who had claimed illness to avoid the event. Military protocol dictated that such transactions be conducted between officers of similar rank, so Washington directed O'Hara to Militia General Benjamin Lincoln, his second-in-command. The backcountry militiamen were thrilled that one of their own was the focus of the symbolic gesture. Regardless of his previous politics and military efforts, Lincoln's name was thereafter spoken with a new admiration, and many locations throughout the young nation were christened with his name as a tribute to the part he played in the Surrender at Yorktown. One of the first and most substantial sites to be named for General

Benjamin Lincoln was a large tract of Fincastle County, Virginia, that was to be divided into three sections—Fayette, Jefferson, and Lincoln counties.

The Houstons of Augusta County found themselves divided by new county lines, with Rockingham formed to the north in 1778 with its county seat at Harrisonburg, and Rockbridge to the south of Augusta, with its county seat at Lexington. Captain George Huston led his men, including his brother John Huston, who served as a Second Lieutenant—on the expedition against native tribes on the Ohio River in 1778 and 1779. In March of 1794, George Huston married Susannah Snapp, a daughter of a large landowner in the area named John Snapp. By 1790 Snapp was the owner of the late John Stephenson's Meadow View Plantation, and in 1792, he was granted a tavern license that allowed Meadow View became a public inn. It was there that George and Susannah Huston raised three children: Archibald W. Huston, Nathan Huston, and Mary Huston. Mary was wed to Philip Pitman in 1821. Nathan died in 1871 and was buried in Cross Keys Cemetery. Archibald W. Huston married Peggy Reagan, and they had six children: Mary B., George W., Lucy J., Margaret Melinda, Lavina, and Archibald W. Huston, Junior.

George W. Huston—like the grandfather he was named for—was called to military service as a rebel. George W. Huston served in the Confederate Army as part of the Virginia 33rd Infantry Regiment during the Civil War, enlisting on June 22, 1861 at his hometown of Harrisonburg. He quickly found himself in action. A Union army under Brigadier General Irvin McDowell was moving from near Washington to Bull Run, or Manassas, Virginia. After a five-day march to the southwest, they were severely defeated by Confederate forces under Generals J.E. Johnston and P.G.T. Beauregard, who pushed McDowell and his men back to the Potomac River. George W. Huston was cited by General T.J. Stonewall Jackson for gallant conduct at Manassas, and was promoted to Major on April 21, 1862.

In 1863, with General Joseph Hooker in charge of the Union Army of the Potomac, an offensive was launched in which the Union force greatly outnumbered the Confederate Armies of Robert E. Lee and Stonewall Jackson. They met at Chancellorsville on May 2, and fought over three days, until Hooker was defeated and his assault ended. George W. Huston was shot and wounded during the second day of fighting, but recovered. He was promoted to Lieutenant Colonel on March 21, 1864 and was serving under General Lee in May when Union General U.S. Grant crossed the Rapidan River in Virginia and met Lee's force in the two-day Battle of the Wilderness (May 5–6). While Lee's Confederates stopped Grant, the Union commander did not withdraw his position as his predecessors had done in previous losses. Two days later, he tried a flanking move at Spotsylvania Court House, and then at Cold Harbor on June 3, he unsuccessfully attempted a frontal attack of Lee's position.

Finally, Grant crossed the James River in a move to the side that caught Lee off guard. Action by General Beauregard and a group of reserves saved Petersburg—considered the key to Richmond, the Confederate capitol—from capture by the North. Grant had his men dig trenches in a siege of Petersburg, to which the Confederates responded with their own long lines of trenches. On July 30, Union engineers tunneled under the Confederate lines and set off an explosion, but the attacking Union army was trapped in the resulting crater and suffered heavy losses. The siege of Petersburg lasted through the winter and into the spring of 1865. By that time, Lee's force was stretched so thin it could no longer hold the position. Just weeks before the Confederate Army gave up their position, George W. Huston was killed in action February 6, 1865, in fighting near Petersburg. His body was returned to Rockingham County, and was buried in Woodbine Cemetery at Harrisonburg, not too many miles from the Meadow View property that had belonged to his grandfather.

David Kyle owned the plantation by then, having purchased it from John Snapp. Kyle was a merchant who operated a store at the intersection of Port Republic and Keezletown roads, and kept the house and property until his death in 1845. The property was divided in 1858, and brothers Edward S. Kemper and William M. Kemper bought the lower tract of land, including Stephenson's plantation house. Edward Kemper raised a family at Meadow View, and his young sons Charles and James were seated on the front porch in June of 1864, when sixteen-year-old Henry Bowman rode wildly by, just ahead of a trio of Confederate soldiers on horseback. The soldiers fired their guns, but missed. When Bowman was finally overtaken, he was escorted back to the main body of the Confederate company, under the command of General David Hunter, who asked Henry why he hadn't stopped as he had been ordered. He told the General that he was afraid his horse would be appropriated for the army, which Hunter reasoned was a valid enough excuse to send him on his way—with an official military pass.

Like the Rebellion of the South, the plantation house of John Stephenson would not last to the next decade. By 1870, Meadow View—the home of the first to settle in the Mill Creek Valley—had taken its place among the colonial-era relics relegated to memory.

To the south in Rockbridge County, Samuel Houston was the principal heir of Robert Houston, and came into possession of the Houston estate at Timber Ridge. He had served with the Virginia Rifle Brigade under Daniel Morgan, whose company fought in major battles at Cowpens and Guilford Court House in North Carolina, and was present when Burgoyne surrendered at Saratoga. Samuel returned home as Major Samuel Houston.

The Paxtons were another prominent Scots-Irish family that settled early in the area. Like most of the devout Presbyterians of the time, John Paxton had little trouble mixing his religion with his line of work. By the end of the war, Paxton had owned a tavern on the Indian Road for some twenty years, and that led most to assume John Paxton was the richest man in the county. His daughter Elizabeth married Samuel Houston and they settled at Timber Ridge. Major Samuel Houston returned from the war but stayed in the military, spending much of his time away from home. Their youngest son Sam spent much of his time hunting and scouting in the woods but joined the other children at the field school near Timber Ridge, a country school in the same building that at one time housed the Liberty Hall Academy—which is said to be the forerunner of Washington and Lee University. Sam preferred the woods to the classroom, but dutifully learned to read and write during his sessions at the school. Even more difficult was the time spent on Sunday at New Providence Church, founded by his great-grandfather John Houston, some fifty years before. The church house was adjacent to Timber Ridge, and Sunday mornings found more than one bench filled with the Houston family; along with Major Sam and Elizabeth were Paxton, Robert, James, John, Sam, William, Isabella, Mary, and Eliza.

In front of the church and Timber Ridge was the Indian Road that ran from northern Virginia, south through the Shenandoah Valley, past the front of Meadow View and John Stephenson's horse racing track in Rockingham County, through Augusta and into Rockbridge County. Fifteen miles further south was the estate of Matthew Houston, who operated a general store from his house on the road, and a mill on Cedar Creek. Once past Matthew Houston's Red Mill, most travelers were inclined to stop nearby and look at the Natural Bridge, a geological marvel that spanned Cedar Creek. In 1775, Thomas Jefferson bought the natural rock foundation and the 250 acres surrounding it, calling it "the most sublime of Nature's works." Even the most brazen of those who visited the site were inclined to drop to hands and knees at the top, and then crawl to the edge to peer down at the flowing creek—215 feet below.

In 1807, Major Samuel Houston died while on an inspection tour and while staying at an inn about forty miles from Timber Ridge. His death predicated even more dramatic changes; as a militia officer, Major Houston was required to pay his own expenses, and it had caused a substantial drain on the family finances. His widow Elizabeth, facing the prospect of raising a large family alone, chose to sell Timber Ridge and buy land at Maryville in East Tennessee.

Tennessee had joined the Union as a state in 1796, and the Scots-Irish were among those who served the cause in its infancy. Robert Houston was sworn in as Knox County Sheriff in 1793, and James Houston had established a settlement in Blount County thirteen years before statehood. Houston Station was near Maryville, and was one of the primary reasons Elizabeth Houston moved her children to that location. The heavy log stockade at Houston Station weathered an assault of more than one hundred Cherokees in 1785. James Houston was one of the Blount County representatives to the Constitutional Convention in 1796 that led to statehood, and also served as a member of the early Tennessee Legislature.

Elizabeth Houston settled on Baker's Creek near Maryville, and it was there that young Sam Houston disappeared for weeks at a time. Once, after his brothers had searched for Sam more than a week, he was discovered on Hiwassee Island near present-day Dayton Tennessee, living with a band of Cherokees. Sam told his brothers he preferred living in the forest with the natives and that they should just go home without him. The chief was named Ooleteka, and became a surrogate father of sorts to Sam, allowing him to live in the midst of the tribe, which Sam did for nearly three years. He returned occasionally to visit his mother, but did not leave his adopted family in the woods until he was nineteen years old. It was shortly after his return to Maryville that the United States declared war on the British.

Sam Houston enlisted in 7th Regiment of Infantry in Tennessee, as did his brother Robert. By 1813, Sam was an ensign in the 39th Regiment, serving alongside Thomas Hart Benton and David Crockett. By February 1814, Houston held the rank of third lieutenant and was serving under Andrew Jackson at Fort Strother in Alabama, when he was hit in the thigh with an arrow, and ordered out of the fighting. As the Creeks began to retreat, Jackson called for volunteers to give chase and Sam grabbed his musket and led the charge toward the river. He was five yards from the hidden band of Creeks when he suffered two gunshot wounds. The other men fell back as the firing began, and Houston dropped to the ground unconscious. When the brush was set on fire, the Creeks moved toward the river, allowing for Houston's recovery. He was bleeding heavily when they carried him back to a surgeon, who removed one of the rifle balls. The second was left when the doctor assumed Houston could not survive.

Sam Houston lay on the wet ground all night, with an arrow wound in his thigh and twin rifle wounds in his shoulder. Sometime during the night, the bleeding halted. When the sun rose, he was still alive—but barely. Rather than leave a dying man on the ground when the troops moved out, a litter was constructed on which Sam was placed and carried back into Tennessee. He was too sick to walk and was carried on a stretcher or dragged on a litter over the next two months as he was moved back across the state, intended for his mother's house at Maryville. There, his comrades would leave him to either recover, or die. When the wounded man was presented to Elizabeth, she did not even recognize him as her son. He was little more than a skeleton of a man, pale and still deathly ill from his wounds. The doctors brought to attend Sam diagnosed his wounds as mortal, and offered their condolences to Elizabeth. Some months later though, Sam felt somewhat stronger and eased himself onto a horse and rode to Washington, where he hoped to find a doctor that could restore his strength.

The second rifle ball was eventually removed, but the wounds Sam suffered would trouble him for the rest of his life. He returned to active duty and served until 1818 before turning to a new career as a lawyer and politician. The day after Christmas in 1821, the *Nashville Whig* carried an advertisement for his new practice.

Sam Houston attorney at Law. Having removed to an office second below A. Kingsley's Esq. on Market Street, can be found at all times where he ought to be.

While Andrew Jackson was maneuvering toward the Presidency, he and the governor of Tennessee selected Sam to run for the 9th Congressional District seat in 1823. Jackson had followed the progress of the young Houston, who had been injured in battle under his command, and who was now following in Jackson's own steps by commanding the Tennessee militia—as Jackson had done. With such influential backing, Houston did not draw an opponent in the election, and Sam found himself inside the operations of Andrew Jackson's political machine. October 1, 1827—after two terms in the House of Representatives, and again with the backing of Andrew Jackson—Sam Houston was sworn in as the sixth Governor of Tennessee.

Seemingly throughout his life, Houston was a lightning rod for controversy, and while there were times in his life when others held his actions in disdain. Such was the case with his marriage and separation from Eliza Allen. He had taken office as a bachelor, and married the niece of a fellow congressman in January of 1829. It was his political undoing. Eliza was barely out of her teens and had been in love with another man, but both she and her family were flattered by a marriage proposal from the Governor of Tennessee. Sam Houston, her elder by sixteen years, still bore the ravages of injuries that refused to heal. Some months after their marriage, when it was apparent to Sam that their union was less than satisfactory, a discussion between the two ended with Eliza's return to the house of her father. Despite Sam's pleas and assurances that whatever had been said between them had been resolved to his satisfaction, she declined to return to him.

April 16, Sam Houston resigned as governor. It was a time when accusations between a man and his wife—particularly a man in elected office—were the subject of much public attention. His friends urged Sam to tell what had caused the difficulty, to set the story straight and salvage his political career, but he not only declined, but threatened harm if anything was said that might impugn Eliza. He would not explain his side of the story, he would not answer the rumors being spread, or speak unkindly against Eliza despite her actions. Nearly two weeks later, Sam Houston departed the state of Tennessee under a self-imposed exile that led him to Fort Gibson in present-day Oklahoma. For the remainder of his life, and even among his closest friends and relatives, Sam Houston refused to discuss what had come between he and Eliza. Years later, when he finally remarried, his bride-to-be's relatives, who knew of both the scandal and his devotion to his betrothed, told Houston that unless he told them the details of the incident, the marriage would be called off. Sam told them that they should at least enjoy some dancing since the wedding musicians had already been paid. Even after moving to Texas, he encountered an old friend who pressed him repeatedly for details about the scandal in Tennessee. Finally, Sam leaned over to his friend and whispered, "Can you keep a secret?" When the friend nodded, Sam Houston replied, "I can too," and changed the subject. Although there was a good deal of speculation that Houston had accused Eliza of loving another man, Sam Houston never spoke of the matter. Many of his detractors, who had at first demanded explanations from him, came to view his silence and the protection of Eliza's privacy as the actions of a true and sincere gentleman.

At Fort Gibson, Sam was reunited with Ooleteka, his adopted Cherokee father. It was a bittersweet reunion for Sam, who had reached a low point in his life. Decades earlier, Ooleteka had given Sam the name *Kalanu* or The Raven. Sam had been at Fort Gibson only a short while before his Cherokee brothers began referring to him by another name—Big Drunk.

He fell into a despair that lasted long enough that Sam embarrassed his friends through his frequent writings and occasion misdeeds, which were widely reported in newspapers throughout the country. During his stay with the Cherokees, Sam did manage to accomplish a few things for Ooleteka, and although he was not officially divorced from Eliza, he lived as man and wife with Tiana Rogers, the niece of Chief Ooleteka. When Sam finally pulled himself out of his despair, it was to return as an emissary of the Cherokees to Washington.

SAM HOUSTON

By 1832, Houston had decided to move to Texas, in typical Scots-Irish fashion. Texas was the site of a new frontier and settlers were taking up land along the border south of the Red River. Within three years, with a new law practice in Tejas, Houston was able to accumulate some thirty thousand acres on the Trinity River. October 13 of that same year, Stephen Austin was leading a force of rebellious Texas volunteers to take on the Mexican Army. A month later, Sam Houston was named commander-in-chief of the Texan forces involved in a full-fledged revolution against Mexico.

Things were desperate for the Texans as Santa Ana began marching to quell the rebellion. Houston ordered the evacuation and burning of the Alamo— orders that were disregarded, later resulting the Alamo massacre.

The force under Sam Houston had dwindled to fewer than four hundred men, and was retreating from Santa Ana, moving as quickly as possible given the circumstances. Entire families were joining the march for the army's protection. Since the men, women, and children were looking to Sam Houston to protect them from the advancing army, he felt compelled to slow his movements to accommodate them. On April 20, 1836, after marching all day and all night, Houston's force camped at a peninsula bounded by the Buffalo Bayou and the Rio de San Jacinto. They had barely begun to prepare breakfast when Santa Ana's troops marched into view less than a mile away and in full battle formation. Scrambling into a defensive posture, Houston ordered his men to wait until the army drew near. At last, Sam gave the order and the shooting began, including the firing of the Twin Sisters—as they called their two cannons. Enough confusion resulted that Santa Ana ordered his army to stop their advance, and he set up camp directly across from the Texans. From where Santa Ana stood, the Texans were boxed in with their backs to the water and the Mexican army in front of them. Santa Ana, believing he could take the Texans whenever he chose, opted to wait.

The next morning, the Mexican commander ordered groups of his men to march into camp, and then fall out and march in again. The clever ruse served to trick Houston's scouts into believing that another 500 reinforcements had arrived and as a result, had the Texans outnumbered two to one.

Sam Houston met with the officers to consider their thoughts on whether to attack or wait for Santa Ana, then walked among the troops to gauge their morale. He decided to attack. The decision came by mid-afternoon, at a point so late in the day that Santa Ana determined it was too late to expect anything from the Texans, and his entire army was at ease. He had not even placed a picket line facing the Texans.

At four o'clock, Sam ordered the cannons fired and shouts of "Remember the Alamo!" went up throughout the force as they stormed over a low rise and into the midst of the Mexican camp. Santa Ana was caught completely off their guard and the Mexican army scattered wildly before the advancing troops. Finally, Santa Ana's lone cannon was fired, and it hit its mark; Houston's horse buckled and fell beneath him. He quickly mounted another, but by the time he did, the Mexican rifles were trained on him. His second horse was killed, and a musket ball shattered his ankle. He was bleeding into his boot, but continued the fight, finding another horse and rallying his men. Eighteen minutes after he led the charge, the Mexicans began attempting to surrender. In a scene that resembled actions of the Scots-Irish mountain men during the British defeat at King's Mountain, the

Texans—having retreated for so long from Santa Ana—lost all control. Houston and his officers were unable to stop the killings, which continued even after the Mexican troops had thrown down their weapons. Finally, a Mexican colonel, realizing that individually they stood no chance of survival, gathered four hundred men near the San Jacinto River and surrendered en masse.

In less than half an hour, Sam Houston had taken an outnumbered force of tired, ragged Texans who held no opportunity for retreat, and vanquished Santa Ana and his trained army.

Houston managed another major victory when he received nearly 80 percent of the vote on September 5, 1836, in the election for President of the Republic of Texas. A year later, the Texas government was moved to the new city of Houston, which was named for Sam, located near the battlefield at San Jacinto where independence had been won. At the same time, holding the presidency of the United States was Sam's old friend and political mentor, Andrew Jackson. It was Sam's belief that the country he was leading could survive only if annexed into the United States, which he hoped Jackson might quickly accomplish. Texas was nearly bankrupt. The 35,000 or so men, women, children, and slaves who made up the new republic had little hard money to begin with; two of the four ships that constituted the Texas Navy were impounded, since the country had no money to pay the repair bills. There were few rations for the troops, fears among the residents that a subsequent attack by the Mexicans was forthcoming, and a national debt of over a half-million dollars. It seemed to Sam Houston that annexation by the United States was the only way Texas could achieve stability.

There were a number of problems associated with bringing Texas into the Union, the least of which was the reaction by European countries to a move that would be to the detriment of Mexico. The major debate among the states was slavery, and efforts were being made to maintain an equal balance between those favoring a continuation and those that had ended the practice. The result was a delay in annexation, and a need to continue on their own, which Texas did for nearly ten years.

Sam recruited a kinsman from Mississippi named Felix Huston to assist him in military operations in Texas. Felix Huston was the son of Joseph Huston and Mary Kelsey of Breckenridge County, Kentucky—a family of some prominence by the turn of the century. Joseph was an early member of the Kentucky legislature and the father of Eli, Felix, and Eliza Huston. Both sons suffered the effects of their Scots-Irish temperament, and although they were clear-headed enough to have established law practices as very young men, they were given to rash behavior. Eli challenged and engaged a man in an illegal duel, which resulted in his disqualification from the practice of law in Kentucky. As a party to the incident, Felix Huston found himself disbarred as well. The two brothers moved to

Mississippi and quickly established successful practices in that state, and some years later, Eli was appointed as a circuit judge of Natchez district, where he lived until his death on June 12, 1835. Felix did not swear off the practice of dueling, despite his previous experiences with it, and was present at several high-profile incidents. He eventually was brought to the attention of Sam Houston, who offered Felix the supreme command of the Texas army. The position obviously did not hold the same esteem as it once had, and in addition, the provisions of Houston's offer required that Felix Huston bring with him two regiments of men to join the Texas army. When Felix complied, Sam placed him in temporary command of the Texan forces.

The young commander jumped in with both feet. He began exercising the troops with a decidedly different perspective than that of his kinsman. Brigadier General Felix Huston wanted to make his mark with an invasion of Mexico, which President Houston opposed. In addition, Felix decided the town of Bexar could not be adequately defended, so he ordered its residents evacuated and the town razed. It was apparent to Sam that he had made a mistake, and he appointed a Scots-Irishman named Albert Sydney Johnston to replace Felix Huston. When the replacement arrived, Felix would not surrender the command, and naturally, he challenged Johnston to a duel. Felix prevailed, and Johnston suffered a serious enough wound that he could not take command.

Taking his case to the legislature, Huston lobbied congress to be outfitted with several thousand men to prepare an invasion. It was the last straw for Sam, who decided that Huston might remain as commander, but would have no army to lead. He sent a messenger with orders that furloughed all but six hundred men, who were divided into several units and sent to separate areas along the coast.

By the time word reached the capital, the action had already been carried out, and there was nothing Congress or General Huston could do about it. Although Sam's methods angered most of the legislators, his instincts were correct. Residents were wary of large standing armies that tended to requisition and procure from the citizenry. They reluctantly conceded Sam's position that a smaller army was not only safer, but more economical. Brigadier General Felix Huston, having retained the title but not the troops, left Texas and removed to Louisiana, where he returned to the practice of law.

The Texas Constitution limited Sam Houston to a single term, and Vice-president Mirabeau Lamar succeeded him in office. At Lamar's inauguration, the feisty Houston delivered a farewell speech that lasted over three hours—by which time Lamar felt so upstaged that he had another man read his inaugural address.

With the country's troubles in the lap of Lamar, Sam left Texas pm a mission to interest investors in land speculation opportunities. At Spring Hill, Alabama, he met twenty-year-old Margaret Moffette Lea. After spending some days in

Alabama, Sam made a return to Tennessee to visit Andrew Jackson. From the home of his old friend, Sam wrote several letters to Margaret, who had been quite taken with him, despite their age differences. Sam Houston was forty-eight. When he left The Hermitage and former-President Jackson, Sam returned to Alabama and proposed marriage.

His marriage to Margaret was to change his life in numerous aspects. There was little time for carousing, as the bachelor-president had done so often. He was devoted to Margaret even to the point that he attended an occasional church service with her. She moved to Texas with him and settled into their modest house that she either ironically or appropriately named *Ben Lomond,* which was taken from Sir Walter Scott's novel about Scotsman *Rob Roy.* Margaret did not enjoy politics, but respected Sam's attentions to the needs of the country. Eventually, their home was a busy place; Margaret and Sam were the parents of eight children. The home became the Presidential Palace on September 6, 1841.

Sam's supporters had been beating the drums for his reelection, almost since he had left office. Many of the troubles he had left behind were still there and some were even worse. Sam received seventy-five percent of the votes cast and his first actions indicated the direction the republic would take. There would be no public celebrations of his elections, the beginning of a new era of austerity for Texas. When Sam left for the capital at Austin, Margaret stayed behind. Sam was a bachelor-president once again, but this time he avoided the trappings the situation might have afforded. He again worked toward the annexation of Texas by the United States, and eventually saw such an agreement brought to a vote, only to be defeated. The slavery issue was still too difficult to overcome. When his term of office expired and Sam delivered a farewell speech before the inauguration of Anson Jones, the address was short and to the point. Having twice been rejected by the United States, Sam Houston told his countrymen that the great Republic of Texas would not subject itself to being spurned again, and that the subject of annexation to the United States would only come about if Texans were asked to join as a state in the Union. Sam also inferred that there were other nations interested in making arrangements with Texas; his remarks were made primarily for the benefit of the United States, which Sam secretly hoped would be spurred toward annexation.

As a private citizen of the Republic of Texas, Sam Houston returned to a law practice, and supervised some farming on his land. In a break from his wild past, he dutifully avoided liquor, with only the occasional lapse, and even went so far as to speak before several temperance groups, although it may have been primarily to satisfy Sam's love of public speaking.

In February of 1845, the US Congress passed an annexation bill to bring Texas into the Union. It was a sentiment that the majority of Texans agreed with, having heard so many times from President Houston the many benefits of such a move. Unfortunately for President Anson Jones, he had just negotiated a treaty with Mexico that would secure peace between the two as separate nations. The people of Texas would not hear of it, and neither would the legislature. A special session called by Jones to consider independence or annexation resulted in a unanimous vote in both houses for annexation. The final Congress of the Republic of Texas adjourned June 28, 1845. When the newly recognized state sent its Senators to Washington, one of them was Sam Houston.

On the floor of the Senate, Sam again found an audience for his oratory flair, but again his words brought controversy. Texas was a southern state, and states across the south were increasingly reacting to calls for the abolition of slavery. Although he lived his entire life in the south, Sam Houston found his greatest supporters in the North, and many of his most vocal detractors in the South. His position was that the Union should remain preserved, and although he recognized the issues pressed by the South, Sam Houston felt that the integrity of a unified Nation should prevail. At a time when emotions on both sides were running rampant, his conservative position angered most of the Southern delegation. After 13 years, Sam returned to Texas, ending his career in the Senate without being able to successfully sway his opposition.

Across the country, the elections of 1860 were being dreaded. Emotions were high and the threat of violence was imminent. Texans were looking for a familiar name to lead the state through the latest difficult times. Sam Houston was elected Governor. Shortly afterward, a convention drawn to consider the secession issue voted to secede. Houston balked at allowing the Confederacy to take charge of military installations in Texas, and it brought about an order from the legislature to have all state officers swear allegiance to the Confederacy. Sam refused and he outlined his reasons in a letter:

Fellow-Citizens, in the name of your rights and liberties, which I believe have been trampled upon, I refuse to take this oath. In the name of the nationality of Texas, which has been betrayed by the Convention, I refuse to take this oath. In the name of the Constitution of Texas, which has been trampled upon, I refuse to take this oath. In the name of my own conscience and manhood, which this Convention would degrade by dragging me before it, to pander to the malice of my enemies......I refuse to take this oath.

...I have seen the patriots and statesmen of my youth, one by one, gathered to their fathers, and the Government which they created, rent in twain; and none like them are left to unite it once again. I stand the last almost of a race, who learned from their lips the lesson of human freedom. I am stricken down

now, because I will not yield those principles, which I have fought for and struggled to maintain...

The death of the Union was almost too much for Sam Houston to bear. When he refused to swear allegiance to the Confederacy, the Governor's office was declared vacant, and Sam Houston again returned to his wife and children as a private citizen. He was an aging man, and the old wounds of his youth began to bother him again, as did the current wounds to his pride. The South had begun to decline in its struggle against the North when Sam finally gave in to pneumonia on July 26, 1863, and died at his Texas home with Margaret at his bedside.

CHAPTER FOURTEEN

Life at the Cross Roads

BENJAMIN LOGAN WAS ONE of the instigators of the idea of statehood for Kentucky, and several conventions were held concerning the proposal. Those meetings were held in the summer of 1784, when Logan had heard rumors to the effect that a major assault on the Kentucky settlements was planned by one of the Tribes in the area; as a matter of caution, he called together as many of the influential men on the frontier to consider some measures for defense. As it turned out, the rumors were false, but the meeting at Danville gave the men an opportunity to discuss among themselves the situation they were in, primarily the number of miles to the seat of government in Virginia, and steps that might be taken to secure protection for their families. Statehood for Kentucky had widespread appeal and a local government that understood the frontier ways might better serve the settlers.

Some twenty-five men had gathered in Danville in December of 1784. They were men from each militia company, sent as representatives to a gathering that had no legal authority, but hoped to move toward that end. Samuel McDowell led the convention, which included a great number of spectators in addition to the militia company delegates. Another gathering was held the following May and the men prepared five resolutions regarding statehood for Kentucky; they voted to urge separation from Virginia, to prepare a petition stating the proposal, to publish an address to the people of Kentucky regarding separation, to call for election of delegates, and to meet at Danville in August.

While some of the men were eager to get on with the push for statehood, the items they proposed were inherently difficult. Attacks on the settlers had begun again, and there were few opportunities to gather to discuss who should attend a convention as a delegate. In addition, the proposal to publish an address to the citizenry required that the address be written by hand, since there was no printing press in all of Kentucky. In August of 1785, the third convention was held at Danville, although little had been accomplished since May. During the following winter, the settlers did manage to have their petition presented before the Virginia legislature, which responded favorably, on the condition that the majority of Kentucky's residents supported the separation. To determine the sentiments of the frontier families, another convention was set for September, but when the date finally arrived, most of the men were gone, having volunteered to serve under General George Rogers Clark in an expedition to Ohio. Nearly a year passed before the issue of statehood could be presented for a convention vote.

The men from the Dick's River valley were anxious to move forward. Riding from the area of present-day Stanford, Benjamin Logan, Nathan Huston, William Montgomery, and Willis Green hurried to meet Isaac Shelby at Traveler's Rest before heading on to Danville. From those five representatives of Lincoln County who gathered with the others delegates in Danville that day in 1788, came one who would assume the responsibilities as the new state's first governor.

Members of the Convention in 1788, held at Danville

Jefferson County	Fayette County	Lincoln County
Richard Taylor	James Wilkinson	Benjamin Logan
Richard C. Anderson	Caleb Wallace	Isaac Shelby
Alexander S. Bullitt	Thomas Marshall	William Montgomery
Abraham Hite	William Ward	Nathan Huston
Benjamin Sebastian	John Allen	Willis Green
Nelson County	Bourbon County	Madison County
Isaac Morrison	James Garrard	William Irvine
John Caldwell	John Edwards	George Adams
Philip Phillips	Benjamin Harrison	James French
Joseph Burnett	John Grant	Aaron Lewis
James Baird	John Miller	Higgason Grubbs

Mercer County
Samuel McDowell
John Brown
Harry Innes
John Jouett
Christopher Greenup

It was the first day of June in 1792 that Kentucky was admitted to the Union, and four days later when Isaac Shelby of Lincoln County was sworn in as the first governor. He had little opportunity to celebrate, since a number of issues required immediate attention. On the fourth of June, Shelby and the members of the first legislature assembled at Lexington to be sworn into office, and that same day Commissioners Henry Lee, John Allen, John Edwards, Robert Todd, and Thomas Kennedy settled on Frankfort as the seat of government. Among the other issues facing Shelby was the need for suitable roads, a topic affected the more than 70,000 people who were now living in the state.

The federal government had established a postal service in 1789, but the mail did not extend into Kentucky, partly due to the rugged nature of the journey. Shelby intended to improve the road from his farm near Danville through the Holston Valley and onward toward Virginia. The young state had no money, so Shelby began a private fund with a small contribution of his own, then asked for donations from his acquaintances and friends around Danville and Stanford. 116 of Shelby's neighbors contributed amounts, and Colonel William Whitley promised to provide bacon for all the workers on the road.

John Logan and James Knox supervised the construction, and took men along the Wilderness Trail from Crab Orchard to the Cumberland Gap. Trees were trimmed or cut down, overgrowth was hacked away, and the trail was widened as the workers tried to make the path look more like a road. Even with the recent attention, the crude road was still occasioned by ambushes and thefts, both by whites and bands from local tribes.

When the Revolution had ended, the British eventually began to pull troops from the outposts they held in the Northwest Territory, leaving behind the tribes who had done much of the British fighting along the frontier. US leaders hoped to force the tribal nations to terms of defeat, but the tribes maintained that they were independent from Britain and retained their autonomy. Partly as a matter of prideful assertiveness in frontier territorialism, members of various northwestern tribes staged infrequent raids against the white settlements. The nature of business dealings between settlers and their tribal neighbors had also changed in the wake of the Revolution. Since many tribal nations had been allies of the British, those settlers who previously might have negotiated the purchase of lands, and reached a mutually recognized agreement to land rights, were now inclined to acquire land by force and without treaty from those still viewed as the enemy.

Stephenson Huston Plantation House, Hustonville Kentucky
Built by Stephenson Huston on the Hanging Fork of Dick's River. The town of Hanging Fork was settled between this and the identical home of Nathan Huston, built to the east in 1792.

The torrid pace with which the migration of new families to the frontier continued quickly hampered the movements of resident tribes. The attacks on settlers were not part of a widespread, unified effort, but were singular incidents that occurred sporadically and unpredictably along the frontier. In response to calls from the frontier citizenry, the government ordered a series of armed reprisals. Since the Continental Army had been disbanded the troops consisted of young men who lived along the frontier, along with a small Regular Army that was called specifically to battle the Frontier Wars, which amounted to a series of skirmishes that continued against the tribes during the period after the Revolution and before the War of 1812, largely confined to the years 1790–1796.

One of the objectives of the frontier army was to lessen the opportunity for violence to occur; those families who had settled on recognized tribal lands were ordered out, although some merely moved to new locations on other tribal lands. Another government objective of the army was to create a Federal presence on the frontier that might serve as a deterrent to tribal attacks on white settlements that were springing up along a line from Lake Erie in western Pennsylvania, along the south bank of the Ohio River, then down through present-day West Virginia, Tennessee, and Kentucky.

Where the earlier settlers were wary of the dangers of the wilderness, and were inclined to find shelter in stockades or forts, the post-Revolution wave of frontier families were inclined to build a single cabin for shelter. Although the rock structures built by Whitley, Logan, and the Huston brothers were examples of traditional construction transplanted to the frontier, most of the early cabins were simple homes of stacked tree trunks. The majority of the rustic cabins were heated in a single room, since stoves were non-existent on the early frontier, and fires were maintained only in the main family room. Fireplaces came later, as did plaster walls constructed of straw and paste-mortar, which was applied to the interior of the log walls in many homes. Paint came much later, and as a result, the houses of the settlers quickly took on a weather-beaten look and were replaced more often than refurbished. Many of the farmers were also slave owners, and often when the farmer's family moved into a new house, the old house was outfitted for the slaves.

Many of the settlers were skilled with their hands, but most men worked farms as a matter of practicality. Many of them left behind comfortable homes in the East and their wives and daughters struggled to achieve some small degree of comfort. Dirt floors were commonplace in the earliest cabins throughout the Dick's River valley, although there were floors of unsanded split logs called puncheons, which lessened the mud, but easily splintered. William Poague built a loom by driving posts into the ground, which allowed cloth to be woven from flax or buffalo wool, and Ann McGinty brought her spinning wheel, which may have been the first on the frontier, and she used it to spin coarse linen from nettles. As a rule, the daily wear of the earliest frontier families was less than fashionable, and would remain so until after the attacks on Kentucky settlements ended.

On July 15, 1793 Nathan Huston was commissioned as Major with a battalion under Major General Charles Scott. His troops were to take part in an expedition into Indian Territory, to quell attacks on farms.

Major David Caldwell was commissioned July 15 as commander of a battalion that mustered October 31, 1793, with Major William Shannon, Adj. Jesse Cravens, QM George Horine, Sgt. Major Robert Dougherty, QM Sgt Morgan Forbes and Corporal Archibald Huston.

———

General Major Scott's Command
Kentucky Mounted Volunteer Militia
Wayne's War, 1793

Lieutenant Colonel Horatio Hall	Regiment, Field and Staff
Lieutenant Colonel William Russell	Regiment, Field and Staff
Lieutenant Colonel John Adair	Regiment, Field and Staff
Major David Caldwell	Battalion Field and Staff
Major Nathan Huston	Battalion Field and Staff
Captain Joseph Bane	Company Caldwell's Battn.
Captain Henry Bartlett	Company, Hall's Rgt.
Captain John Cochran	Company, Caldwell's Battn.
Captain Robert Floyd	Company, Adair's Rgt.
Captain John Forsyth	Company, Russell's Rgt.
Captain George Frazier	Company, Russell's Rgt
Captain Henry Grider	Company, Adair's Rgt.
Captain John Hall	Company, Hall's Rgt.
Captain Ezekiel Hayden	Company, Hall's Rgt.
Captain Benjamin Howard	Company, Russell's Bttn.
Captain David Kennedy	Company, Caldwell's Bttn.
Captain Simon Kenton	Company, Huston's Bttn.
Captain James Lanier	Company, Hall's Rgt.
Captain William Lewis	Company, Russell's Rgt.
Captain Nathaniel Rawlings	Company, Russell's Rgt.
Captain John Steen	Company, Adair's Rgt.
Captain Richard Taylor	Company, Adair's Rgt.
Captain John Wilkerson	Company, Caldwell's Bttn.
Captain Jonathan Logan	Company, Huston's Bttn.
Captain Robert Modrall	Company, Huston's Bttn.
Ensign Christopher Clarke	Company, Huston's Bttn.
Ensign Thomas Davis	Company, Huston's Bttn.
Ensign David Foreman	Company, Huston's Bttn.

Major David Caldwell's Battalion
Captain Joseph Bane's Company

Joseph Bane, Capt.
James Hunter, Lt.
Jacob Lindar, Cornet
Aron Bobbit, Sgt.
John Crutcher, Sgt.
Charles Grundy, Sgt.
Isaac Thomas, Sgt.
Jacob Duffner, Corp.
Jeremiah Gaugh, Corp.
Vincnt Goldsmith, Corp.

Allen, William
Ambrose, Lewis
Ashby, Stephen
Ashby, Thompson
Berry, Richard
Carter, Joseph

Chaffer, Abner
Chambers, Ahimas
Colvin, John
Comes, Benjamin
Dyer, John
Eaglin, John
Ferguson, William
Froman, John
Harned, Edward
Haycraft, Joshua
Hobbs, Zachariah
Holliday, John
Irwin, James
Lee, John
Login, Robert
Luce, William
Masterson, Hugh

Mattingly, John
McColgin, James
McCullock, James
Miller, Nicholas
Newgent, John
Perkens, John
Pursell, James
Pursell, James, Sen.
Reave, Samuel
Row, Adam
Samuels, Robert
Smith, James
Spencer, Richard
Silkwood, Baizil
Snyder, John
Stephens, Solomon
VanWinkle, Jesse

Major David Caldwell's Battalion
Captain John Wilkerson's Company

John Wilkerson, Capt.
Allemander Pope, Lt.
George Hughs, Sgt.
William Felding, Sgt.
John Nevel, Sgt.
Hugh Gilbreth, Sgt.
Wm. Survants, Corp.
Charles Logan, Corp.
Archibald Huston, Corp.
Jsph McCollister, Corp.
Abraham Bledso, Corp.

Allstotts, Daniel
Bright, Wm.
Bledsoe, Elijah
Cravens, Jesse
Duncan, John

Forbes, Morgan
Horine, George
Hughs, Birket
Higanbautham, Jas.
Hutchins, Thomas
Harris, Samuel
Hunter, Samuel
Hughs, Francis
Hewey, Epherum
Jackson, Joel
Lawson, David
Logan, Matthew
Long, Banjamin
McCarter, Robert
Noaks, Thomas
Nelson, Abraham
Nash, John

Nash, Maruk
Patton, James
Patterson, Wm.
Purkins, David
Porter, Samuel
Queen, John
Reynolds, George
Stemmans, Henry
Smith, David
Shutes, David
Smith, Christopher
Southerland, Wm.
Sutton, Roland
Thurman, John
Turner, Stephen
Woodrum, Wm.
Whitten, Elijah

Sixth Regiment, Kentucky Militia, Frontiers of Lincoln County
Sergeant David Allen's Detachment

Allen, David	Magill, Hugh	Payton, Daniel
Caton, Jesse	Moore, Joshua	Low, Thomas
Gay, Alexander	McFerren, James	Williams, Samuel
Lawrence, James	McFerren, Thomas	Wright, Jonathan
Marshall, John T.	McCormack, Daniel	Rutherford, Dudley

Sixth Regiment, Kentucky Militia, Frontiers of Lincoln County
Ensign Christopher Clark's Detachment

Clark, Christopher	Christenson, Thomas	Grayson, Uriah
Wagoner, John	Cox, James	Huffman, John
Christenson, William	Eliot, George	Short, Moses
Baley, Ruben	Emmerson, John	Smith, Christopher
Brite, William	Feland, James	Sharp, George
Byars, John	Givens, Samuel	Whitton, Elijah

Sixth Regiment, Kentucky Militia, Frontiers of Lincoln County
Ensign David Foreman's Detachment

Arbuckle, Samuel	Gay, John	McKinney, Eban
Berry, Joseph	Horine, Jacob	Pettit, Benjamin
Embry, Elisha	Jones, Gabriel	Rodgers, William
Foreman, David	McKinney, Daniel	Simpson, Joseph

Major General Charles Scott's Command
Major Nathan Huston's Battalion, June 13 to Oct. 26, 1794

Major	Nathan Huston
Captain	Edward Terrell
Captain	Samuel Moore
Captain	Jesse Richardson
Captain	William Kavanough
Lieut.	James Finney
Lieut.	Abraham Miller
Lieut.	James McAllister
Lieut.	William Jennings
Ensign	Asa Learey
Ensign	Smith Mounts
Ensign	Samuel Potter
Ensign	William Lawson

The same militias helped protect postal riders when a route was finally established throughout Kentucky on August 20, 1792. Thomas Barbee of Danville was named the first postmaster, and was placed in a position to listen to the many citizen complaints; business was not always as regular as the residents had hoped, but there was a great excitement when the government hired express riders to carry mail into Kentucky. Their arrival was eagerly announced at each town along the trail, since the riders not only carried mail, but also delivered the latest news from the East, in a more timely and regular fashion than had ever been possible. People along the frontier were able to keep up with the latest events from the rest of the country, only days or weeks after they had occurred. The riders, always having ridden many miles between stops, were invited to rest at the tavern and share the news and the company.

Public Houses along the road offered food, drink, and lodging to travelers, and although the custom of the time was to open the doors to strangers who needed to stop for the night, the risks involved with that practice on the frontier reduced the number of willing hosts. One of the indicators was found on the door itself; a rope or heavy cord was threaded through an opening in the door, which when pulled from the outside, would lift the latch inside and allow the door to be opened. To keep people out, those inside would simply draw the cord back in through the door opening, effectively locking the door. Inns and "rooms" were able to create a profitable enterprise for the owners who kept the latchstring out for travelers.

The arrival of a horse was generally noticed inside the house, but if the door remained closed, the rider would call out a request for accommodations. "Get down and rest your saddle," was the common reply to such requests, even if there were no longer spare beds. The beds and straw beds went to the early arrivals, leaving the latecomers to sleep on the floor, which was still preferable to sleeping outdoors.

On Christmas Day in 1797, a posse led by Capt. Joseph Ballenger arrived at Hanging Fork. He was called Devil Joe by the settlers and had a store in Stanford. His posse had tracked a group of people to the Hanging Fork area. Ballenger arrested two men and three women described as heavily tanned, between twenty and thirty years of age. The leader was a big man with dark, curly hair and heavy eyebrows. The other man had red, curly hair and was slightly smaller in size. All three women were pregnant, and the entire crowd wore clothing that amounted to little more than rags.

When asked, the men replied that they were brothers—Micajah and Wiley Roberts—and that the women were sisters. Susanna and Sally Roberts were the wives of the two men, and the third woman was Betsy Walker. Ballenger bound all five at the wrists for the trip from Hanging Fork back to the jail at Stanford. The men were wanted in the murder of Thomas Langford, whose body was found hidden under a pile of brush and leaves, an apparent robbery victim.

The two suspects were later identified as the infamous Big and Little Harpe, whose escapades in North Carolina were the talk of the frontier. They were sons of a Tory farmer and had terrorized the countryside with their robberies, horse thefts, ambushes, and murders. Deaths along the Wilderness Road that coincided with the arrival of the Harpe brothers were also attributed to them. On March 16, 1798, ten days after the second woman gave birth in jail, the brothers managed to escape their chains and overpower a jailer.

The Harpe brothers left the women and their babies behind, and as time passed, the people of Danville began to worry about the families being held in their jailhouse. The Harpe women convinced the town they were not involved in their husbands' crimes and that they were sorry for everything that had happened. Convinced, the residents took up a collection, bought clothes for the women and babies, found a donated horse, and outfitted them with enough supplies to take them back to their home in East Tennessee. Once the women reached Crab Orchard, however, they slipped off onto a rarely traveled trail, made their way to the Green River, and traded the mare for a boat. The three women and their infants paddled more than seventy miles along the Green and Ohio rivers until they reached a place called Cave-in-Rock, where river pirates and desperadoes kept out of the reach of the law. There, they were reunited with Big and Little Harpe. The women might have regretted the move; the infants proved to be a difficult addition to the movements of the wanted men, and in a fit of rage, Big Harpe murdered Betsy's daughter.

One of the largest and wildest manhunts in early-day Kentucky ensued before Big Harpe was finally tracked down and shot. His trackers took a sword to the criminal's neck and the head was placed on top of a trimmed sapling in Hopkins County, Kentucky. The place where the skull remained as a grim reminder was for many years referred to as "Harpe's Head." Little Harpe's fate, although less grisly, was similar to his brother's. He moved from Kentucky to Mississippi territory, where he continued living the life of an outlaw, until he was finally caught and executed.

The death of Big Harpe came on July 22, 1799—the same day a convention of men gathered in Frankfort to consider revising the constitution. Much had occurred in the seven years since statehood; the legislature had met at the new capitol city at the home of Major James Love, a new newspaper had begun publication in Kentucky, and a line of Ohio "packet boats" began making trips from Pittsburgh, Pennsylvania to Cincinnati, Ohio with stops at Maysville, Kentucky. Several major engagements involved militia under General Anthony Wayne against tribes in Ohio. The legislature passed an act in 1795 that required each white male over sixteen years of age to kill a certain number of crows and squirrels every year.

The Scots-Irish continued their interest in public office and public education with new ventures in Kentucky. The Scots-Irish Presbyterians of Lincoln County established the first chartered school in Kentucky. Reverend David Rice applied for and received a charter to conduct a school in his home in Danville under the name of Transylvania Seminary. It was later moved to Lexington and removed from the auspices of the Presbyterians, which prompted church leaders to solicit some $10,000 in endowments, including contributions from President George Washington and vice-president John Adams, for the establishment of Kentucky Academy.

Benjamin Logan served three terms in the Virginia General Assembly, but was unsuccessful in his bid to succeed Isaac Shelby as the state's chief executive. James Garrard was elected as Kentucky's second governor in 1796. Benjamin Logan's brother John, who had served as a member of the first Senate of Kentucky, had been selected to serve as the first State Treasurer. He kept the state books at his office at Robert Megowan's tavern on Main Street in Stanford until the legislature picked a permanent site. After the capitol was moved to Frankfort, John Logan in 1793 left his Scots-Irish neighbors for a new home to the north. Jane McClure Logan kept house for her husband and family, including son David and six daughters—Jane, Mary, Elizabeth, Theodocia, Letitia, and Sarah. John Logan served sixteenth terms before his death in 1807.

The new nation was of considerable interest on foreign shores, and numerous correspondents reported from the frontier. J.P.B. de Warville roamed the countryside beginning in 1788, and noted in his writings that the people of the United States still lacked a national identity.

> *The national features here are not strong…; we still see the liberal English, the ostentatious Scotch, the warm-hearted Irish, the penurious Dutch, the proud Germans, the solemn Spaniard, the gaudy Italian, and the profligate French…*
>
> *I have just returned from a tour of ten days into the interior of Kentucky…thickly settled with excellent well built farm houses, and raising wheat and corn. I mounted my horse and continued the road to Lexington…a mere buffalo track, following skillfully the ridges of hills and mountains. Lexington is composed of upwards of three hundred houses ranged into streets intersecting each other at right angles. They are built principally of brick. The public buildings consist of a University, Court-house, market, Hall, Bank, and four Churches…one Lutheran, one Presbyterian, and two sects of Methodists.*

The inhabitants shew demonstrations of civilization; but at particular times,
on Sundays and market-days, they give a loose to their dispositions, and exhibit
many traits that should exclusively belong to untutored savages...

I found the country exceedingly well-timbered...numerous farms chequered
this rich scene, producing wheat, corn, oats, flax, hemp, tobacco, cotton, and
vegetables of all kinds...I stopped at the house of a cultivator...a log one, fitted
up very well...the dinner consisted of a large piece of salt bacon, a dish of hom-
slie, and a turreen of squirrel broth...the Kentuckyan ate nothing but bacon,
which indeed is the favourite diet of all the inhabitants of this State, and
drank nothing but whiskey.

Just before Christmas in 1797, Kentucky Academy agreed to merge with Transylvania Seminary, and the resulting institution was to be called Transylvania University. In the meantime, studies would be done among delegates considering changes to the state constitution, which would be taken up the following summer. Nathan Huston and William Logan represented Lincoln County, and many of the delegates were former neighbors. Alexander S. Bullitt headed the delegation, while Benjamin Logan represented Shelby County with Abraham Owen. Caleb Wallace and William Steele represented Woodford County. William Casey, a man familiar to most everyone from the Green River to the Dick's River valley, was elected as a delegate from Green County. Colonel Casey had founded Casey's Station near Hanging Fork.

By the turn of the century, the population in the valley of Dick's River and Carpenter Creek had increased immensely, as had the towns of Stanford and Danville. Archibald Huston married Sally Gay in 1792. She was the daughter of Thomas Gay, who had recently moved into Lincoln County. The Gay family migrated from the Ulster Plantation of Northern Ireland and settled first in Pennsylvania before the Revolution. A number of the brothers later moved to Augusta County, Virginia and settled in the "Calf Pasture" section, before moving to Kentucky. Meanwhile, Mary Huston, the daughter of Stephenson Huston, married Matthew Slaughter, the nephew of Kentucky Governor Gabriel Slaughter. They named their first son Stephenson Huston Slaughter.

General Sam Houston is said to have stopped on his travels to visit at Hanging Fork with the Slaughters and Hustons, and extended an invitation to move to Texas. Stephenson H. Slaughter gave up his medical practice in Lincoln County to move to the Lone Star state. Stephen Huston's daughter Clarenda married John Wright and named their son Thales, for her brother Thales Huston. Thales Wright married Martha Helm, another name well known in county politics. Thomas Helm served as Clerk for Lincoln County and his signature validated many of the early-day marriage licenses. The Harvey Helm house in Stanford was one of the first structures of the town and survives as a library and museum, as testimony to the influence of the Helm family in the area since colonial times.

Nathan Huston died in 1806. He had lived as a pioneer in the valley, a builder, and a protector. He had represented the area as a delegate to several conventions concerning statehood and the constitution, and as an under sheriff, he worked to make the Wilderness Road and the Dick's River Valley a safer place for its residents. A plot of land was set aside on the hill where the Huston Plantation looked out over the meandering creek, a spot less than fifty yards from a field where the town's residents later created a cemetery. The Huston family cemetery became the final resting place for Nathan Huston and others who lived at the plantation at Hanging Fork. The plantation house survives, but the cemetery markers fell victim to vandals and the trees and grasses have long since reclaimed the graves of the Huston pioneers.

———

The population of Lincoln County, Kentucky by 1810 was a mix of pioneer families, primarily from Western Pennsylvania and the Scots-Irish settlement in Virginia. There is no simple method for determining the origin of that populace, and the results of any study can be little more than estimates without a complete tracking of each of the approximately 937 heads of household for that year. Understanding that last names can be traced to specific regions of origin allows for some amount of conjecture, although there are a number of factors that must be considered. The Ulster Plantation was a settlement of both Scots and English, and would contain surnames indigenous to both locations. The lowland Scots largely bore names based in middle and old English rather than Gaelic. Spelling was not standardized until much later, and literacy was not as widespread as in later years, allowing for spelling variations by both family members and those recording the names. Additionally, some of the handwritten records are difficult to read.

Comparing the 1810 US Census for Lincoln County to lists and references indicates a sizable percentage of Scots-Irish in the county. The comparison makes several assumptions—for example, that the name listed as Diar was intended to be the same name as Dyer—but indicates that of the 937 named heads of households 289, or 30.8%, are names found in a listing of lowland Scots recorded in the first half of the 16th Century. The Aberdeen Registry was not a complete census of the lowlands. Additionally there are known Scottish names that are not included in the Aberdeen Registry that are also known Scots-Irish in Ky. The simple inclusion of those names beginning with the Scottish patronymic indicator *Mc* and a conservative addition of known Ulster Scot names brings the percentage of Scots-Irish to 35.8% of the 1810 Lincoln population. However, there are

673 surnames listed in the so-called Scotch-Irish Settlement in Augusta County, Virginia that appear in the 1810 Lincoln County, Kentucky census, or 71.8%. Even a median figure between the high and low estimates places the number of Scots-Irish at over 50% of the population.

In the list of 1810 Heads of Household, an * indicates the surname is among those found in the Aberdeen Registry, a + indicates the surname is known to be of Scottish origin, and an = indicates the name was among those listed in the indexing of the Augusta County, Virginia court records for the period when it was considered to be settled mainly by the Scots-Irish.

———

Lincoln County Heads of Household
1810 US Census

Adams, Daniel * =
Adams, Thomas * =
Akin, John * =
Alford, Charles =
Alford, James =
Alford, John =
Allen, Rebecca * =
Anderson, Thomas B * =
Anderson, Walter * =
Arington, James * =
Arnett, David *
Arvin, William
Ashlock, John
Ashlock, Richard
Bailey, Elijah + =
Bailey, James + =
Bailey, John + =
Bailey, Thomas + =
Baker, Patsy =
Baldock, Ann
Baldock, Levi
Baldock, William
Ball, Daniel =
Ball, Thomas =
Ball, William =
Banton, William
Barnett, Ann =
Barnett, James =
Barnett, John =
Barnett, Robert =
Barren, Amy + =
Basck, Even
Bayley, James + =
Bayley, John + =
Bayley, Ralph + =
Baylor, David =
Beady, Thomas A * =
Beard, Sam =
Beedles, Rue =
Bell, John * =

Benedick, John *
Benley, Jeirrse
Bennedick, Jacob *
Bentley, John
Bentley, John
Bently, James
Berden, Thomas
Berry, Jesse + =
Bersion, Isaac
Bess, W +
Bettan, James
Bettiss, John
Bewley, Nathan
Bibb, Thomas =
Binjaman, Henry
Birnaugh, Taliafero *
Birnaugh, William *
Bivins, John =
Blackburn, James =
Blackwood, Joseph + =
Blacky, Rentsen *
Blain, Alex * =
Blain, Alexander * =
Blain, Ann * =
Blain, John * =
Blain, John * =
Blain, Joseph * =
Blankenship, Geo. =
Blanks, Lydia
Blevins, Daniel =
Blevins, John =
Blevins, Sam =
Blevins, Samuel =
Bly, David =
Boatman, John
Boley, Isaac *
Bosley, Abraham
Bosley, Thomas B
Bosly, Gidian
Bost, David

Bost, John
Botten, Sally =
Boughman, Henry =
Bowers, William =
Boyd, Hugh =
Bradly, John
Bradly, Johnson
Bridges, Absalam
Briggs, Benj. =
Bright, David =
Bright, Henry =
Brisco, William =
Brown, Elijah * =
Brown, Ezekial * =
Brown, Mary * =
Brown, Stephen * =
Broyles, Elizabeth
Bruce, William * =
Bryant, David =
Bryant, Robert =
Bryant, William =
Burch, Benjamin
Burgess, William =
Burks, Mathew =
Burrough, Thomas =
Burton, Archibald =
Calvin, John
Calvin, Joseph
Calvin, Moses Sr.
Calvin, Solomon
Calvin, William
Cammell, Joseph =
Campbell, Samuel =
Campis, Thornton
Carpenter, Conrad =
Carpenter, George =
Carpenter, Henry =
Carter, Charles =
Carter, Collins =
Carter, Edward =

Carter, Jesse =
Carter, John =
Carter, Peter =
Carter, Solomon =
Carter, Stephen =
Casey, Levi =
Casick, Christopher
Cass, Hannah =
Cass, Thomas =
Casy, Stephen =
Cauldwell, Josiah =
Chandler, Rankin * =
Chapman, Daniel * =
Chapman, James * =
Chapman, Job * =
Chapman, Richard * =
Cheatham, Leon *
Clampett, Moses
Clark, Henry * =
Clark, John Sr. * =
Clark, Reuben * =
Clayton, Hank =
Clemands, John =
Clemons, David =
Cloyd, Faithful =
Cloyd, John =
Cochnell, Lewis
Cockrun, James =
Cole, Benett =
Cole, John =
Collier, Moses =
Collins, Alex * =
Collins, Jacob * =
Combs, John =
Combs, John =
Combs, Stephen =
Combs, William =
Comes, Richard =
Coock, Anthony * =
Coock, George * =
Coock, John * =
Coock, John * =
Coock, Lewis * =

Cook, David * =
Cooper, Caleb * =
Cooper, James * =
Cooper, James * =
Cooper, John * =
Coos, Margeratt
Cornett, Park =
Cox, Edward =
Cox, Richard =
Cozall, John
Craig, Elizabeth * =
Craig, William * =
Cramer, Peter =
Cristopher, Elizabeth
Crought, Susanah
Crow, Andrew =
Crow, James =
Crow, Walter =
Crow, William =
Crown, Rebecka =
Culbersson, David =
Culbertson, David =
Cullison, Joseph
Daniels, William
Darnold, Joseph
Davidson, George * =
Davidson, Samuel * =
Davison, Elijah * =
Daviss, James =
Daviss, James Sr. =
Daviss, John =
Daviss, Joseph =
Daviss, Nathan =
Daviss, Sam =
Daviss, Thomas =
Daviss, Thomas =
Day, Francis =
Day, Valentine =
Dean, Mary =
Defoe, Stephen
Denton, John =
Denzashy, William
Deshaies, Charles

Devin, James =
Diar, Reuben =
Dickerson, James =
Dickin, John =
Dinaway, William
Dinwiddie, William =
Dinwidie, John =
Doalin, William
Dobbin, Patty =
Dodds, John =
Dodds, John =
Dollins, William
Dollins, William
Donnally, Ephraham =
Dooly, George =
Downing, John =
Downs, James * =
Downy, William * =
Dudggins, William
Dudgins, William
Duggin, Mary
Duggins, Alexander
Dunaway, William
Duncan, Benjamin * =
Duncan, George * =
Duncan, Sam * =
Duttsy, Samuel
Dyer, Abraham =
Eads, Thomas =
Eames, John
East, Joseph =
East, Neal =
Edwards, Clayburn =
Edwards, George =
Edwards, Henry =
Edwards, John =
Edwards, Thomas Jr. = .
Edwards, Thomas Sr. =
Elder, James
Elder, Mathew
Eldon, Thomas
Eliot, Daniel =
Elisarse, Elijah

Elmore, John
Elmore, Mathew
Elway, Abraham
Emberson, Samuel
Embsee, John
Emmerson, John
Epperson, Amos =
Epperson, David =
Epperson, John =
Eubanks, John
Eustis, Thomas
Evins, John =
Fain, James =
Falconbury, William
Fariss, James Jr. =
Fariss, James Sr. =
Fariss, William =
Farris, John Jr. =
Farriss, Gilbert =
Farriss, John =
Farriss, Johnson =
Feland, Andrew
Feland, Ann
Feland, James
Fenton, Zacuriah =
Findly, Samuel * =
Finley, William * =
Fisher, Matthias * =
Fisher, Thadeus *
Flack, John =
Flack, William =
Fletcher, Joseph * =
Flint, Martin
Floyd, Benjamin =
Floyd, Singleton =
Floyd, William =
Forbes, Montgomery * =
Forbis, Jonathan * =
Ford, John =
Forsythe, Elial * =
Forsythe, James =
Foster, William =
Francis, John =

Fresh, Benjamin
Funk, Gabriel =
Gabbard, Mathias =
Gabbins, Jacob
Gains, Richard =
Gains, William =
Gallbird, George
Gams, Francis
Garland, Anderson =
Garret, Francis =
Gay, Alexander * =
Gay, John Esq. * =
Gay, Thomas * =
Gellott, Jonathan
Gentry, Esham =
Gentry, John =
Gibson, Catherine * =
Gibson, Catherine * =
Gilbert, John =
Gilbert, Mary =
Gilbert, Thomas =
Giles, Lucinda =
Gilmore, George =
Gilmore, James =
Givens, Alexander =
Givens, George Jr. =
Givins, George =
Givins, James =
Givins, James =
Givins, John =
Givins, Robert =
Givins, Robert Jr. =
Givins, William =
Glenn, Nehemiah =
Goff, John =
Gooch, Dabny =
Gooch, Logan =
Gooch, Thomas =
Gooch, William =
Good, Benjamin =
Good, Elizabeth =
Goodnight, Ford
Goss, Kinnard

Grayham, William =
Green Willis =
Greenwood, Barkley =
Grimes, Margarett =
Grisham, John =
Grisham, John =
Grisham, Tab =
Guthrie, David * =
Hackman, James
Hains, James =
Haley, Bartlett =
Haley, Benjamin =
Hall, Andrew =
Hall, John =
Hall, John =
Hall, Joseph =
Ham, Drury =
Hambleton, John * =
Hamilton, William * =
Hammond, George =
Hammond, John =
Hampton, George =
Hannah, William =
Hansell, Lawrence =
Hardin, James =
Harper, Henry =
Harrington, Joseph
Hart, Jack =
Haslin, George =
Hay, Kinnard *
Hayly, Benjamin =
Hays, Hugh * =
Hays, William * =
Haywood, Christopher
Hazlewood, Benjamin
Hedrick, George =
Helms, George Jr. =
Helms, George Sr. =
Helms, Joseph =
Helms, Marcus =
Helms, Marcus =
Hensley, Daniel =
Hensley, John =

Luse, John =
Luse, Marshall =
Macey, James *
Magill, Hugh * =
Magill, James * =
Magill, William Jr. * =
Manfred, Polly
Marshall, John =
Marshall, William =
Martin,—* =
Martin, Edward * =
Martin, John * =
Martin, John * =
Martin, Selvanns * =
Mason, William =
Masse, James * =
Masterson, William =
Matherly, Israel
Matherly, Samuel
Mattox, William =
May, Jacob Jr. =
May, Jacob Sr. =
May, Nancy =
May, Roland =
McBride, David * + =
McCann, George * + =
McClure, Robert * + =
McCormack, Daniel * + =
McCormack, John * + =
McCormack, Joseph * + =
McCormack, William * + =
McCulla, James * + =
McElhany, Patrick * + =
McElwee, Ann * + =
McFerrin, James * + =
McGill, John * + =
McGill, William * + =
McIntosh, Joseph * + =
McKensey, Alexander * +
McKinley, Alex * +
McKinney, Abraham * + =
McKinney, Alex * + =
McKinney, Collin * + =

McKinney, David * + =
McKinney, James * + =
McKinney, John * + =
McKinney, William * + =
McKinny, Abenezer * + =
McKinny, Archibald * + =
McKinny, James * + =
McKinny, Jany * + =
McMullin, J. * + =
McMurray, Thomas * + =
McNutt, George * + =
McPherson, M. * +
McRoberts, Andrew * + =
McRoberts, Isaac * + =
McRoberts, John Jr. * + =
McRoberts, John Sr. * + =
McWhorry, Daniel * +
Middleton, Charles *
Middleton, Charles *
Middleton, E. *
Middleton, Henry *
Middleton, Honly *
Miller, Abraham =
Miller, David =
Miller, Jacob =
Miller, John =
Miller, Joseph =
Miller, Mildred =
Miller, Thomas =
Miller, William =
Millin, Alexander
Mills, Armstead =
Miner, Coleman =
Miner, George =
Miner, Josia =
Minnifie, James
Minsan, John
Montgomery, Ezekiel =
Montgomery, James =
Montgomery, John =
Montgomery, William =
Moody, Alexander =
Moon, A =

Moor, Jonathan * =
Moor, Mordeca * =
Moor, Samuel * =
Moor, Samuel * =
Moore, William * =
Moorhead, Abner =
Moorhead, Daniel =
Morris, Benjamin =
Morris, John * =
Morrison, Ezra * =
Mouzy, John
Mumford, William *
Murphy, Gabriel * =
Murphy, John * =
Murphy, Richard * =
Murphy, William * =
Mussick, George
Myers, Benjamin * =
Myers, David * =
Myers, Jacob * =
Myers, Michael * =
Nash, Arther * =
Ness, Adam
Newgent, Edward
Noaks, George
Noel, Joel =
Noel, Lott =
Norcutt, John
Norcutt, Roy
Nowell, Hugh =
Oliver, William =
Oskers, Henry
Owsly, Anthony
Owsly, Daniel
Owsly, Henry
Owsly, Thomas Jr.
Owsly, Thomas Sr.
Owsly, William
Owsly, William Sr.
Page, Dillard =
Paggette, Ephraim =
Pain, John =
Painter, Joshua =

Pankey, Phillip =
Parks, John =
Parks, Samuel =
Parks, William =
Parson, Joseph =
Patton, William =
Paxton, John =
Payne, Reubin =
Payne, Reubin Sr. =
Payton, Martin *
Payton, Randolf *
Payton, Valentine *
Peak, Spencer
Pemberton, Thomas
Pence, Emanuel =
Pendleton, John =
Peniman, Jenny
Penix, James
Penix, John
Penix, William Sr.
Pennill, Henry
Pensill, William
Perkens, Reuben =
Perrin, Archabald
Person, James
Phillips, Lewis * =
Phillips, Samuel * =
Pickard, Peter
Pigg, John
Pigg, Paul
Piner, William
Pines, Judith =
Pleasents, Edward
Plummer, George =
Poe, Isaac
Poe, John
Pope, George Sr. =
Pope, John =
Potter, Benjamin * =
Potter, Benjamin * =
Potter, Moses * =
Potter, Thomas * =
Pratt, James * =

Purdum, William
Purnelle, Susanah
Ray, Joseph * =
Ray, Nathaniel * =
Read, Francis S. * =
Ready, William * =
Reed, James * =
Reed, Jonathon * =
Reed, Margerat * =
Renalds, James * =
Renalds, Robert * =
Renfrow, Isaac =
Renn, John
Rennalls, John
Rennells, Fountan
Rice, Anderson =
Rice, Mathew =
Richards, Abm. * =
Richards, Felix * =
Richards, John Sr. * =
Richards, William * =
Richardson, David * =
Richardson, Isaac * =
Richardson, John * =
Ridgeway, Elijah
Ridgeway, Mary
Ridgeway, Osburn
Ridgeway, Samuel
Riggs, Samuel =
Riggs, Zadock =
Rigney, John
Riley, Alex =
Riley, George =
Riley, John =
Rinnix, James
Roberts, Hiram =
Roberts, John =
Roberts, John =
Roberts, Sarah =
Robertson, Duncan * =
Robertson, H * =
Robertson, Luke * =
Rogers, John =

Rowten, Elizabeth
Rowten, William
Rudner, Henry
Rudner, Reubin
Runnells, Joseph
Rupe, Barney
Russell, Joseph =
Russell, Joseph Sr. =
Russell, Sanders =
Russell, William =
Rutherford, James * =
Ryley, John =
Sampson, William =
Sampson, William =
Sanders, John =
Sandridge, John
Sandridge, Larkin
Sconce, Nicolas
Scott, James * =
Scott, James * =
Scott, Peter * =
Scott, Thomas * =
Scott, William * =
Scrutchfield, Nathaniel
Seaton, Thomas
Senten, James
Shackleford, Edmund =
Shackleford, Sam =
Shaffer, John =
Shanks, William
Shannon, Absalam * =
Shannon, Thomas * =
Shelby, Evin * =
Shelby, Isaac * =
Shelton, Jeremiah =
Shiply, Samuel
Shiply, Thomas
Shockly, James
Shockly, Levi
Shoemaker, John =
Short, George =
Singleton, Christopher
Singleton, John

Singleton, Mary
Singleton, Richard
Skelsen, George
Skidmore, Joseph =
Slaughter, Mathew * =
Smack, Gadlip
Smith, Arther * =
Smith, Charles * =
Smith, D * =
Smith, James * =
Smith, James * =
Smith, Jesse * =
Smith, John * =
Smith, John * =
Smith, John * =
Smith, Reubin * =
Smith, Scarlet * =
Smithson, David =
Snow, Frostin =
Snow, Leonard =
Snow, Nicodemus =
Snutchfield, Art
Snutchfield, James
Snutchfield, Terry
Southerlin, Enos =
Spar, James
Sparks, Robert =
Spears, Christina =
Spears, David =
Spears, Jacob =
Spencer, John * =
Spinggins, Josie
Spires, John
Spires, William
Spoonaman, Fred
Spoonaman, Henry
Spragins, Nathaniel
Spratt, William =
Spraul, Joseph =
Sprowal, Joseph =
Stephens, John * =
Stewart, John * =
Stewart, Mary * =

Stine, Jacob
Stine, Jacob Jr.
Stine, Jacob Sr.
Stone, John =
Stone, Levi =
Stone, Spencer =
Stone, Thomas =
Stout, Nathaniel * =
Stout, Samuel * =
Striat, Nathaniel
Sublett, A Phillip
Sublett, George
Sugaw, Sam
Sulivin, Mary * =
Suthards, John
Sutton, Edmond =
Sutton, James =
Sutton, James =
Sutton, Joshua =
Swiny, Moses =
Swope, Jacob =
Tanner, Martin =
Tayler, John * =
Tayler, John * =
Templeman, John
Templin, Martha
Tendall, William
Thurmond, Molly * =
Thurmond, Phillip * =
Thurmond, William * =
Tilford, William
Tinsly, James =
Tisdale, John
Tolbert, Richard
Tompkins, Edward
Trotter, Jon =
Turner, Ann =
Turner, Calep =
Turner, Molly =
Vanhock, Thomas
Vantiess, William
Vardeman, Ham
Vardeman, Morgan

Vaughn, Allin =
Vaughn, Eliza =
Vaughn, Thomas =
Vauters, Aron
Veluzat, Francess
Vest, Robert
Wade, Jesse * =
Wade, William * =
Walker, Jesse * =
Walker, Jesse * =
Wall, James =
Wall, Robert =
Wallace, Andrew * =
Warant, John
Ward, William =
Warner, Jacob * =
Warner, John * =
Warner, Peter * =
Warren, Benjamin * =
Warren, Gabriel * =
Warren, John Jr. * =
Warren, William * =
Warren, William Jr. * =
Warrin, James * =
Warrin, James * =
Warrin, John * =
Warrin, John * =
Warrin, William * =
Washington, Thomas =
Waters, Samuel =
Weatherford, Abel
Weatherford, Elijah
Weathers, James =
Weathers, James =
Weldon, John =
Welsh, James =
Welsh, John =
Welsh, John =
Welsh, Joseph =
Welsh, Thomas =
Welsher, John
Welsher, Joseph
West, William =

White, William =
Whitesides, Jane =
Whitly, Andrew * =
Whitly, Solomon * =
Whitly, William * =
Wicker, Thomas
Wilkison, John =
Willhite, Aaron
Willhite, Joseph
Willhite, Lewis
Williams, David * =
Williams, David * =
Williams, Israel * =
Williams, John * =

Williams, Samuel * =
Wiloughby, William =
Wilson, Abraham * =
Wilson, Catherine * =
Wilson, Mathew * =
Wilson, Thomas * =
Withers, John
Wood, Thomas * =
Woodall, Charles =
Woodall, Jesse =
Woodall, John =
Woodall, William =
Woodrum, William =
Wray, Moses * =

Wray, William * =
Wright, James * =
Wright, Jonathan * =
Wright, Joseph * =
Wright, Linsy * =
Wright, Mannix * =
Wright, Nelson * =
Wright, Samuel * =
Wyatt, John =
Wyatte, Rebeca =
Yeager, Joseph =
Yeager, Lewis =
Young, John =
Young, Leah =

CHAPTER FIFTEEN

Frontiers and The War of 1812

ON JUNE 18, 1812 THE UNITED STATES declared war on the British, and in the west the British saw Detroit as a point where the Americans might be vulnerable and enlisted the aid of the Shawnees in attacking the American fort there. Chief Tecumseh had his six hundred warriors march again and again in front of the fort being defended by Brigadier General William Hull, who thought the march was a single stream of incoming warriors, instead of the same men marching several times. Hull believed he was facing overwhelming odds sought terms of surrender August 16 without a fight, and without consulting his officers.

The surrender placed Tecumseh back in charge in the area, and he began leading his army of some fifteen thousand in raids on settlements along the frontier. His fortune quickly changed for the worse, however; his ally was British Major General Isaac Brock, and when Brock was shot and killed and Colonel Henry Proctor as his replacement, proved to be a much less formidable leader. In addition, following Hull's surrender, the northwest forces were put under the command of General Harrison once again, and he called to the Kentucky militia for volunteers for a march to Detroit.

The frontiersmen along the Dick's River valley quickly heeded the call, including some of the well-known fighters who were by now stronger in spirit than physique. Benjamin Logan joined as a private, as did aging soldier William Whitley, who—at sixty-four—had recently told friends that he hoped that when his death came, it was in defense of his country. Isaac Shelby was again serving as Kentucky's governor, and he responded to General Harrison's with an offer to lead the men himself. Shelby called for the militiamen to meet him on July 31, 1813 at Newport, near Cincinnati, where he would lead the men "to the field of battle, and share with you the dangers and honors of the campaign."

Where 5,500 men had been requested as volunteers, some 7,000 arrived ready to follow Shelby in an attack against Tecumseh and the British. Most of the settlers brought their own rifles, as the Scots-Irish had done at King's Mountain. The first division was assembled and placed under the command of Major General William Henry of Lincoln County, and consisted of the First, Third, and Fourth Brigades. Abraham Miller and Michael Davidson led men in Col. Richard Davenport's Sixth Regiment of the Fourth Brigade. Meanwhile, a large body of Dick's River militiamen joined the Scots-Irish from the Hanging Fork area to serve as part of the Kentucky Mounted Volunteers commanded by Colonel Samuel South.

————

Kentucky Mounted Militia
Captain Rowland Burk's Company, September 18, 1812

Rowland Burke, Capt.	Coleman, James	Mitcheltree, George
Abraham Wood, Lieu.	Carson, Robert	Mullican, James
Richard Mason, Ens.	Fare, Absalom	Poulson, Benjamin
Thomas Vandever, Sgt.	Goode, Daniel	Spaw, Jacob
Thomas Mason, Sgt.	Guifford, Joel	Shuck, James
Mathias Coffee, Sgt.	Goard, Gabriel	Shackelford, Reuben
	Harper, William	Vandever, Ashberry
Allen, Robert	Hutchinson, Lewis	Winniford, Norwell
Allen, John	Hickman, Reuben	Whittle, John
Allen, Thomas	Kerr, Thomas	Wood, John
Bell, Henry	Moore, Joshua	

Captain George Murrell's Company, September 18, 1812

George Murrell, Capt.
Abraham Miller, Lieu.
Michael Davidson, Ens.
Thomas Helm, Sgt.
Archibald Burton, Sgt.
Rankin Chandler, Sgt.
Walter Anderson, Corp.
James Mntgomery, Corp.
Gabriel Lackey, Corp.
Levi Owsley, Corp.
James Paxton, Corp.
Sam'l Moore, Trumpeter

Brown, Joshua
Bently, John
Benedict, Jonathan
Briggs, Thomas
Blackburn, James
Bailey, Elijah
Bentley, Ephraim
Carpenter, George
Craig, John
Clemens, Charles
Craig, David
Crum, William
Davenport, George
Duncan, Willis
Dooley, James
Elder, Andrew
Epperson, Jesse
Estis, William
Engleman, Jacob
Embree, Elijah

Feland, Thomas
Forbes, Montgomery
Fleese, Nicholas
Findley, William
Givens, George
Givens, Alexander
Givens, John
Gilbert, Isham
Gray, Hugh
Gilmore, James
Gilbreath, Alexander
Huston, James
Helm, Charles
Huntsman, Benjamin
Hocker, John
Hocker, William
Hazlewood, Reuben
Hughes, John
Hutchinson, Thomas
Harlin, Jeremiah
Harlin, Henry
King, John
King, Robert
Kerr, Thomas
Lee, William F.
Logan, Baty
Lee, Francis
Logan, Allen
Lee, Abraham
Lewis, Jaqualine A.
Logan, Hugh
Lee, Thomas
Logan, Benjamin

Logan, Hugh
Logan, Samuel
Montgomery, John, Jr.
Moore, Samuel
Miller, George
McCormack, William
Minor, Laban
McCormack, Daniel
McGill, James
McKinney, George
Moore, George
Montgomery, Wm. L.
Montgomery, Wm. P.
Myers, George
Norcut, Arthur
Patton, Robert B.
Peak, Spencer
Slaughter, Matthew
Sutton, Joshua
Servant, William
Suddith, Samuel
Stewart, Milton
Tinsley, James
Turner, Josiah
Terrell, Thomas
Wridgeway, Thoams
Willoby, Andrew
Wallace, Caleb
Wilhort, Joel
Warner, David
Williaism, Meshac
Yager, James

Lieutenant-Colonel Richard Davenport's Command
Captain Abram Miller's Company, August 25, 1813

Abram Miller Capt.
Alexander Givens 1Lt.
Joseph H. Woolfolk Ens.
Gabriel Lackey 1 Sgt.
Alexander Gay 2 Sgt.
George Carter 3 Sgt.
John Tinsley 4 Sgt.
Allen Logan 1 Corp.
Thomas Briggs 2 Corp.
Samuel Murrell 3 Corp.
John K. Johnson 4 Corp.

Bailey, Ralph
Barnet, William
Bentley, James
Blakey, Reuben
Carpenter, George
Carter, Britton
Carter, Larkin
Cumberland, Jiles
Cooper, James

Craig, John
Dawson, Elijah
Dodds, James
Downey, James
Elder, James
Ely, Winson
Fielding, John
Fisher, Matthew
Gilbert, John C.
Givens, Alexander
Givens, William
Helm, Charles
Huston, James
Huston, Thales
Johnson, William B.
Jones, David
King, Thomas
McAllister, John
McBride, David
McCormack, John S.
McCormack, William

Miller, George S.
Murril, George
Patton, James
Patton, William
Pemberton, William
Reed, John
Reynolds, Benjamin
Sampson, William
Shackleford, Bennet C.
Shelby, Evan
Skidmore, James
Slaughter, Matthew
Spears, Jacob
Sutherland, William
Upthegrove, Joseph
Vance, John
Warren, Samuel
Warren, William
Wilhight, Joel
Wright, Joel
Wright, Jonathan

———

General John Payne of Kentucky led 670 men near the Rapids of the Maumee, and on January 10, 1813, after being joined by Harrison's force they constructed a stockade which they called Fort Meigs, for Return Jonathan Meigs, the Governor of Ohio.

In the spring, Tecumseh attacked Fort Meigs with British forces under Colonel Proctor, but the stockade held and Proctor decided to maintain a position rather than storm the fort, as Tecumseh wished. In the meantime, some eleven hundred Kentucky volunteers arrived as reinforcements, but nearly half of the men were killed as they arrived. In a move similar to that of Hull at Detroit, Proctor was disheartened by the appearance of reinforcements and ended his siege of Fort Meigs. By summer, he withdrew from his location at Fort Walden and headed to the Canadian side of the Detroit River, a move that further aggravated and disgusted Tecumseh.

Buffalo Spring Cemetery, Stanford Kentucky
Old Presbyterian Section established by Early Scots-Irish

The victory over the British fleet by Commodore Oliver H. Perry allowed the Kentucky militia to build a corral on a peninsula of land near Port Clinton, herd their mounts into it, and cross to Canada by water. Colonel Richard M. Johnson was left at Fort Meigs until the main body set sail, then marched his mounted detail to Detroit. Colonel Richard Riffe of Casey County and a small detail of men were left in charge of the remainder of the horses in the corral.

September 27, the force made for the shore and landed at Hartley's Point, near the British headquarters at Fort Walden, on the Canadian side of Lake Erie. There, they expected to do battle, but Proctor had left Walden in flames and was gone, along with his force of seven hundred men and Tecumseh's force of 1,200 Shawnees. Their departure was determined to be recent—as little as an hour— and the militia force immediately set out to the east. Governor Isaac Shelby, who at age sixty-six anticipated difficulty making the march, found a mount in the only horse left behind by Proctor—a small Canadian pony.

At a site eighty-five miles to the east of Fort Walden, on the Thames River, Tecumseh finally convinced Proctor to take a stand against Harrison. The militia force was in hot pursuit of Proctor and Tecumseh, when they took up a defensive position with the river to their left, a large swamp to their right, and a smaller swamp in between—which they flanked. The British were set in two lines between the small swamp and the river, while Tecumseh's men were posted in the undergrowth between the two swamps.

On October 5, Harrison sent his cavalry headlong into the British lines that scattered immediately, and within five minutes of the first shot the British detachment surrendered. At the same time, a force of some twenty men was sent against Tecumseh's warriors near the swamp. The actions of the volunteers were termed a "forlorn hope" as a diversion that they were not expected to survive. Twenty men volunteered without hesitation, including: William Whitley of Lincoln County, Benjamin S. Chambers, Garrett Wall, Eli Short, Joseph Taylor, Robert Payne, William S. Webb, and John L. Mansfield of Scott County, Samuel A. Theobold of Franklin County, Samuel Logan of Harrison County, and Richard Spurr and John McGunnigle of Fayette County.

Whitley led the diversion, with Colonel Richard M. Johnson at his side, and the party rode toward Tecumseh's army. The shots rang out and fifteen of the militiamen, including Whitley, were killed almost immediately. Four men, including Colonel Johnson, were wounded, and one man escaped injury. The remainder of the militia force waded into the midst of Tecumseh's army as they attempted to reload.

The Shawnee force had little option for retreat, and the fighting continued hand to hand, as Tecumseh shouted words or encouragement to his men; there was blood visible on his face as he fought alongside his warriors against the continuing onslaught of the militiamen. Finally, Tecumseh fell, and without him, the Shawnees scattered.

CHAPTER SIXTEEN

Hanging Fork to Hustonville

AMONG THE KENTUCKY FRONTIER newspapers was the *Lexington Reporter*, which included references to the late war and other activities in the west. At W. Essex's Bookstore at Lexington, the *History of the Late War in the Western Country* offered a full account of "all the transactions in that quarter, from the commencement of hostilities at Tippecanoe, to the termination of the contest at New Orleans."

Benjamin Lanphear, who had previously operated the Boston Coffee House, announced January 1, 1817, that he had opened the Indian Queen Tavern at Lexington, on the corner of Main-Cross and Short Streets, where he intended to devote "his whole attention to accommodate and please those who shall honour him with their custom." The Bowling Green Hotel offered accommodations on "an extensive scale" under proprietor Benjamin Vance. Residents of the "western country particularly" were advised in the February 21, 1817 issue of the Reporter that James A. Lee, the "proprietor of that large and commodious establishment in Howard Street, Baltimore," having formerly lived in the western country, could accommodate business travelers at his establishment of "near one hundred rooms, neatly fixed up as chambers where persons may be quite retired from noise and bustle."

The growing social climate in the young state required services beyond that of the farmer, and Samuel M. Brown offered his expertise in the practice of law "in the Circuit Courts of Fayette and Bourbon counties," who would also "attend the County Courts of Fayette and will be faithful and punctual to all business confided in his care." Doctor Overton moved his practice from his house on Limestone Street in Lexington to Main Street, "above Capt. Postlethwait's tavern," where he could always be found, "except when absent on professional business."

Notices of court actions also dealt with residents far flung from Lexington, as in the case of the Felands of Hanging Fork, who were named in a notice posted by Jonathan Forbis.

NOTICE

Messrs. Thomas Feland, James Feland, and Wm. Feland, heirs of James Feland decd. Jesse Emberson, Eliza Rowton, widow and relict of Samuel Rowton decd. James Wallace, guardian for the heirs of Jesse Walker decd. William Wade, guardian for thei heirs of Polly Sutton decd formerly Polly Walker, Wm. Wade and Sukey his wife, Robert Settle and Rhoda his wife, James Dawson and Phoebe his wife

TAKE NOTICE

That I shall attend by myself or agent, at the house of Jno McRoberts Esq. in the county of Lincoln, on the 1st day of April 1817 (between the hours of 10 A.M. and 5 P.M.) to take the depositions of Linney McRoberts, wife of said McRoberts, and others, to be read as evidence in a suit in Chancery pending in the Lincoln Circuit Court, wherein the heirs of Richard Jackman decd are complainants and you are defendants. Respectfully yours,
JONA FORBIS, Agent

Money was a problem for some businesses. To receive "Oranges, Cocoa Nuts, Claret &c. just received by the Steam Boat Washington, arrived at Louisville from New Orleans," the grocer would accept only notes from the Commercial Bank of Lake Erie, the Western Reserve Bank of Warren, the Columbia Bank of New-Lisbon, the Bank of Mount Pleasant, the German Bank of Wooster, the Bank of Steubenville, and notes on all the chartered Banks of Ohio. John W. Hunt had offerings from the same steamboat, but his merchandise was ready-to-wear "Coatings, Dimities, Velvets, Fancy Prints, Cotton Checks...and crates of Queensware, well assorted."

While cash rewards were being offered for the return of runaway slaves like Kitty, who had vanished from William McClanahan's farm at Richmond, and

Luc, who had left the Baton Rouge, Louisiana plantation of A.C. Beauregard, some business owners hoped to train slaves or former slaves in a profession. Brickyard owner S. Chipley placed an ad in the *Reporter* for "NEGRO MEN AND BOYS to work in my Brick yard, and attend to Brick Layers...as Apprentices to the Brick Laying business." Even in earliest America, the subject of slavery brought emotional, and often violent, responses, and on many occasions both sides of the issue were present within bodies of a single organization. By the end of the decade, there were 126,732 slaves in the state of Kentucky, representing an increase of more than 57 percent over the last census of a total population of 564,317. Many of the Scots-Irish were caught in the middle of the debate, including the Hustons, who by 1850 held more than 60 slaves on their combined plantations.

The primarily Scots-Irish Presbyterian Church in America began to swell its ranks during the extensive church revivals that swept through Kentucky and other states. During a four-year period from 1826 to 1829, more than four thousand additions were made to the Presbyterian Church alone. It was just previous to the so-called Great Revivals that a Presbyterian Church was founded at Hanging Fork, and as Elders of the Hanging Fork Congregation of Presbyterians, Stephenson Huston, Benjamin Briggs, Robert Givens, and John Blain acquired land and built a meeting house for the church. Some time later, when the church members had not received a deed to the property, the four went to the County Courthouse to file papers that would finalize the transfer of property.

...entered into this eleventh day of May in the year eighteen hundred and twenty five between Samuel Shackfod of Lincoln County, Abraham Vance, and Sarah his wife, late Sarah James, and Jacob Curtner and Leah his wife, late Sarah Leah James of Mercer County parties of the first part by Thomas Helm Commissioner appointed by a decree of the Lincoln County Circuit Court and Stephenson Huston, Benjamin Briggs, Robert Givens, and John Blain & their successors who may be duly appointed by the Hanging Fork Congregation of Presbyterians in trust for the use and benefit of the said Hanging Fork Congregation of Presbyterians, party of the second part...

...Witnesseth that whereas by a decree of the Lincoln Circuit Court pronounced at the January Term thereof in the year eighteen hundred and twenty four in the Suit in Chancery pending in the said Circuit Court...it was among other things decreed and ordered that the said Samuel Shackleford, Abraham Vance, and Sarah his wife, Jacob Curtner and Leah his wife should on or before the first Monday in April last past convey to the said Stephenson Huston, Benjamin Briggs, Robert Givens, and John Blain and their successors...all the

right title claim interest and demand which they the parties of the first part have of in and to the following tract or parcel of ground lying and being in Lincoln County on the Hanging Fork including the meeting house of the Hanging Fork Congregation…

Just months after the court action was filed, the name of the church no longer matched the name of the community in which it was located. Hanging Fork had been earlier been referred to as Cross Roads and was officially changed to New Store, Kentucky in 1826. Church members at the Hanging Fork Church joined other congregations across Kentucky on November 17, when the Presbyterian Churches of Kentucky declared the day be set aside and observed as one of thanksgiving, humiliation, and prayer.

Thales Huston listed himself as a manufacturer when asked by the census enumerator, since no specific category existed for distiller. He had moved from Hanging Fork to Stanford, enjoying the life of the bachelor, and running up a number of debts that he may have assumed his father would cover. There were still a good many Hustons at the west end of New Store, Ky. Including Dr. Matthew Slaughter, his wife Mary, and children Stephenson Huston Slaughter, Matthew Jr., Eliza, Oliver H.P., James, Jane, Tabitha, and Minerva Ann. Eleven-year-old Polly died of an illness in 1827 and was buried along with the Huston pioneers in the family graveyard behind the Plantation House. There were other Huston grandchildren living at other farmhouses. Archibald, the youngest of the Huston brothers to settle at Hanging Fork, had a grandson, Thomas, in addition to a granddaughter by his son George before 1830, and at the same time had two granddaughters by his son John.

Last of a true Scots-Irish line, L to R; Elsie, Clara, Rosella, Edna, Eula, Ambrose, and John Huston. At front, Mary Huston, circa 1918.

In the summer of 1830, Stephenson Huston drew up his will, which is typical of the early Scots-Irish wills of Lincoln County, Ky.

> *In the Name of God, Amen. I, Stephen Huston, of the County of Lincoln and State of Kentucky, being of strong mind and memory, do make and constitute this my last will and testament. It is my will and desire that all my just debts be paid and that all my funeral expenses by paid.*
>
> *Item 1st. I give to my beloved wife Jane Huston 3 Negroes to wit: Dinny, a girl about 20 years old and her child about 1 year and 6 months and Sam about 40 years old during her life or widowhood. I also give to my said wife 1 bed and furniture, 2 work beasts and also my Narris mare, also 2 cows and calves and 1 bureau. At the death of my said wife the said Negroes and their increase together with the other property is to be sold by my Executors and the proceeds thereof to go to my 4 Grand Daughters (to wit) Jane, Eliza, Tabitha, and Minerva Ann Slaughter, when they arrive to the age of 21 years old.*
>
> *Item 2nd. I give and bequeath to my two Grand Sons Stephen H. Slaughter and Matthew Slaughter the tract of land whereon I now live to be equally divided between them, the said Stephen is to have the part the*

dwelling house stands on in consequence of him have to take care of my wife, She having a right to live in the said house as long as she shall live, and to have all the priviliges as if it was her own, and the other part is to be rented out for the benefit of the said Matthew until he arrives at the age of 21 years old, and if he should die before he arrives to the age of 21 years old, then and in that case, the said land is to go to Stephen H. Slaughter by him paying to to James and Oliver H.P. Slaughter, two thirds of the value of said tract of land, and if the said Matthew should die before the said James and Oliver arriev to the age of 21 years old, then the said Stephen is to execute his note to my Executor hereafter to be appointed, made payable in a reasonable time.

Item 4th. I give and bequeath to my other two grand Sons James and Oliver H. P. Slaughter, the Tracts of land on Carpenter Creek and Green River in Casey County containing about 400 acres to be equally divided between them when they arrive at the age of 21 years old, but it is to be understood that Matthew Slaughter the father of the said James and Oliver is to use and occupy the said tract of land for the purpose of raising my grand children without paying rent and if the said Slaughter think proper to remove off said tracts of land, then the said Executors hereafter to be named should take possession of the same and to rent it out for the benefit of the said James and Oliver, and should either of the said James or Oliver die, the other shall pay to Stephen and Matthew two thirds of the value of the half.

Item 5th. I give to my said wife Jane Huston $100 in case to be paid by my Executors when she may want it.

Item 6th. It is my will and desire that my Executors make sale of all my personal property of all kind and description and also of all my Negroes that is not heretofore divised, and the proceeds of the same to go to my 4 grand Daughters to wit: Jane, Eliza, Tabitha, and Minerva Ann Slaughter, My Executors to have the control of the same by placing it out on interest until they arrive at the age of 21 years old. I also give to my said grand Sons and Daughters aall the Debts due my estate after all my Debts are paid. It is my will and desire that Stephen H. Slaughter rent out the Shop lot and house that stands on the Shop Lott and the house opposite the Tavern House and the proceeds to be applied to his own use and benefit for the term of 10 years. It is my will and desire that my Executors rent out the Tavern house in the Village of Hanging Fork together with all the outhouses, Stables, and lotts, together with the pasture lot until my youngest grand child shall arrive to 21 years old and the proceeds to be applied to the Schooling of my grandchildren.

And lastly, I appoint Archibald Huston, Stephen H. Slaughter, and Thales Huston my Executors to this my last will and testament, hereby revoking all other wills heretofore made, as witnessed my hand and seal this

26th day of June 1830. Signed, Sealed and delivered in the presence of John Montgomery, A.H. Garvin, George Huston

On Monday, the fourteenth day of February 1831, the will of Stephenson Huston was produced in Court at Stanford, in the presence of his nephew George Huston and neighbor John Montgomery. Stephen Huston Slaughter declined as executor, and the court named Thales Huston and Archibald Huston. It was two and a half years before an inventory of Huston's property was presented to the Court. In August of 1833, the sale was held and many of the neighbors joined family members as the property was auctioned. George Carpenter bought a black steer for $8.50, the same price William Masterson gave for a cow and calf. The horses brought considerably more: Thomas Purdon paid $60 for a single roan horse, while Ellis Brown gave $36.50 for a bay. Through the day, items were sold, such as bedding, furniture, plows and other farming implements. John Huston bought a hogshead of rye for just under six dollars, and another sold later for just under four dollars. William Bailey bought a hogshead of oats for $2.62. Livestock was paraded out, including red heifers, white faced cows, black cows, black horses, sorrel horses, and a gray filly. There were kettles and pots, shovels and tongs, blacksmith tools, saws, barrels, candle stands, chests, and bags of cotton. In a fashion typical of the time, his widow Jane was required to buy back personal items. She bought back her saddle for $5, and a skillet for fifty cents, a kettle for $2, and spent another $1.25 for two pots.

Not too many years earlier, the "rifle gun" likely would have been specifically listed in the will as a valuable tool and coveted possession. Stephen Huston Slaughter bought his grandfather's rifle gun for $7, while his brother Matthew bought a gunstock and a set of shoemaker tools for under a dollar.

The sale inventory and prices fill more than five pages of the Lincoln County Court book, and contain the names of many of the Hanging Fork relatives and neighbors who were present at the sale:

John Allen	Samuel Blain	Charles Crutcher
William Anderson	Benjamin Briggs	George Culley
Frederick Bailey	Ellis Brown	Milton Dixon
William Bailey	Joseph Caits	Willis Duncan
Capt. Baker	George Carpenter	Isaac Ellis
Nathan Barnett	George F. Carpenter	John Feland
Robert Barnett	John Carpenter	B. Fitzpatrick
Skyler Barnett	B. Cauthon	John Fitzpatrick
Edward Bartow	James Clarkson	A. Garrett
Samuel Baxter	William Cooper	Archibald Garvin
Francis Ben	Morris Cotter	James Garvin

Micah Gerlaw
Lorenzo Good
Micajah Good
Timothy Good
David Grimlee
Dry Griton
George Griton
Stephen Griton
Frederick Haifley
Samuel Harrison
Jane Huston
John Huston
Samuel Huston
Jacob Johnston
Nate Jones
Abraham P. Lee

George Lee
J.A. Lewis
James Lineberry
William Masterson
John McGee
George Miller
Robert Miller
William Minshaw
John F. Napier
James Patton
Horatio Penn
Major Powell
Thomas Purdom
Joshua Richards
Doct. Ray
Pullum Sandridge

I.A. Sevier
A. Shannon
William Shields
James Slaughter
Jane Slaughter
Stephen H. Slaughter
John Spears
Noah Snow
William Truman
Fleming Tucker
Henry White
John Whittle
D. Williams
Thomas Williams

There were mixed blessings for the slaves of Huston Plantation regarding the sale day. The death of a slave owner always brought uncertainty for those who could not control their own destinies. In his will, Huston indicated that forty-year-old Sam should stay with his widow Jane, along with twenty-year-old Dinney, and an infant child. While Huston recognized the need for the infant to remain with its mother he made no mention her two other children, which likely would have caused the family to be separated. Later, Jane Huston made an arrangement with James Lineberry agreed to keep them as a family, and their move was finalized previous to the date of the scheduled sale. For many women the idea of having slaves was somewhat of a paradox, even concerning slaves born on the farm and raised alongside the slave owner's children. There were women who relied on domestic help for everything from cooking and cleaning, to raising the children, and for them, learning to perform the same tasks for themselves seemed a daunting proposal. There were women who released their slaves, or had them sold, who later mentioned in correspondence how difficult a job it was to raise the children, or to keep up with the housework without help. The relationships between slaves and their masters varied from plantation to plantation, but widows could rarely maintain the type of interaction to which the slaves would have become accustomed. In addition, many women were morally opposed to slaveholding, but had little say concerning the issue while the husband was alive, and it was only after the husband's death that the widow was free to make choices.

Jane Huston did not keep Sam, as had been outlined in the will. At the same time Dinney and her children moved to the Lineberry farm, Sam moved to the

Casey County farm of her grandson, James Slaughter. For Dinney and her three children, James Lineberry paid the estate $720, and for Sam, James Slaughter paid $155. The rest of the slaves were sold during Stephenson Huston's public vendue, scattered among the farms of Hanging Fork, although two were sold to Huston's relatives. Stephenson Slaughter paid $177 for Jim; a young girl patriotically named America was sold to Dry Griton for $255, while a girl named Panthy went to the home of George Griton, for $305. Cinthia was sold to Archibald Garvin for $331, Samuel Huston bought Lewis for $360 and Grim (Green?) was sold to Doctor Ray for $201.

Following the death of his father, Thales Huston found himself without an

inheritance and reliant on his brother-in-law and his nephews in regard to the Huston's business interests. His cousin Samuel had recently married Elizabeth Lee, one of the many Lee daughters on the several neighboring farms run by the Lee families. Elizabeth had a sister, Jane, a sharp woman who had been left considerable land following the death of her father Richard Lee. Thales and Jane were wed the second day of December 1831, not quite a year after the death of his father.

The couple returned to Thales' house in Stanford, and for the next few months Jane was to discover the facts about her husband's finances, and just ten months after their wedding, she was deathly ill. She wrote her will October 8, 1832, placing the estate that she had brought to her marriage into a trust to be run by her brother and her sister's husband. William M. Lee and Samuel Huston were placed in charge of Jane's property, a two-hundred-acre tract of rich farmland and another 150 acres of "knob" land in Lincoln County, and another large tract of land in Casey County. William F. Lee sold lands to her father, Richard H. Lee, of which Jane was a one-seventh owner, along with her siblings. She was also one of the largest slave owners in the county, and she directed Samuel and William to be in complete charge of the 25 slaves, who would continue to assist Thales should he require it. Jane had grown up alongside Charity and Usley, and when Jane had come of age, her father had placed the two on "loan" to her. Charity and Usley would be in the care of William and Samuel as well.

Her wishes were explicitly written regarding the debts that Thales owed. Not a cent of her estate was to be spent toward those obligations, and should her brother or Samuel believe that Thales was trying to raise money for that purpose, they were to immediately take charge of the estate to prevent any such action. In addition, since her father's estate had not been completely settled, she was also expecting a sizable amount of cash. Jane directed in her will that "no portion of said money" should be applied to the payment of any debt created by Thales previous to their marriage. He could have the use of the property or the use of the money, for any purpose—excepting his bachelor-debts.

After Jane's death, Thales returned to the life of a bachelor for nearly nine years before he remarried. When Thales did remarry, it was not to a frail woman of means. The day after Christmas in 1840, Thales married Lydia Root, the forty-two year old daughter of Timothy Root, one of the early preachers in the county. Ten years later Thales and Lydia were caring for the eight-year-old son, and five-year-old daughter of Lydia's younger brother, a widower who was unable to simultaneously keep up with both his children and his work. Thales distanced himself further from Huston Plantation when, some years later, he removed his family to Harrodsburg.

———

The Scots-Irish brogue was diminishing, and in the rolling hills of Kentucky each generation of children helped replace the rolled consonants with a colloquial dialect. It was a new sound for words, developed as a result of their continued remoteness from distinct speech patterns in the East, the mixing of ancestries and heritage through marriage, and the influence of a closer-knit society that was predicated by neighbors and public schooling. There were still pockets of isolationism, and although marriages consisting of true Scots-Irish heritage could conceivably extend the window of the Ulster influence on early America into the twentieth century, it would be the exception rather than the rule.

By the mid-1800's, when the wave of true Irish immigrants began to appear in the United States, the Scots-Irish might still be distinguished by their speech or their temperament, but in general, they had been on the continent for a century, and many families who comprised the earliest of the Great Migration waves from the North of Ireland had been in America nearly 150 years. They were regarded as long-time neighbors, the sons and daughters of pioneers, and contributing citizens in the American Society. When the Irish potato famine brought boatload after boatload of impoverished Irish to American shores, those who had come earlier from the North of Ireland began pointing out that they were Scottish, "by way of Ireland," and not to be confused with those recently arrived.

Typical of the Scotch-Irish in early Kentucky were the Hustons at Hanging Fork. Stephenson Huston was the influential and brash family member whose business dealings placed him in contact with many of the residents and visitors to the area. His brother Nathan served the public as a law officer and twice as a state convention delegate. Archibald, the youngest of the three Huston brothers who settled at the Hanging Fork on Carpenter's Creek, was a farmer. Recognizing the contributions to the area made by the brothers, the citizenry chose to rename the town Hustonville.

Main Street, Hustonville KY, circa 1909
3rd from left: J. H. Hocker in door of National Bank, 4th from left: Wesley Hocker, at curb: Smith Yowell, bldg. to right: Jerry Adams Drug Store

Stephenson Huston was recognized at Stanford, when a plaque honoring the Revolutionary War patriots from Lincoln County was placed at the Court House. Nathan's name is included among the historical references to the early conventions of Kentucky, including the convention for statehood at Danville, and the Constitution Convention of 1799. The contributions of brother Archibald were strongest in the area of family and community, and his legacy lives in the number of Hustons who are able to trace their ancestry through the valley of the Hanging Fork. When Archibald died in 1857 at age 83, he left behind a sizable estate to be divided among his ten children; Polly—who had married James Gay, George, John, Elizabeth—who married John Gilbert, Samuel, Nathan, Patsey—who married Isaac Gibson, Ambrose Lee, James A., and A. Thomas Huston.

William Henry Huston and Maggie Lee Quaite Huston
30th Wedding Anniversary, October 1, 1915, Cass Co. MO

The Scots-Irish as a race might have been waning as an influence, but its influence was still strong for Ambrose Lee Huston, who had been renting a farm for $100 per year from his father-in-law. At the death of his father, Ambrose received a one-tenth share of the estate, enough money to buy land out west where his sons could have farms of their own. He gathered his family and all the belongings that could be carried in their wagons, and set out on the road to start anew in Missouri. It was typically Scots-Irish. Just as his father had moved west to begin a new life, so would the son. As the grandfather had moved from the Cumberland Valley to the Shenandoah, so would the grandson, from Kentucky to western Missouri. Just as his great-grandfather had caused a second move within a matter of years, so would the great-grandson, landing first in Holt County near the jumping-off point for the Pony Express at St. Joe, then moving once more before finally settling for good on a farm south of Kansas City. Like most of the Scots-Irish, Ambrose headed a large family as the wagons rolled westward to their new home, including Washington Huston, Abraham Lee Huston, Permelia, Mary, James, Samuel, Matilda, Richard, Sarah, Archibald, and William Henry Huston.

When King James opened the Ulster plantation to the Scots, they brought their religion with them to Northern Ireland, and when they arrived in America, they quickly transplanted their Presbyterianism to their settlements. John Houston founded the Timber Ridge Congregation in Virginia, and his son Robert later contributed land to the church. Archibald Huston and his father-in-law John Stephenson were among the founders of the Peaked Mountain Church in the upper Shenandoah Valley. In early-day Kentucky, Stephenson Huston helped found the Hanging Fork Congregation of Presbyterians. True to his heritage, Ambrose Huston and his wife Elizabeth, along with five neighbors, founded on August 14, 1881, the Sharon Presbyterian Church near Drexel, Missouri. They farmed the land, and celebrated the good times; they hoped hard times would pass. They were buried near their church house. It was the Scots-Irish way.

Index

Huston, Joseph, 68, 136, 153, 168
Huston, Joseph Jr., 153
Huston, Lavina, 161
Huston, Lucy J., 161
Huston, Margaret, 161
Huston, Mary, 113, 161, 213
Huston, Mary B., 161
Huston, Matilda, 213
Huston, Melinda, 161
Huston, Nathan, 42, 90, 113, 124, 136,
148, 149, 150, 151, 155, 158, 161,
174, 176, 177, 178, 180, 184, 185,
211, 212
Huston, Neil, 136
Huston, Patsey, 212
Huston, Permelia, 213
Huston, Peter, 136, 153
Huston, Polly, 212
Huston, Richard, 213
Huston, Samuel, 77, 136, 153, 208, 209,
212, 213
Huston, Sarah, 113, 213
Huston, Stephen, 90, 112, 113, 145, 146,
148, 150, 151, 155, 157, 158, 184,
205, 207, 211
Huston, Stephenson, 71, 90, 122, 124,
136, 147, 158, 176, 184, 190, 203,
204, 205, 207, 209, 211, 213
Huston, Thales, 184, 198, 204, 206, 207,
209
Huston, Thomas, 204
Huston, Washington, 213
Huston, will of Stephen, 205
Huston, William, 21, 137, 153
Huston, William Henry, 212, 213
Huston's Station, 153
Hustonville, KY, viii, 147, 154, 176, 201,
211
Hutchens, James, 190
Hutcheson, John, 77

Hutchins, Benjamin, 190
Hutchins, Thomas, 179
Hutchinson, 10, 196, 197
Hutchinson, Lewis, 196
Hutchinson, Thomas, 197
Hutchison, Alexander, 20
Hutchison, James, 20
Hutchison, Joseph, 190
Hutchison, Thomas, 190
Hyatt, Benjamin, 190
Hyatt, John, 190
Hyatt, William, 190
Hyatt, Wilson, 190
Hyde, Benjamin, 28
Hyde, James, 28
Hyde, John, 28
Hyeth, Frederick, 190
Hynds, James, 60
Hyrons, Joseph, 44
Hyrons, Saml., 43
Hyrons, Samuel, 43
immigration, 15
Indian Road, 39, 118, 163
Ingleman, Samuel, 190
Inless, 10, 20
Inless, Abraham, 20
Inman, William, 190
Innes, Harry, 175
Inyard, John, 190
Iredell County, NC, 53, 55, 135, 154
Ireland, ix, 5, 7, 8, 9, 10, 11, 12, 13, 14,
15, 16, 18, 19, 37, 52, 60, 73, 86,
102, 108, 184, 210, 213
Ireland, John, 60, 73
Ireland, northern, 13, 15, 210
Ireland, Northern, vii, ix, x, 11, 12, 14,
18, 19, 102, 184, 213
Ireland, William, 60, 73
Irish Settlement, 54, 87, 89

978-0-595-35914-1
0-595-35914-0